Library of
Davidson College

Democratic Liberalism and Social Union

DEMOCRATIC LIBERALISM
AND
SOCIAL UNION

Terry Pinkard

TEMPLE UNIVERSITY PRESS
PHILADELPHIA

Temple University Press, Philadelphia 19122
Copyright © 1987 by Temple University. All rights reserved
Published 1987
Printed in the United States of America

The paper used in this publication meets the minimum
requirements of American National Standard for Information
Sciences—Permanence of Paper for Printed Library Materials,
ANSI Z39.48-1984

Library of Congress Cataloging-in-Publication Data

Pinkard, Terry P.
  Democratic liberalism and social union.

  Includes index.
  1. Social contract. 2. Justice. 3. Liberalism.
4. Democracy. I. Title.
JC336.P56 1987   320'.01'1   86-23088
ISBN 0-87722-458-7 (alk. paper)

To my parents,
J. L. P. and E. L. P.

Acknowledgments

MANY PEOPLE HELPED me along with this manuscript. My debts to them are so great, I could not even begin to acknowledge them fully. Friends and colleagues have patiently listened to the things being said here and have just as patiently saved me from making even more grievous errors than I no doubt already have. Indeed, when I look over the manuscript, it sometimes seems as if what is good in it comes from them, and my contribution consists only in the deficiencies that remain.

Several people read the manuscript through from start to finish and gave me a number of helpful comments and suggestions for revisions, along with criticisms that I hope I have answered. In many ways, the book is the result of a kind of extended conversation with Klaus Hartmann over several years. Without his advice and input over that period, I would not have even known where to begin. He read an earlier draft of this and kindly offered a detailed account of just where he thought that I had gone wrong. Because of his criticisms and suggestions, a large part of it substantially changed. Daniel Robinson offered more suggestions that found their way into the book than I could ever begin to note. Norbert Hornstein offered an abundance of criticisms and suggestions for alternative ways of putting things; his cajoling and advice caused me to change the manuscript quite a bit. I owe him a great intellectual and personal debt. Sherman Cohn first got me thinking about a lot of these issues, patiently listened to various versions of the theses that pop up in here, and just as patiently pointed out where they were in need of more development or (sometimes) abandonment. Winfried Brugger helped me think out a number of ideas here and led me to some literature in the field that would otherwise have escaped my attention. John DeGioia, Simeon McIntosh, and Mark Tushnett read over parts of the manuscript and made a number of helpful suggestions. David Hite helped with some of the crucial details of getting the manuscript ready. I have also borrowed liberally from conversations with many friends; they will recognize many of the discussions we have had reflected in these pages.

Over the last few years, I have also had the opportunity to associate with a remarkable bunch of people at the Kennedy Institute of Ethics at Georgetown University. They all endured earlier versions of this and offered more help and suggestions than it is possible to note here. Their high standards and camaraderie have been a splendid example of what the phrase "academic community" is supposed to mean. Special thanks to Tom Beauchamp, whose conversations and help over the years are particularly appreciated.

The first draft of this book was written while I was a Fellow of the Alexander von Humboldt Foundation at Tübingen University in the Federal Republic of Germany. I would like to thank the foundation for their generous support. The Dean of the Faculty of Philosophy at Tübingen University, Professor Rüdiger Bubner, helped make my sojourn in his department a very enjoyable and productive one. The generosity of the Graduate School of Georgetown University in the form of some Summer Research Grants permitted me to get the final draft of the manuscript completed.

The readers for Temple University Press made a number of suggestions that improved the manuscript quite a bit. Jane Cullen and Doris Braendel of Temple University Press also made a number of helpful suggestions; their good humor and support was appreciated throughout the process.

Vicki Boyle's emotional support and encouragement got me through it all. Thanks.

Table of Contents

Introduction, xi

CHAPTER ONE: Autonomy, Social Union, and the Common Good, 3

I. Freedom and Autonomy, 5
II. Self-Identity and Social Union, 15
III. Respect for Persons and Respect for Choices, 32
IV. Distributive Justice and Social Union, 38

CHAPTER TWO: Moral and Legal Principles, 53

I. Sovereigns and Rules, 54
II. Are Rules Enough?, 63
III. Principles and the State, 68

CHAPTER THREE: Civil Obligation and Social Union, 79

I. Contract and the Strategies of Distributive Justice, 81
II. Sharing and Fairness, 96
III. Risks and the Balancing of Principles, 121
IV. Balancing and Cost/Benefit Analysis, 130

CHAPTER FOUR: Basic Principles, Basic Rights, and the State, 137

I. The Minimal State as a Social State, 138
II. The Political State and Basic Rights, 141
III. Welfare Rights and Property Rights, 151
IV. The State, Society, and the Constitution, 158
V. Real Rights and Ideal Rights, 171
VI. A Note on Crime and Punishment, 176

Notes, 185

Index, 215

Introduction

THERE HAS BEEN a remarkable renaissance in political theory in Anglo-American philosophy in the last few years. We now have both a substantial literature on analysis of the concepts of justice and of rights and a substantial, growing literature on the relations among various basic kinds of ethical claims and issues in public policy and professional ethics. One need not look far to find some reasons for this upsurge in political theory; one clear impetus for it has been John Rawls's *A Theory of Justice*. However, one of the curious things about the present debate concerning theories of justice is that, with few exceptions (one thinks of Robert Nozick's *Anarchy, State, and Utopia*), there has been little reflection on one of the classical themes of political theory, that of the nature of the state and its relation to society.[1] Rawls's theory, for example, has no theory of the state in it at all, no entry for it in the index to the book, and only a couple of passing references to it in the text. This is perhaps all the more curious in that it was the theory of the state that was the cornerstone of much modern political philosophy, including the social contract theory, which Rawls has so effectively revived. Nor does there seem to be an expressed view in the relevant literature that whatever problems there were in the classical theories of the state have been resolved, leaving room for creative thinkers to apply their energies elsewhere.

The distinction, moreover, between the state and society is important in distinguishing between economic and political models of rights. The point of liberal society, I shall argue, is the realization of each individual's liberty to pursue their own interests; the point of the democratic liberal state is to create and maintain conditions assuring respect for the dignity of each individual in society. Society is a sphere of economically modeled rights; these are pieces of property over which individuals have disposition. The state is a sphere of politically modeled rights; these are not tradeable any more than one's dignity is tradeable. Without a theory of the state and society, liberal political philosophy cannot make the distinctions that are necessary for understanding its own basic claims.

This is, however, more than just a failure to include some things that should be considered. It cannot be remedied by simply tacking on a theory of the state at the end of the leading treatises on the subject. There are deeper and, I think, inadequate assumptions shared by both Rawlsians and others that lead them to what I shall argue is a faulty characterization of the relation of state and society. One is the tacit assumption that the state is only an instrument of society to pursue ends that society on its own cannot. Another is the tacit acceptance of Kant's identification of respect for persons (what he calls respect for their dignity) with respect for their autonomy; this leads to the mistaken identification of respect for persons with respect for their capacity for choice. Nozick offers a radical version of what accepting this identification entails. Rawls takes it seriously enough to fashion a theory that rests on what people would choose in an appropriate situation.

These assumptions, along with others, have led critics of liberalism to the claims, variously, that liberalism is inherently incapable of taking seriously such ideas as character, that it presupposes an atomized, alienated set of social relations, and that it has a shallow view of the self and its relation to others.[2] None of these views are, I shall argue, inherent to democratic liberalism. The democratic liberal ideal of state and society depends on a set of shared self-understandings to be found in democratic liberal social union and a kind of ideal of personality that the critics claim is impossible in democratic liberalism.

The mistaken identification of respect for persons with respect for their choices partially helps to explain the ongoing appeal of social contract theory as a paradigm of democratic liberal thought. Now, it would be foolish to deny that a major part of the current appeal of social contract theory, of course, is just the sheer power and range of Rawls's reconstruction of that theory. Rawls's book is a masterpiece of philosophical reasoning, breadth, and subtlety and is the basis on which virtually any contemporary discussion of political philosophy must proceed. However, like many theories of democratic liberalism, it stresses one element—choice—at the expense of other equally central aspects of a democratic liberal social order, such as mutual trust and reliance and the virtues proper to a democratic liberal social union. Social contract theory, I shall argue, is the wrong vehicle to use to reconstruct the kind of shared self-understandings of democratic liberalism, even if Rawlsian principles turn out to be adequate expressions of the ideals of democratic liberalism.

There are also good historical reasons for the appeal of social contract theory as a form of liberal theory. From its inception, liberalism has often presented itself as a kind of ahistorical view of the world. The questions liberal theorists have often posed are indeed the ones found in the social contract tradition: "What would rational people, outside of any tradition, authority, or social organization, choose as the proper form of government?" Early liberals often understood themselves to be throwing off the yokes of what they understood as medieval superstition, and thus it was natural for them to present their views as the result of dispassionate rational choice rather than the working out of certain movements in their own cultures. However, because of this stress on ahistorical rational choice, liberalism has often been portrayed by both its defenders and its critics as blind to the very traditions that gave rise to it. Its critics have accused it even of being hostile to the elements in the culture without which it cannot long maintain itself.

Liberalism, as a doctrine that stressed material prosperity, intellectual progress, and limited government, became respectable when it was married to democratic government. Democracy, which had been discussed at least since Plato and Aristotle as a form of government equivalent to mob rule, became legitimate only after its marriage to the liberal theory of limited government and individual rights. The union, democratic liberalism, was the rational result of different historical traditions, ranging from the ancient Germanic *Schöffen*, which led to the English tradition of trial by jury of one's peers, to the construction of ideas of individual rights as defenses for individuals from encroachments by a sovereign authority. In each case, democratic liberalism was able to provide solutions to the practical problems posed by its predecessors that they themselves could not provide within their own conceptual resources. I shall argue that this marriage is not an unhappy accident. The principle of respect for individual dignity that provides a rationale for a liberal theory of limited government pushes liberalism into the form of *democratic* liberalism. Democratic liberalism is able to resolve some internal problems of liberalism *per se* not by abstracting itself out of history but by providing solutions that are latent within liberal theory and tradition itself.

This tradition, however, does not immediately appear as consistent. In particular, the marriage of two very different lines of thought—democracy, with its tendencies to equality, and liberalism, with its insistence on individual rights and liberty—has produced what is in some ways a kind of fragmented tradition. It is possible to pick up on parts of that tradition and stress them to the detriment of other elements. This has indeed been done with some current theories of liberalism. Such a stress would be, however, one-sided; it neglects equally central elements of the tradition and thus falsifies its picture of liberal democracy. Of course, it remains to be shown that a consistent and coherent account can be given of this fragmented tradition in such a way that the fragments can be pieced together. To say that the tradition does not have an immediately apparent consistency is not to say that it is in fact inconsistent; it is only to say that the consistency must be shown, not assumed.

To see liberalism in this way is to understand it not just as the result of dispassionate rational choice but as a historical achievement and a rational development of certain crucial themes in our culture. It sees liberalism, as it were, as a learned affair, not something latent in the *a priori* structure of reason itself. Although he is hardly ever taken to be a liberal, Hegel held that much of what early liberals counted as "mere" tradition and custom could be understood as rational answers to problems that arose in predecessor forms of life and in earlier political theories. Consequently, the marriage of liberalism and democracy might itself be seen in the same light. Part of the view that I will be attempting to articulate here is the reintegration of what I would take to be the Hegelian legacy for democratic liberalism. Hegel's reflections offer a good springboard for an explanation of what I take to be the type of social union that is democratic liberalism.

Hegel was correct, I think, in his criticism of classical social contract theory as misunderstanding the relation of the individual and the state, and the more streamlined versions of the social contract that have recently appeared repeat those mistakes.[3] Unfortunately, Hegel's own proposal has often been taken to be substantially worse than the ills it sought to counter. Nonetheless, some themes found in Hegel's works supply what is missing in many current theories that claim to be versions of some kind of democratic liberalism. They would be: (1) the devaluing of the Kantian voluntarist element in political and moral theory, with the conception of acknowledgment instead taking center stage;[4] (2) the rejection of Rawlsian claims about the primacy of justice without an undermining of the importance of justice in what Rawls calls the well-ordered society; (3) the contextualism of content for morality without (I hope) any commitment to an objectionable moral relativism; (4) the necessity of some conception of social union and the various ideals of character within it to explain why certain rights and ideals are important.

Central to the Hegelian conception of political philosophy is the belief that one cannot understand political and moral principles outside the social and historical context from which they draw their life. Philosophical theories do not arise in a vacuum; they arise against a background of pressing political and social problems and against a background of shared assumptions. Because of this, political philosophy must be at least in part a theory of social unions, and such a theory, I shall argue, sets into clearer relief the basis and framework for the types of democratic liberal claims that Rawls's theory of justice involves. Rawlsian justice (unlike Rawls's own theory), I shall argue, does not depend on mistaken ideas such as identification of respect for persons with respect for choices. A theory of the kinds of social unions that make up a democratic liberal state and society does not therefore replace Rawls's own theory but supplements it in ways not available within the ambit of Rawls's own framework. Now I know that this will go against the grain of many contemporary critics of democratic liberalism. They have used Hegel as the perfect foil to argue that Rawlsian principles are insupportable. Nonetheless, strange as it might sound to those critics, a Hegelian theory of social unions is precisely what Rawlsian justice needs in order to meet their objections.

Taking a cue from Hegel, I shall call this a speculative theory, in the sense that it offers one explanation (among the many possible) of how things such as rights or claims to justice can be possible. The theory views philosophy's subject matter as the explanation of possibilities.[5] This view has two parts: A philosophical *problem* on this view is one of difficulty in seeing how two sets of basic beliefs (both of which one has good reason to consider true) can in fact both be true. For example, it is a philosophical problem that we seem to be free, and the world seems to be determined, and it seems that we cannot be both free and determined. A philosophical *theory* is an attempt to provide an explanation of the problem. Philosophical theories typically take one of two tacks: they either deny that one or the other set of beliefs is in fact true (they deny, for example, that we are free, or they deny that determinism is the case); or they argue that a more adequate understanding of the matter shows that the apparent incompatibility is *only* apparent, that a proper theory shows that the two seemingly incompatible beliefs are actually compatible with each other. A philosophical theory is then the attempt to explain how something is even possible, given other basic assumptions that would rule out its possibility.

This is true not only of metaphysics and epistemology but also of political philosophy. Many of the great concepts and theories of political philosophy have been framed around problems such as whether it is possible for individual liberty to be compatible with the state's authority; or whether it is possible to have a state that fully realizes the true good; or whether a kind of human flourishing is possible in a certain type of society (or in what kind of society human flourishing would be possible). The critics of democratic liberalism have been concerned with such problems of possibilities. Is it possible to have an adequate understanding of virtue in a democratic liberal individualist culture? Can liberals value anything more than a mere capacity for choice in people?

Such an understanding of the role of political philosophy as the explanation of possibility does not obviate the fact that it is always framed in terms of the felt social and political problems of its time. Many of those problems are in fact themselves ones of possibilities, of what things are open to us in the future if we hold on to current assumptions, of what needs to be true if an adequate pursuit of human goods is to be possible. The problems of possibility that belong peculiarly to philosophical reflection do not isolate it in any proverbial ivory tower, remote from human concerns. The problems of liberalism discussed by its critics are real ones for us who live in democratic liberal societies. The alternative resolutions of these problems have a practical, not just a theoretical, significance.

There is another reason for calling the type of theory presented here a speculative theory. One can distinguish two different approaches to philosophy in the Western tradition. Let us give them the crude labels of the Aristotelian-Hegelian model and the Kantian-critical model. In the latter, one approaches philosophy and particularly the history of philosophy as resting on some kind of basic, deep, and fundamental *mistake*. For Kant, this was the failure to recognize the limits and nature of pure reason. Kant claimed that all metaphysics prior to him had failed to become a science because of this error. He believed that once this had been seen for what it was, philosophy would be on the sure path to becoming as rigorous a science as any other. Other theories, however great they had been, belonged to the pre-scientific stage.

Kant is certainly not the only philosopher who has held to this critical paradigm. Others have also claimed to have found the basic, underlying error of all past philosophy, the correction of which is necessary if any real progress is to be made in the field. Even a short list turns up some well-known ones: the failure to appreciate the conditions under which propositions can be verified; the failure to understand the priority of ordinary language; the mistaken assumption that there were such things as "mental events" or "representations"; the failure to understand the priority of phenomenological description of experience and the phenomenological reduction; the forgetfulness of being. (One can add one's own personal favorites to the list.) On the Kantian-critical view, the history of philosophy usually turns out to be a series of well-intentioned (even well-executed and exceptionally intelligent) errors based on this one crucial mistake, whatever it is taken to be. Since most all past philosophy is basically mistaken, all that one can appreciate in past philosophical theories is basically the beauty and elegance of their execution. The Kantian-critical model's appreciation of alternative philosophical theories therefore becomes generally only a kind of aesthetic one.

The Aristotelian-Hegelian model, on the other hand, sees the alternative theories as alternative explanations of some subject matter; it does not look for some kind of basic, underlying error in the theories. The goodness of a theory lies in its being a better explanation, not on its avoidance of the crucial mistake. Aristotle, for example, began his *Metaphysics* with an overview of his predecessors' theories. He certainly thought that there were explanatory shortcomings in those theories, but he did not apparently believe that they were just confused about some very deep but nonetheless false assumption. On this Aristotelian-

Hegelian model, if a particular theory is a better theory, it is so because it offers a better explanation than its alternatives. Thus, I will not be arguing that social contract theory rests on some kind of basic error, nor will I be arguing that there is some feature of life for which it cannot in principle account. The intent is to construct an alternative theory that explains some things better.

My strategy for constructing this kind of theory of social unions has the following general form. Since the major focus of the book is the construction and defense of a non-Kantian theory of social unions as a basis for a democratic liberal theory of justice, the first chapter is concerned with the construction of a non-Kantian theory of autonomy, respect for autonomy, and the relation of both conceptions to a theory of social unions. The result, I argue, is compatible with a generally Rawlsian conception of justice and also shows that a Rawlsian theory is neither dependent on indefensible Kantian conceptions of the self nor blind to the role of communitarian elements in our sense of self. The second chapter forms a bridge between the first chapter and the third and fourth chapters, taking up some issues in legal philosophy as a way of introducing the theory of society and the state that form the basis of the third and fourth chapters. Consideration of some of the issues in contemporary jurisprudence shows that one cannot understand the role that democratic liberal principles play except as solutions to historically framed problems. (My rationale for using this chapter as a bridge also includes the belief that a democratic liberal theory will essentially involve some conception of rule of law, and this is best introduced as a separate chapter rather than in bits and pieces in other chapters.) The third chapter tries to provide an explanation of how civil obligation is possible. Its point of departure is a treatment of the way in which a democratic liberal theory of law functions within the social union of "society." This chapter considers the application of principles of justice to areas of contract and tort law; here I wish to argue that the ideals of personality found in democratic liberal social union make an essential appearance. The fourth and final chapter is a theory of the state as a form of social union and the implications of such a theory for conceptions of rights and the nature of a constitution (along with the nature of constitutional adjudication). It is argued that such a theory is necessary to make the application of Rawlsian principles of justice work.

I hope that the arguments and suggestions found in this strategy are convincing. A sober view of one's own theory, however, will most likely find that, whatever the charms of that theory may be, they will be well matched by the charms of other theories, and whatever shortcomings appear in other theories will also be well matched by shortcomings in one's own. The theory presented here is a speculative theory in the sense of the Aristotelian-Hegelian model. Although I speak of various shortcomings of the social contract theories, I see them as alternative models of explanation. It would be nice, of course, to think of my own views as fully complete, explaining all that the alternatives do and doing it so much better. It would be nice to think that I had resolved all the problems that needed to be resolved. It would also be a little silly to believe it.

Democratic Liberalism and Social Union

CHAPTER
ONE

Autonomy, Social Union, and the Common Good

FEW CONCEPTS ARE used as much in modern ethical theory as the notion of the autonomy of the individual. Associated particularly with the idea of Kantian ethics are the related claims that autonomy is a condition of morality and that the conditions of respecting the autonomy of the individual are therefore the conditions of morality itself. This emphasis on autonomy as the crucial concept of ethics, however, goes beyond the bounds of Kantian theory alone. In much contemporary philosophical and legal literature, there is great emphasis placed on something called "respect for autonomy." Many justifications of social policies found in the contemporary literature often proceed on the basis of some claim that such and such policy is necessary in order to "respect autonomy." Often respect for autonomy is taken to be respect for something like an individual's choices, even if those choices are believed to be inimical to the individual's interests. There is some discussion as to which kinds of choices should be respected (all choices? only the rational ones? and what sense of "rational"?).

Running throughout the discussion are the assumptions that we are indeed autonomous beings and that being autonomous is of great value. Some would say that this fact is almost always of overriding value. But is it even for the most part a fact at all? Think of the myriad actions that one performs each day. One decides to have a cup of tea instead of coffee. One drives to work. One asks Norbert for advice on the most efficient route to somewhere in town. One consents to a physician's routine request for a test of blood pressure. One decides to buy a newsmagazine. These are all free actions—are they also 'autonomous'? Do they deserve 'respect' even if they are not autonomous? Are we even clear what we are asking when we pose such questions? Until one has at least some idea about what autonomy is, one cannot know what exactly one is being urged to respect or how respect for autonomy is different from, say, merely respect for free choice or respect for rational choice.

In fact, one often finds two very different conceptions of autonomy at work in the various discussions of it.[1] There are *will*-oriented conceptions of autonomy in which one is concerned with whether the choices made by individuals are really their own or are under the governance or dominating influence of other persons or conditions. Will-oriented conceptions have their classic expression in Immanuel Kant's writings. There are also *action*-oriented conceptions of autonomy, in which one is concerned with the latitude that should be given to individuals with regard to what actions they choose to perform. Action-oriented conceptions have their classic expression in John Stuart Mill's work. What will count as respect for autonomy will be different in both cases. In will-oriented conceptions, one respects autonomy when one respects choices that the individual makes that are his or her own choices, and one worries about the kinds of influences on the person's choices. In action-oriented conceptions, one respects autonomy when one does not interfere with the individual's chosen course of action, and one worries about various legal and institutional impediments to individual action. These two different conceptions of autonomy thus lead to two different ideals of what would constitute respect for it.

A complete theory of autonomy should do at least five things: (1) it should tell us what autonomy is; (2) it should explain how autonomy could be possible; (3) it should explain what would be valuable about it, what makes it worth respecting; (4) it should give us some idea of how valuable autonomy actually is; and (5) it should show how the concept of autonomy fits in with our other moral concepts—show, that is, what role it plays in the moral world. With regard to the fifth point, it should also tell us what the relation between freedom and autonomy is.

Because of the importance of the concept of autonomy in liberal theory, I shall begin with it. As I hope to show, this is not because I take autonomy to be foundational for liberal theory. Quite the opposite. On the other hand, I do hope to show just what importance the concept of autonomy actually has for liberal theory. My strategy will be to construct first of all a non-Kantian conception of autonomy in Section I; to do this, I shall first show what I take the Kantian conception to be and then develop the alternative. In Section II, I hope to show how the Kantian conception is flawed and how the alternative conception adumbrated in Section I can be put to use in a theory of social union. In Section III, I will show how the Kantian conception of the importance of autonomy has serious flaws in terms of our conception of what counts as respect for persons. In Section IV, I will then show how this cashes out in terms of a reinterpretation of Rawls's notions of distributive justice.

I
Freedom and Autonomy

"Autonomy" means most generically to be self-determining. An autonomous person is a free person in a special sense: he or she is capable of *determining him or herself* in both thought and action. Historically, the notion of autonomy has always been linked with that of freedom and self-choice. It originally applied to political communities to indicate that they were free from foreign rule. Kant extended this notion to the self, choosing a legislative, political model of the self as his model of the autonomous person. We can note three things about this model of the autonomous person. First, to act autonomously, in Kantian terms, is to act according to one's idea of law, not merely in conformity to it. Thus, like the autonomous political community, the autonomous person legislates for him or herself. Kant contrasted this with what he called heteronomy, determination of the will not by oneself but by other persons or conditions. Second, in acting according to his or her idea of law, the autonomous person is said to act according to principles that can be willed to be universally valid for every rational agent. Laws, after all, are general, not particular. Only a will that acts according to such self-given but universally valid rules can be said, according to Kant, to be autonomous. Third, only an autonomous person qualifies as a *moral* person at all. On Kant's view, autonomy is not just a component of morality; it is the condition of morality itself.

Much more can be said about Kant's conception of autonomy. For now, let us just note one small curiosity in it. This *self*-determination is, oddly enough, not a matter of *personal* choice in any ordinary sense. A personal choice is one that is somehow expressive of oneself as an individual. In Kant's model, however, the self that determines these principles is not the idiosyncratic empirical self but the rational (in Kant's metaphysics, the noumenal) self. Indeed, for Kant, to be free is to be autonomous and to be autonomous is to act according to self-legislated rational principles, those chosen by the rational self in accordance with its nature as a rational self. The free, autonomous person is one who acts not out of what would normally be taken to be personal choice but out of a kind of *anonymous* choice—a choice that any rational agent would make. To act autonomously in this sense is to act without any consideration of what we would normally take to be our selves; the self-determining person would be one who acted in a non-individualistic fashion. The *self*-determining person on the Kantian view is one who acts universally, without consideration of him or her*self* in the personal sense.

It might seem paradoxical that one acts in a self-determining manner only when one's choices are determined by things that abstract completely from all the personal idiosyncrasies of the self—that one acts in a *self*-determining manner only when one abstracts from all that is peculiar to one*self*. One might think that, intuitively speaking, a person would be self-determining only if they did the exact opposite. An autonomous person would be one who acted according to his or her own sense of self, of what *he or she* in particular valued, not in terms of what people in general valued. A train buff, for example, would be acting autonomously if he collected railroad timetables, caught the last runs of various lines, and so on, not merely if he acted as an anonymous rational being in general. What reasons would someone have for believing otherwise? What view of the person and their relation to their actions would make such a Kantian position possible?

The Kantian position is not paradoxical if one assumes two things: (1) that the rational self is the essential (or true) self and the idiosyncratic self is a contingent (or false) one; and (2) action that is expressive of our true self is autonomous action. Take the first assumption: acting anonymously would be acting according to determinations posited by the essential, not the contingent, self. If we identify the person with his or

I. Freedom and Autonomy

her essential self, then (because of the second assumption) acting according to the determinations posited by that self would be acting autonomously. Anonymity and autonomy would merge. This seems indeed to be Kant's view: one acts autonomously when one acts according to maxims laid down by one's rational (essential) self, not one's empirical (contingent) self. It should not therefore be surprising that a latter day Kantian such as John Rawls can propose in a thoroughly Kantian spirit that to act autonomously is to act according to principles that express our natures as rational agents.[2] At the least, such a view seems to be the presupposition of a conception of autonomy such as Kant's. If so, then it would seem that the conceptions of our *nature* and of its *expressions* are prior to our conception of autonomy. Is this enough to capture what autonomy is, and will it tell us what is valuable about autonomy?

Let us generalize this point a bit. If the two assumptions explain why anonymous action would be autonomous action, then the difference in varying conceptions of autonomy will simply be a function of the extent to which they differ over conceptions of our essential self and of its expression. Contrast, for example, this broadly Kantian view with what would be a broadly Aristotelian one. (This is, of course, an anachronism, since Aristotle had, strictly speaking, no theory of autonomy.) On this broadly Aristotelian view, an act would be autonomous if it flows from the person's character. A person's character, however, is more than merely their rational self; it is also composed of their desires, emotions, and the types of motivations that make up the person's various dispositions (not all of which have rational origins). This different conception of the essential self also implies a different conception of what counts as autonomous. What for an orthodox Kantian would be a non-autonomous action (one done from motivations other than pure or rational ones) would be for this kind of Aristotelian an autonomous action. Take the difference of two people, W. and V. Since W. is not the suspicious type, her unreflectively loaning you five dollars would express her character and would count as an autonomous action. On the other hand, V.'s asking you to sign a note for the five-dollar loan would, since it expresses her non-trusting nature, also be an equally autonomous act. If one sees emotionally based motivations as belonging to the true self (or to our natures), then even actions that spring from pure emotion will be autonomous. If not, then the actions will appear as non-autonomous and in the extreme case even alienated. It all depends on what you see as essential and inessential to who the person is.

An extreme position would be one that would see neither reason nor emotion nor desire as part of our essential selves and instead would view the essential self as merely a kind of metaphysical point that originates action without itself being the causal result of anything else. On this extreme view, autonomous action would be one that is independent of *any* rational or emotional motivations. (This is not necessarily to say that this view makes very much sense, although it comes close, I would argue, to the kind of theory that Sartre advances in *Being and Nothingness*.)

This makes any theory of autonomy derivative from a theory of what is and is not essential to a person's self. I think that there is something valuable in this way of putting the issue, but I also think that the Kantian conception is on the wrong track to capture what that value actually is. On this conception, autonomous action is one that expresses our essential self. What is the overarching conception of self that is common to our essential and our contingent selves?

One way of marking the distinction of the essential from the contingent self would be by reference to a set of valuations. Here one must distinguish between *valuing* and *desiring*. The distinction amounts to being a characterization of two different types of motivations.[3] To value anything is to hold it to be *worthy* of appreciation, desiring, or action; to desire something is merely to *want* it. It is clear that the two can clash; one can desire to do something without holding the action to be worthy of doing. Likewise, one might find oneself appreciating things that one holds are quite unworthy of appreciation (a confirmed and delicate aesthete finding to her horror that she actually likes punk rock and feeling ashamed of herself for doing so). Or one might have desires that one feels are unworthy (a fundamentalist minister finding that he has developed a fondness for the "Emmanuele" movies). The extent to which this kind of clash can put one into a quandary is well attested in everyone's everyday life and fills the waiting rooms of psychiatrists.

Since both desires and valuations can have the same objects, the felicitous state of affairs would be where both desire and value completely coincide, that is, where we both desire and value the same things. It would be a happy state, since we would only want what we believe to

I. Freedom and Autonomy

be worthy. Where the two clash, however, it is a clash within ourselves, and it is often expressed as a clash of the essential self and the contingent one (or it may be expressed as the clash between the true or real self and the false one, as when someone complains that it was not 'really' him or her that wanted to do something naughty). The compulsive smoker or gambler who wishes he were not is a person who is alienated from his own actions. People who find themselves in this quandary often see themselves as driven by motivations that are not properly their own; their essential self seems powerless to effect any change in their actions. The popular music industries from tin pan alley to country and western music have grown fat chronicling this kind of clash within people's selves.

This distinction of valuing and desiring is one interpretation of the sense of expressions such as "desires of *mine*—which are not my *own*." At first blush, this seems perhaps to be a trifle nonsensical. How is it *possible* that some desire be mine yet not my own? Nonetheless, the expression and the belief that something true is being said are common enough. How would it be possible that this common expression would be true?

First, note that "mine" and "my own" can express different things. A desire can be mine in the sense that it is ascribable to me as a self-identical being over time—what we can call our *numerical* identity—but not be mine by not being ascribable to my self—what we can call our *character* identity. Our character identity involves the ascription to ourselves of various roles and the like, whereas our numerical identity is not such a predicative matter. Second, to act out of character is also sometimes expressed as acting from something not really one's own, from motivations not part of one's self. Among all the predicates that can be ascribed to us, we will identify some set of them as constituting our essential self, who we really are. Now, what criteria could we use to distinguish our essential character from our inessential character?

Take the proverbial repentant compulsive gambler. He loves to gamble, but he wishes he did not. When asked to describe himself, he identifies him*self* with his non-gambling desires ("that's the real me"). In doing so, he dissociates himself from his compulsive desires to gamble. What is he doing? He clearly values not gambling, but nonetheless desires to gamble ("I want to go gambling, but I wish that I were not burdened with such dead-end desires"). We could take him to be ascribing some desire to himself as an identical being over time, but dissociating it from his character identity; or we could take him to be distinguishing his essential from his inessential character. The grounds of the distinction in both cases would seem to be valuational. His unsuccessful repentance is best captured by the distinction of valuing (what he holds worthy) and desiring (what he actually wants). This person is not an autonomous person. Is he even, in this respect, a free person?

Our valuational system constitutes to a large part our point of view on the world. If nothing else, our values express what we take to be the satisfying and fulfilling life, for they determine what things will in our eyes count as worthy of appreciation or action. What we identify as the essential self, as properly our own, greatly depends on this system of valuations. I have not, of course, specified how this identification is to be done, nor do I intend to suggest that the process of distinguishing what is one's essential self from one's contingent self is a fully conscious or even completely rational activity. These distinctions only demarcate an interpretive framework both for understanding the distinction of the two and for giving that distinction some intelligibility. Let us take it as giving us a preliminary determination of a sense of "freedom" (*not* "autonomy"): a free person is one who acts on the basis of motivations that are expressions of his or her essential self. Our compulsive gambler, in this sense, is not a free man.

But what if the compulsive gambler truly held that gambling was, say, the highest form of life? He would then be a free man. Would he also be autonomous? Not necessarily. Since free action is that which expresses our essential self, and the essential self is demarcated from the inessential one by a process of valuation, the capacity for freedom comes down to being a capacity for making our values effective in our lives. A free choice is one where what actually motivates one to act is consistent with what one holds to be valuable; it is a motivating act expressive of the essential self. However, a free choice need not necessarily be an autonomous choice. An autonomous choice is one in which a certain amount of reflection on those values is present. Respect for freedom is respect for those choices that express a person's essential self; respect for autonomous choice, however, would be respect for those choices that display at least a minimal amount of reflection on those values. This difference can be highlighted by noting that, on this view, being free

I. Freedom and Autonomy

would be compatible with being manipulated (which I shall without argument assume is different from being coerced). One may be manipulated into accepting a set of values, or one may be manipulated into choosing something that one otherwise might not have chosen. But surely an autonomous choice is not one that is the result of manipulation at all.

What then is the difference between freedom and autonomy? A *free* choice is one that is *mine*: it is the choice of *my* self. An *autonomous* choice, on the other hand, is one that is not only *my* choice but also involves a certain critical reflection and evaluation of those values. This can be formulated as the condition of *independence*.[4] An autonomous choice is one that is independent of external elements; this captures, I think, the idea that an autonomous choice could not be a manipulated choice. If this is true, then autonomy can be a matter of degree; one can be more or less autonomous.

An example of a free but nonetheless manipulated choice may be found in the phenomenon of entrapment, where a person who would not normally seek to do a particular wrong thing is provided an opportunity to do just that thing (and does it). This phenomenon shows, I think, that although we hold it to be valuable that people be independent, we also hold independence to be enough of an ideal so that all we can sometimes legitimately demand of people is that they be free. To hold that entrapment does not make a person responsible for something is to say perhaps that although he *should* have been autonomous enough to resist the temptation, it is assumed that the other person was wrong into manipulating him into a free but wrong choice. Our intuitions on the way in which we might not be held morally responsible for free but not autonomous choices are, however, not clear. Adolf Eichmann might be said to have done the murderous things that he did freely but not autonomously: there is little evidence that he ever reflected on what he was doing. What is, of course, demanded of people like Eichmann is that they be a bit more autonomous. One can hold a person blameworthy for not developing a greater sense of autonomy. He was free to become more independent, he did not, and he was therefore responsible for what he did. Our conceptions of what is and is not important about autonomy thus seem to be more complex than the Kantian conception would have it.

What follows if we accept this conception of autonomy? It has the important consequence that autonomy would turn out to be not so much a *condition* of moral choice (as Kantian theory has it) but a moral *ideal*. Full autonomy would be a limiting case of this ideal. A person would be fully autonomous if that person could truly say of his or her choices, "They are my own choices," in the following sense. The choices are *mine*: they are the choices of my essential self. This condition may be called (following Heidegger, Sartre, and Gerald Dworkin, among others) *authenticity*, the identification of the essential self as the locus of the choice. The condition of authenticity requires one to be able to consciously mark out who one is and is to become, and to assume full responsibility for those choices. The condition of authenticity gives us the dimension of a free choice. For a choice to be fully autonomous, a second condition is required: the choices are to be my *own*. For a choice to be one's own, one must be capable of avoiding being manipulated into making decisions because of one's ability critically to reflect on and to evaluate one's motivations. This is the condition of *independence*. A fully autonomous person would thus be one who is completely authentic and independent in their choices and in their appreciations. This gives us a conception of autonomy, thus answering our first question ("What is autonomy?"). It also begins to give us an answer to our second question ("Of what value is autonomy?"): full autonomy would be an ideal of personal development, not a condition of moral choice itself. It is most likely also an ideal to which few, if any, people attain.

The Kantian conception of autonomy thus turns out to be misguided. It is the conception of freedom, not autonomy, that depends on the distinction of the essential from the non-essential self. The autonomous self is a free self of a particular sort, namely, a reflective, independent free self. How important an ideal is autonomy? To be fully autonomous would be to be able critically to reason through all one's choices. Not being a condition of morality, the autonomous self is instead an ideal for people living within a particular cultural and social order in which such a goal of independent personal choice is valued. This ideal and its actualization, however, rest on assumptions of shared forms of life. Full autonomy is by no means a self-evident ideal. Pre-modern societies certainly did not put a great deal of emphasis on it. In Confucian China, for example, the goal of personal development was not autonomy but a

I. Freedom and Autonomy

sense of acting in accordance with the order of things (with the Tao). Not only was full autonomy not an ideal for Confucius, he would no doubt have regarded the introduction of such an ideal as something that would have been morally harmful.

The extent to which autonomy is an ideal, therefore, depends on other considerations than just what is necessary to morality. It also depends on socially construed ideals of personal development and the role that an ideal of independent choice plays within a particular kind of moral world. Hannah Arendt's thesis about the banality of evil—that the source of evil is found not so much in the demonic powers that are part of our human nature (one of the classical views of the source of evil) but rather in the human capacity to refuse to *reflect* on matters— highlights the importance of full autonomy as a moral ideal, since that ideal remains a check against the possibility of evil in a particular type of culture.[5]

One possible misconstrual of this position should be mentioned before we go any further. This conception of freedom as an expression of the essential self does not commit one to a distinction between *ideal* and real selves. There is a tradition of thought (often identified with Rousseau, often with Plato) that holds that free choices are those made by the ideal self (or the 'real' self, as it might be called). An actual choice need not be a free choice since the person choosing may be, for example, alienated from their ideal self. (The true or ideal self may not be recognized as such by the ideal self.) In many brands of Marxism, a worker who would reflectively choose to work in capitalist conditions would not be said to be making a free choice because he or she would be alienated from her true self. A real self theory, on the other hand, holds that the actual, existent self is the true self. Different conceptions of respect for free choice emerge in these two theories. In the ideal self theory, free choice is not necessarily what the person does choose but what his or her ideal self *would* choose; one need not respect, therefore, what might otherwise be seen as a free choice. Whatever the merits of an ideal self theory might be, I understand the theory of freedom and autonomy presented here to be a real self theory. A free choice is one that expresses the essential self, but that is the real, not the ideal, self. One decides what the essential self is by reference to the agent's values, but that does not make the self ideal (in this sense). An autonomous choice is one that is expressive of a reflective, free self, which again is the real, not the ideal self.

Full autonomy as an ideal of personal development—as an ideal of what is a guiding *telos* for one's life, what would be the life worth living—leads quite naturally on certain assumptions to an ideal of autonomy in the action-oriented sense of the term. If it is true that people learn to be autonomous only when they are given a wide amount of latitude in making their own choices, then the ideal of autonomy in the will-oriented sense will support the action-oriented ideal of autonomy. The best way to promote the growth of individual autonomy (the will-oriented sense) will be to allow great latitude of free action (the action-oriented sense). This of course rests on a weighty empirical assumption about how people develop into autonomous persons. This assumption is certainly not universally shared. Many Marxists, for example, reject this, holding that only in a developed communist society could full autonomy be realized. Now, this is not the only reason why one would support a right to autonomy in the action-oriented sense of the term; but it surely functions as an important support for it.

This conception of autonomy is, moreover, consistent with an understanding of moral judgments as objective. If freedom is linked with expressing one's self, then acting according to objective principles is consistent with one's freedom if one identifies with those principles. What we identify as our self will be a function in part of what values we hold. This occurs in a process of the self-ascription of both personal and role character-predicates, and this is possible only in an intersubjective world in which we participate with other agents. Any concrete argument about this will be one that turns on which kinds of roles one can identify with, which itself (as a matter of valuation) turns on arguments about what kinds of intrinsic and extrinsic goods attach to what roles. Disputes about freedom and autonomy are ultimately disputes about what form the self should take, which in turn are either linked to or are themselves disputes about the kind of social world with which one can identify. Arguments of this sort in the everyday world are the concrete echoes of the abstract arguments of philosophy; they are about possibilities, and they move from the kinds of relationships in which we encounter each other to the considerations of what specific type of social world is a condition of proper self-identification.

To answer our original questions: (1) What is autonomy of action or thought? It is the conjunction of independence and freedom. (2) How is autonomy possible? It is possible because of our capacity for reflection. (3) What is valuable about it? It is an ideal of personal development within a kind of social and cultural order. (4) What is the relation between freedom and autonomy? Autonomy is an independent free choice. Nonetheless, one question remains unanswered: Just how valuable actually is autonomy? To answer that, we need to go further.

II
Self-Identity and Social Union

The Kantian conception of morality sees autonomy as a condition of the possibility of morality itself. Yet autonomy, rather than being a condition of morality, emerges as at best a moral ideal of sorts. Would the Kantian argument perhaps work just with freedom as the condition of morality? Most likely not. If the above reconstruction of the idea of freedom is correct, then more basic than the notion of freedom is the notion of the self. However, our idea of the concrete self is a valuational and hence a social conception. In fact, our understanding of ourselves in terms of who we are and are to become is made up of these social values, roles, and so on. Kant explained the possibility of morality by recourse to a rather radical notion of freedom. Rather than seeing this kind of radical freedom as the condition of morality, I would propose that we see the possibility of morality in general as resting on a view of ourselves as co-members of a common world, of seeing each as 'one of us.' The fundamental notion in morality, therefore, is that of a reciprocal acknowledgment by a community of rational selves. On the other hand, *ethics*, as the doctrine of the *concrete* rights, duties, virtues, and ideals of personal development, rests on a unity established between people that in its most abstract form is the expression of a shared form of life.

This gives us the lineaments of a different explanation from the Kantian one. It breaks moral inquiry down into two spheres: the moral and the ethical. In particular, it gives us the possibility of explaining morality in general by appeal to an ideal community of mutually acknowledging selves and of explaining concrete ethics in terms of what I will be calling social union, rather than explaining both in terms of the Kantian metaphysics of the free will. More specifically, it explains autonomy not as an element of morality in general but as an ethical ideal of a particular form of social union. Following this distinction, I shall here be concerned not so much with moral theory (in the sense of abstract morality) as with ethical theory.

There are three items on which one can focus in ethics: the self, its actions, and the consequences of its actions. Each leads to a different kind of ethical question. Take the kinds of questions raised when one ethically focuses on the self: Is this life the best life? By acting this or that way, what kind of person am I becoming? Or consider the kinds of questions that arise from a focus on the actions themselves: Are these actions in accordance with some general rule or principle? Do they express some type of relationship to the other as a person? Finally, consider the types of ethical questions that arise from a focus on the consequences of the actions: Do they produce more rather than less good? Do they inflict costs more than they provide benefits?

It is characteristic of moral theories that they focus only on one of these elements or make one of them basic and the others derivative. Obvious examples are classical utilitarianism and deontological theories. Classical utilitarianism, for example, focuses exclusively on the consequences of the actions, determining their rightness according to whether they maximize some form of happiness. Within utilitarian theory, the elements of the self and of principle are then derivative from the more basic questions about the outcomes of actions. Deontology, on the other hand, holds that the right thing to do is determined independently of the goodness or evil of the consequences of the action. Deontology either makes the elements of the self and the outcomes of actions completely unimportant or at least allots them only a derivative status. (On some readings, Kant is the paradigm case of this view: he is taken as holding that all moral value is derivative from the will's willing in accordance with self-legislated universal law.)

Such a focus on one of the elements of ethics to the detriment of the others is, however, only a one-sided approach to things; it ignores the equally valuable aspects of the other sides. This idea, that both deontology and utilitarianism are only one-sided views of the elements of ethics, is typically associated with Hegel's views.[6] Hegel held that each of these was important on its own, and an adequate ethical theory must

II. Self-Identity and Social Union

provide some balancing of these in a way that does automatically give precedence to one at the expense of the others. However, on Hegel's view, there is no way in abstract morality to provide anything other than an arbitrary balancing of these three elements. Even if a formal balancing structure could be derived, any concrete balancing would have to come from some particular social structure or role in that structure. It was partially for that reason that Hegel came to believe that ethics must attend to the spirit of its culture to provide a balancing of these three elements and that only a doctrine of what I shall call social categories can provide the rational basis for evaluating ethical claims.

In order to develop this idea, I need to introduce some more or less Hegelian conceptions necessary for explicating the conception of ethics being used here. These will be the idea of the spirit of a culture and the idea of a common good. Together these notions will allow us to construct a conception of social union. I will argue that Kantian conceptions of autonomy are inconsistent with an adequate understanding of the common good as so conceived.

Following Hegel, we can call the interconnected set of basic ideas, ideals, and norms by which a given culture understands itself the *spirit* of that culture. This governs things like the idea of the proper relationships between men and women, the relation between subordinates and superiors, ideals of courtesy, the understood norms governing when formality is and is not appropriate, conceptions about who owes what to whom, and so on (the listing could obviously go on for quite a while). It is the spirit (in this sense) of a culture that gives content to the abstract idea of a shared form of life; these ideals and conceptions of relationship are the forms in which people acknowledge each other and establish their self-conceptions. More importantly, the spirit of a culture gives content to an idea of a common *good* for that culture.

The idea of a common good is one of the most easily misunderstood political notions. Indeed, it often seems impossible that in a liberal, pluralistic society there could be anything like a common good in any save a sparse sense (or that anyone who argues for one is on the slippery slope to authoritarianism). One might think that if there is a *common* good, then it must be a good that is the *same* (at least formally) for everyone. Classical hedonic utilitarianism is in some ways an expression of this view in that it argues that something like happiness is good for everyone. Thus, the classical utilitarians (particularly Mill) could argue (1) everyone regards happiness as a good; (2) a rational treatment of it demands that we attempt to maximize it; and (3) maximizing the common good sometimes involves the sacrifice of individual happiness for the sake of producing more overall of it. For such utilitarians, the common good is not necessarily something that is good *for* everyone, but is something that everyone regards as good. Or one might argue that there is one good that is somehow preferable or superior to all other goods. (Mill tried a version of that line too.)

None of these offer any full-bodied sense of the common good. But how would a common good that is none of the above be possible? One vehicle for explaining how this common good would be possible is the Hegelian notion of the spirit of a culture. On this view, the common good is seen as the interrelated set of various goods; the good is really just the ordering and unity of various other goods. In order to show how this conception works, I shall first consider some possible grounds for skepticism about the possibility of this kind of common good.

Skepticism about the very possibility of something like a common good comes from two quarters, which I shall call the "Kantian autonomy" and "anti-authoritarian" objections to it. These two bases of skepticism are, moreover, linked. The objection based on Kantian autonomy has two components: first, it believes in a basic, perhaps overriding right to personal liberty, which puts considerations of the common good out of bounds; and, second, it subscribes to a view of individuals as self-determining in the sense that they legislate for themselves. I shall consider the rationale of the idea of individual liberty in Section III; for now, I wish to concentrate on the idea of individuals as self-legislators.

Consider the link between freedom of choice and pluralism. Our society is ineluctably pluralistic. Now, in such a pluralistic society, individuals have different and often competing conceptions of what is good. This means, however, that there is no *common* good at all; there is only a *plurality* of (most likely) incommensurable goods. A common good would have to be one that would be common to everyone—but there is no such good (on this view) and, almost by definition, there can be none. Besides, even if there were such a common good, it would still be wrong for something like the state to make its decisions on the basis of that, because individual liberty is of such overriding importance.

II. Self-Identity and Social Union

The anti-authoritarian objection goes hand in hand with this view. Since there is no such good, it would only be by possibly draconian authoritarian political measures that such a good could even come to exist, much less be held in force. Only by the conscious suppression of pluralism could there be anything like a common good. The existence of a common good would imply at the least a homogenization of life that would only be possible through an authoritarian suppression of conditions that would spawn competing conceptions.

Let us look from a different angle at the Kantian conception of autonomy. For Kant, autonomous action was literally that: self-legislating actions, that is, those that are *auto*-nomos. To act autonomously is to act according to one's own idea of law, to be the legislator for oneself. This distinguishes autonomous action from all other sequences of naturally related causal events. All non-arbitrarily occurring events share for Kant the characteristic of being governed by laws that can be expressed in the form of rules. The essential difference between autonomous action and natural causal sequences is precisely the self-imposed nature of the rule in the case of autonomous actions. For the rule to be *self*-imposed, the self must in some sense be prior to the rule that it imposes. To the extent that the rule is imposed from without, the self is not self-legislating, that is, autonomous. The autonomous self is thus conceived as an analogue of a political community: the question is whether the laws governing the community are given to the community by itself (in which case it is self-legislating) or are imposed on it from without.

Kant drew a radical conclusion from that: the self cannot be autonomous if it acts according to rules that express means toward some pre-given end—what he called heteronomous action. Our essential self, on the Kantian view, is the rational self. Our desires, however, are not part of this rational self; they are determined by our physical and social makeup, which are contingent to us. Hence, rules that express means to the pre-given ends of desire cannot be self-imposed in the requisite sense, since they express only means to pre-given ends. The self must therefore act according to rules that do not express a means to some desired end but determine the ends themselves. Only rules that are universally rational could possibly do this. Thus, we act autonomously only when we act according to our idea of universal law, when we act as a rational agent in general would act.

What Kant clearly saw was that this idea committed one to the notion that autonomous action is taken in accordance with purely formal laws of reason. What he did not so clearly see—and what has become a common ground of dispute about his theory—is that such a view has no hope of generating content for ethical judgments.

The reason for this is Kant's failure clearly to grasp the distinction between morality and ethics. In Kantian morality, the right thing to do is identified with acting in accordance with some rule that would be valid for all rational agents in general. Unfortunately, rules of this type will always turn out to be empty; a rule that applies to *any* rational agent will not be able to generate any particular ethical content for specific people. This was the argument made by Hegel in his Berlin days against Kant.[7] In such Kantian theories, an action is moral only if the agent can self-consciously formulate a universal rule, one that is valid for him or her and for all others, and can make this the rule upon which he or she acts (that is Kantian autonomy). Since moral action is autonomous action, this makes moral action into anonymous action. What, though, is anonymous moral action? To the extent that I am capable of taking up an anonymous standpoint on my interests, I am capable of considering my own welfare from a completely impartial point of view, taking the interests of nobody in particular as my standpoint. How, though, can the universalized rule be a *good* reason for the particular agent's acting? Beyond the impartial reasons for acting that a universal rule would give him or her, the agent must also have a personal reason for acting—not merely a reason for *one* to act but for *me* to act. A "good" reason for acting must be one that the agent as an individual can find good, that expresses an agent's essential self. A consideration of a person's action that focuses only on whether it was done in accordance with a reflectively formulated impersonal rule leaves out the actor's interest in the action.[8]

Kantian morality cannot support the agent's finding some individual interest in the action unless one identifies the essential self with the rational, anonymous self. If one makes this identification, however, then one is left with an account of moral willing that cannot explain why the particular agent should prefer the anonymous concern with the welfare or rights of all over his or her own welfare, especially when that anonymous concern strongly conflicts with his or her own particular welfare.

II. Self-Identity and Social Union

At this level of moral explanation, there remains the unexplained move from the agent's rational, intentional, reflective concern with his or her own welfare to his or her concern with the welfare of all. It leaves us with the gap between the anonymous self and the particular individual.

In order to answer this objection, the logic of Kantian morality leads to the conclusion that the moral good cannot be anything but a universal rule that, if it is to be consistent with a sound theory of moral motivation, must include some reason for particular people to *want* to will this universal rule. Kantian moral theory must then postulate that the moral good *is* that universal rule that is also in the interest of the agent, as a rational agent in general, to will. It is this part of Kantian morality that leads to an empty conception of both the agent and the moral rules that it tries to promulgate. There simply are no such things as rational agents in general; a rational agent in general would have no interests, or at least none that could serve as the grounds for moral motivation.[9]

The upshot of the Kantian views of ethics and autonomy is thereby a complete dissociation of the autonomous self from its concrete ends, the objects of willing. Since the Kantian autonomous self is a self capable of acting on formal rules, no particular end is congenial to it except the purely formal one of universalizability. But even granting that the Kantian ethic might be able to generate some set of ends of action, the *autonomous* self still becomes the *anonymous* self, the self of nobody in particular—the "abstractly universal self," as Hegel might put it. The ends of action chosen by this "abstractly universal self" will be only general ones. There is really no way out of this conclusion for Kantian morality. For Kant, the object or end of an autonomous will had to be determined by the will itself, and it had to be internally linked to the act of willing; the object of autonomous willing could not be just any arbitrarily chosen object. A view of autonomy that sees it as self-legislation, as prescribing rules for itself, must see the object of the autonomous will as the rule itself—and only a very abstract rule will then suffice. Simply free willing itself (acting according to universalizable rules) becomes the moral good, and the common good can at best be conceived only in utilitarian terms.

The Kantian conception of autonomy rests on a very thin theory of the self.[10] What is morally important about the Kantian self is its capacity for autonomy, but this can yield no determinate moral content for the concrete self to choose. This view of moral personality is, as it were, a juristic one. The actual makeup of the self is not important, nor are any particular facts about it; it is the anonymous, "universal" self that is important from the moral point of view. The self is prior to its ends but has no content on its own. In versions of this conception of the autonomous self such as those offered by Sartre, this self ends up being called exactly what it in principle is: nothingness. It becomes equivalent to mere agency (assuming that to be a coherent notion). Indeed, Sartre's self is just the Kantian self deprived of its only redeeming quality, the capacity to give itself rules.

The Kantian argument seems to presuppose two things. First, in a rather juristic fashion (of a positivist stripe) it assumes that moral obligation can exist only where there is some rule specifying the obligation. Second, it assumes that if the will is to be free, it must choose the rule that fixes the obligation. (If the rule has its obligatory force outside of its being chosen, the will cannot be free. In fact, this seems to be one of the basic presuppositions of this view.)

Such a view of the moral self has difficulty explaining the possibility of real moral choice because it cannot supply the self with any direction. Instead, we are left only with the model of a self *choosing* to legislate a rule to guide its action. An adequate phenomenology of our real moral life, though, shows that our values are not simply *chosen* by us; the moral authority of some things is not dependent on their being voluntarily assumed.[11] This is the case with many role responsibilities. A father has an obligation to look after the welfare of his child because he is a parent, not because he chooses to look after the welfare of the child. The physician has many obligations to her patients, not because she chooses these obligations, but because she is a physician and they are her patients. It is also true of a great many other moral values that are not rolebound *per se*. Gratuitously insulting a person is wrong not because you or I have chosen for it to be wrong but because it *is* wrong. (We often loosely speak of "society's choosing" certain values, but that is simply a loose way of speaking of the values as not necessarily holding for all societies. For an innumerable set of ethical values, there is no real 'choice' that occurs in society at large to make them such values—no primordial societal 'vote' ever put insults on the list on don'ts.) But this cannot be the case for the Kantian conception of the moral self. If the

II. Self-Identity and Social Union 23

freedom of the self is seen as its capacity to give itself rules, then any end that is not determined by the rule undermines the freedom of the agent. The priority of the empty abstract self over its ends is necessitated by Kant's view of the self as free in its self-legislation.

This is not, of course, a disproof of Kantian theory, nor is it intended as such. The value of any philosophical conception lies in its explanatory capacity. Often the best that we can do is simply offer up an alternative and see where it takes us, assessing both alternatives in light of their overall capacity to explain the possibility of the phenomena in question. (It is of course impossible to take up at one time all of the different directions that an alternative explanation might take us. Sometimes the full ramifications of what might appear at first to be a better explanation only appear much further down the road.)

Let us consider an alternative model. Since the Kantian model puts the self prior to its ends, we can as an alternative try putting the ends prior to the self. This would conceive the self's freedom not in terms of the model of self-*legislation* but in terms of its choosing the proper *objects* of the will. Freedom would then consist in the person's being motivated to choose certain types of objects. If it works, this alternative would provide a "thicker" conception of the moral self than is found in the rather austere Kantian conception of the self.

This different model of freedom is similar to the view put forth by Hegel. One of the reasons that Hegel had for proposing such a view is the very paucity of the Kantian conception of the self. Kant's view of the rational self puts it prior to all ends (except its own free willing), essentially outside of all contexts. Content ultimately comes from sensibility, but the morality of universalization and freedom cannot on its own supply us with any specific duties or goods. On the Hegelian view, in order to supply such content, we must appeal to the mores and ethos of our culture—to its spirit, in Hegel's terms. One can take Hegel's distinction of ethos and spirit in the following way.[12] The *ethos* of a culture includes its moral ideals, its ideals of character, of proper behavior, of human relationships, of legitimate aspirations, and so on. The *spirit* of a culture, on the other hand, philosophically explains the ethos. The spirit of a culture consists of the interconnections of those ideals in terms of its more basic principles and values. The spirit can remain the same while the ethos of a culture changes. The concept of 'spirit' here plays an explanatory role: it explains the multifarious aspects of an ethos by reference to fewer, more abstract ideals. The relation between spirit and ethos can take several possible forms. In some cases, one would explain certain changes in the ethos of a culture by reference to changes in its spirit. Or one could explain a change in the ethos of a culture by reference to a felt incoherence in its ethos in light of some underlying principle of its spirit. (One might, for example, explain a changing ethos of relations between men and women by appeal to the importance of the principle of equality in the spirit of our culture.) Content for willing ultimately comes from the spirit of a culture as it is embodied in its ethos, ultimately in what can be called social *categories*. These are the basic forms of unity between individuals in that culture; they explain how it would be possible that such and such principles of the ethos of a culture embody its spirit.

This view carries with it a deeper supposition about the source of moral principles. The supposition has two parts, a negative one and a positive one. The negative part is a rejection of any kind of foundationalist view of ethics, of which Kant's theory is a prime example. The Kantian view sees ethics as a hierarchical structure of very general principles gradually yielding more particular principles through some process like deduction. Thus, Kantians typically see the relation of moral principle to concrete situation as one of general principle to instance. "Honor thy parents" becomes seen as simply a specific version of "respect all persons" with some factual content about mommy and daddy thrown in. On the non-foundationalist view, as one moves to the particular cases, one finds new principles that are not mere instances of more prior, very general principles but are genuinely new principles on their own.

The phenomenology of the lived moral life supports this non-hierarchical conception. Consider how often the determination of what will count as a specification of a given end is not the mere application of a more general principle but an act involving a certain amount of imagination. What makes a "good marriage"? What constitutes being "true to your friends" (when do you take their side, when do you not)? How does a professional show respect to the wishes of his or her client? Even the simple utilitarian injunction to maximize happiness requires not merely a calculation as to the best means to do this but also a specification of what counts as happiness. Deciding Tuesday evening to

II. Self-Identity and Social Union

watch more television instead of reading more passages from the *Philosophy of Right* may be justified, but the decision is not well construed as just a specific instance of the injunction "maximize happiness." The fact that the answers to questions such as "How do I as a physician respect the autonomy of my patients?" *may* be taken as specifications of more general principles does not in fact make them merely derivative or less fundamental. Their specification requires what has been called the moral imagination—and moral imagination belongs not to the rational agent in general but to an embodied self in a particular culture.

The positive part of the view is the supposition that these more determinate principles have their source in the types of relationships that people bear to each other and that one can only discover these principles by attending to these types of relationships. It is these concrete principles that I shall call *ethical*. Acceptance of the negative and positive theses would suggest a typology and ordering of principles in something like the following way. Those general claims that others have on us and we have on others constitute a sphere of abstract principles of morality; it is a sphere that is common to all types of relationship, or, as it might be put, to abstract relations between moral persons, not concrete relationships between people. At this level, we could speak of only the most general moral principles holding, such as the principle of respect for persons or that enjoining us to avoid injuring persons; these principles hold for both institutions and individuals. The natural moral duties are more specific, being the kinds of duties we could universalize, duties that we as individuals (as subjects, moral agents) owe to the world at large, such as the duty not to be cruel. Our concrete ethical duties—such as those involved in being a parent, a teacher, a friend, a business associate—are derived from the concrete types of relationships in which we find ourselves. Only these concrete types of relationships would be capable of supplying us with specific objects of the will—with, that is, the concrete duties, rights, virtues, and ideals. Social *categories* explain the possibility of how the basic ideals and principles of a culture (its spirit) can be embodied in its basic forms of social union.

The term itself, "social union," is taken from Rawls.[13] I use it if for no other reason than to avoid all the connotations of the already overworked notion of 'community.' Nonetheless, there are important differences between the view of social unions expressed here and those expressed by Rawls. Moreover, it is not at all clear that Rawls's claims about social union are in fact supportable within his own theory. He says that, in social unions, we value others for their own sake, not as a means to some end. (For Rawls, that distinguishes social unions from arrangements of what he calls private society, where the only glue, as it were, that binds people together is the belief on the part of each that such arrangements best further their own private interests.) Rawls ascribes three vital features to social union. First, social unions are practically necessary because each of us cannot realize all of our own potential, much less all of the potential of humanity at large; to the extent that we value such realizations, we must rely on others to realize some or most of them. Second, in social unions there is a common point of view. (In Rawls's scheme, that is constituted by the system of the principles of justice.) Third, in social unions, there is a common end. (Again, in Rawls scheme, that consists of promoting a just constitutional order in which complementary plans of life can coexist. Rawls calls, incidentally, this relation to each other "civic friendship.")[14]

He illustrates the idea of a common end by an analogy with games. The common end shared by the players of a game is (ideally) that the game be well played; each player is thus necessary if this intrinsic good of a well-played game is to be achieved. Consider a simple, two-person game like, for example, chess and what it might be rational to do in that game.[15] One might play the game solely for some reward for winning the game; the reward would be a good extrinsic to the game. If that were all there were to it, it would be rational for a player to cheat in the game. Even if prudential considerations convinced one that cheating was irrational, it would still not be intrinsically but only situationally irrational to do so. However, if one's end is the intrinsic good of a well-played game, then it would be irrational to cheat, since that would detract from the goodness of the game. (Playing a game to win is, of course, not necessarily equivalent to playing a game for a reward. One can, for example, play a game to win without having a desire to win; one could play to win because one would believe that doing so makes the game better, not because one necessarily cares whether one wins or loses.)

Let us take this idea of an intrinsic and extrinsic good of the game a bit further. Just how important is the other person in the game? Are the other people intrinsic or extrinsic goods in the context of the well-played game? It would seem that they turn out to be only extrinsic goods. We do not value the others for their own sake; rather, we are related extrinsically to them in order to achieve the intrinsic good of the game. It is because of the intrinsic good of the *game* that our relation to others comes about; the others remain simply means to achieving the intrinsic good of the well-played game. They are not "valued for their own sake"; they are valued as means to an end. If I told you that I associated with you only because I needed a good partner in squash, you would hardly feel that you were being valued purely for your own sake. Generalize games to social practices. At best, people might value the social union itself for *its* own sake and people in it derivatively, as necessary components of the union. The Rawlsian view of social union thus falls short of Rawls's claims for it, that in it we value others for their own sake.

Is this all there is to social unions? In some social unions the self-understanding and character-identity of individuals is often *constituted* by their membership in such unions. The union is then not merely a good that the individuals may share but also defines to a large extent *who* they are; it establishes a sense of *shared* identity. The basic types of social union in a culture (its social categories) do exactly that: they define the types of (valued) people in that culture. Whereas some social unions may give rise to various roles and the things that go with such roles, the basic social unions provide roles in which are embedded the ideals of the self for that culture. To understand those social unions is to understand those ideals and vice versa. Only within social unions do we have *ethics* and not just *morality*. It is in social union that the thicker conception of the self emerges: in it we have, along with the set of rights, duties, and permissions, the nexus of ideals of human flourishing, of what is the proper life in that context. That is, in these social unions we have not merely ideals of the person but also of personality.

In such unions we find these ideals of personality expressed as the virtues. It is helpful to distinguish between virtue as a general concept and the virtues as more specific traits of character. In its general sense, virtue is the capacity to exercise correct ethical *judgment*. A person with virtue is capable of recognizing the ethical requirements of a situation and making a judgment as to what behavior is appropriate. (Non-ethical virtues are the same, except that the requirements of the situation are not ethical ones.) It is thus impossible to break down virtue into a series of rules, however tempting that might be to many ethical theorists.[16] Even Kant, who certainly displayed a propensity for rendering an ethical system into a system of rules, recognized that the application of the rules requires judgment, which cannot be itself reduced to further rules.[17] (If there were a rule for applying the rule, then one would need another rule for applying that rule, *ad infinitum.*) Virtue in general is then just that capacity to discern what is ethically required of one in a situation.[18] The virtues (in the plural), on the other hand, are those acquired traits of character—such as patience, gratitude, humility—that over time people with virtue have come to see as being close to indispensable propensities that a person who wishes to be virtuous—to have virtue in the general sense—must have. Any list of the virtues will then necessarily be historical in character. Moreover, it would be impossible to make a systematic list of the virtues by deriving them all from some first principle. (Note too how it takes a virtuous person to know how to practice the virtues; patience is a virtue, but it takes an act of judgment to know when enough is enough and patience is no longer called for.)

This account of the virtues differs from one that defines the virtues as propensities to follow certain moral rules. That view makes the determination of the virtues completely secondary to the prior determination of these rules. Such a view has its advantages. It has the plausibility of making the virtues into conditions of the realization of moral rules. (One must postulate a propensity to follow those rules in order for them to have any effect.) It also has the virtue (as it were) of ordering an account of the virtues nicely into a unitary theory. (First determine what your rules and principles are; then your list of the virtues follows automatically from that.) Unfortunately, it has the vice of being most likely a false account of the virtues. Integrity, for example, as a virtue cannot be nicely correlated with any moral rule, without a lot of pushing and shoving going on around the edges. The same holds for the virtue of patience. With other virtues that could be classified as moral ones, the correlation is easier to make, but by and large this is just for historical reasons. Such virtues would more naturally be the ones that virtuous people have recognized as being traits of character helpful to the making of correct ethical judgment in a variety of different situations.

One possible objection should be met before we go further. Does a view of social unions as sources of our concrete ethical duties, rights,

II. Self-Identity and Social Union

and virtues leave us with no means of criticizing any form of social union? At least three modes of criticizing and critiquing social unions exist. First, we can criticize their coherence with each other. The young Marx did this when he tried to cast doubt on the idea that in bourgeois society one could consistently be the private citizen acting out of self-interest as the market required and also be the altruistic citizen in political matters that the liberal state required. Second, we can criticize them from the standpoint of the spirit of a culture. Third, we might criticize them from the standpoint of abstract morality (although this would generally be effective only in cases where some gross violation of moral principle is occurring).

Thus, we need not be compelled by this account to at least one form of radical relativism. We need not claim that whatever a culture approves (slavery, degradation of some unfavored groups) is for that culture justified, provided only that it is internally coherent and consistent with the spirit of that culture. An analogy will perhaps show this. What may count as a reason at earlier point in time need not count as a reason later. Prior to, say, Einstein's theories, it would have been rational for physicists to accept Newton's theories as the best ones, and it would certainly not have been amiss for them to have failed to take Einsteinian objections into account. However, after Einstein's theories have been introduced on the scene, it would be unjustified in any defense of Newtonian theory to ignore the Einsteinian objections—not that such objection cannot then be met, nor that Newtonian physics becomes thereafter indefensible, but only that a new set of reasons (the Einsteinian ones) now play an essential role in the debate. So in ethics: the rise and demonstrated practicability of new ideals and new challenges to older, accepted norms does not *ipso facto* invalidate these older ideals and norms, but it does mean that advocates of the old order must now, if they are rationally to defend their views, show how these reasons are mistaken or not compelling. Now of course if one denied that there are ever new reasons or new evidence in morals, one could deny all of this. That would mean that one would also have to deny that there is ever conceptual innovation in morals, and that does not seem to be an entirely plausible claim. The new ideals that the major religions of the world introduced into their respective cultures would be examples of conceptual innovations in morals. The modern ideal of equality is another. Not that there have been many such innovations, nor that we have made much progress in morals: only that what counts as an admissible element in moral debate has changed, and where there is change, there is the possibility of rational criticism of it.

Ethical inquiry is thus tied to the spirit and ethos of its times. The delineation of the ethos of a culture is an interpretive, descriptive enterprise; the delineation of its spirit is more of a critical, explanatory enterprise, since such a delineation consists in the construction of the principles and ideals that justify and explain the ethos. Social categories supply the explanatory means by which one moves from spirit to ethos, in the sense that they are construed to be the social unions in which spirit, as it were, finds its embodiment. Since the self is constituted in part by the social unions of which it is a member, the concrete ethical person is one who pursues certain ideals, sees his or her duties and takes his or her aspirations from within the ethos and spirit of his or her culture. Any defensible notion of the common good will then be one that is based in some interpretation and reconstruction of this spirit of a culture. It will not be a good that is homogeneous nor one that is in an egoistic sense necessarily equally to everyone's advantage. It would be a unity of the various goods embodied in the fundamental social unions of that culture. What is *common* in this good is that it is constructed of the various ideals of the spirit of the culture; it is composed of the goods that go to constitute the various senses of self-identity that individual members of the culture have.[19]

This should not be taken as the view that in any social order there will be one single coherent conception of the good shared by all in that society. Such a view is probably factually false. It is all the more likely that what is taken to be the common good will be a complex of ideas, not all of which are perhaps consistent with each other. After all, not all the values that an individual may hold are in fact compatible with each other. There is no reason, outside of a rather rosy view of the world, to believe that the common good would be any different. Determining what the common good is often involves theorizing about what kinds of goods (among the many that are available) are in fact compatible with each other. The common good will consist in part of an ordering of those various goods in terms of priority and compatibility. It will also consist in a sense of shared ends, of shared self-identity. The choices

II. Self-Identity and Social Union

about this ordering and compatibility of goods will therefore also be to some extent choices about who we are to be.

This is not a denial of pluralism. A self-consciously pluralistic society will be one in which one of the goods will be the multiplicity of heterogeneous goods available. That is, it will be held to be objectively better for there to be more goods of a different type than fewer goods (or only goods of the same type) available. Nor is it being claimed here that there is a single homogeneous concept of good that is being maximized, nor are the concepts of rightness being defined completely independently of the good. Rather it is a theory of the proper objects of the will—of the valuations that go to constitute our sense of self-identity—as concretely embodied in the various kinds of social unions. The principles of ethics are discovered by reconstructing them out of these social unions. The very general principle of respect for persons is bound up with the still abstract notion of a moral community as consisting of entities acknowledging each other as 'one of us.' An *ethical* ideal such as autonomy, however, requires the ideal of *reflective* agency as one of the basic valuations of the culture. It requires that we think of ourselves as better people to the extent that we become more autonomous.

While the claims of abstract morality might enjoin us from certain very general actions (such as it being by and large wrong intentionally to harm innocent people), such claims do not take us very far. They will not even get us to the still very general principle of respect for autonomy, unless one establishes some ranking of valuations as objects of the will, as self-definitions. Even the autonomous self turns out to be a socially defined self, if only on a different level (a level that says it is a value to reflect on one's values and choose them according to certain procedures). To move from the principles of abstract morality to even very general principles like the value of autonomy requires a conception of goods and their ranking, and this comes from critical reflection on the ethos of one's culture, done in terms of its spirit. This requires a balancing of the principles of rightness, goodness, and virtue in terms of some theory of social unions, and this latter theory is one in terms of how these unions hang together, of the fit of the unions ultimately with the spirit of one's culture.

One of the theses I will be arguing is that there need be no inherent contradiction between a respect for autonomy and a pursuit of the common good in a democratic liberal form of social union. To show this, however, will require some demonstration that there is a set of shared self-understandings common to democratic liberal culture. One of the ideas held in common among many critics and defenders of democratic liberalism is that democratic liberal societies are so pluralistic that no shared self-understandings are possible within them. I think that this is a flawed understanding of democratic liberalism, and I hope to show that it is so.

III
Respect for Persons and Respect for Choices

There is a long tradition in ethical theory—particularly in liberal political and ethical theory—that identifies respect for persons (often identified as respect for something like their inherent dignity) with respect for their autonomy or their capacity for choice. Kant, for example, completely identified the two: the dignity of individuals consisted of their capacity to be self-legislating (autonomous) beings. Respect for the dignity of persons thus became equivalent in Kantian theory to respect for this capacity for autonomous choice.[20] It is but a short step to move from claiming that respecting persons involves respecting the capacity for autonomous choice to the claim that respecting persons involves respecting the actual choices that people make. The Kantian notion of autonomous choice is, after all, restricted to moral choice. Kant did not seem to consider that ordinary everyday non-moral choices could be classified as autonomous at all. Yet this seems false. To the extent that autonomous choice involves setting one's own ends, it seems that we do this in everyday life as much as we do in morals. We fret over whether a job is the correct one for us. We reflectively refuse to give consent to certain forms of medical treatment. After careful thought, we decide to buy our children a pet cat (or dog or fish or whatever). We decide that some value (following fashion, going to the 'in' restaurant) is not for us. All these choices are non-moral in character. However, they certainly seem to be at least as autonomous as, say, pointing out to the waitress that she gave us five dollars too much in change or helping the man at the department store door with all the packages in his arms (both things involving, respectively, avoiding stealing and the duty to provide aid). Because the

III. Respect for Persons and Respect for Choices

realm of autonomous choice seems to be wider than just that of moral choice, it is natural to conclude that respect for autonomy involves respect for the capacity for moderately reflective free choice itself, not just moral choice. Those who follow in the footsteps of the Kantian philosophy are indeed prone to do this; some go further and argue that respect for persons is equivalent to respecting their choices.[21]

However, the two concepts—the dignity of persons and their capacity for choice—are not the same, nor are the corresponding ethical principles—respect for persons and respect for choices—the same. The language that Kant chooses to express what is usually taken to be his basic principle—treat people as ends and never merely as means—captures this basic confusion. What does it mean to treat someone as an end? Or merely as a means? One plausible reading of this Kantian dictum is that to use someone merely as a means is to use them in a fashion to which they could not in principle consent.[22] That is, treating someone as an end implies in some sense treating them in ways in which their (at least possible) choices are respected. Something like this certainly seems to be Kant's view when he says that to regard persons as ends is to regard them "only as a being who must themselves be able to share in the end of the very same action."[23]

At first, this looks promising. Who wants to be used merely as a means? "Being used merely as a means," however, has a special sense in Kantian theory. It refers not to things to which one actually consents but to things to which one would "in principle" consent. This way of taking this basic Kantian injunction is made more plausible if we think, as Kant apparently did, that respect for dignity is equivalent to respect for the capacity for autonomous choice. That would at least make the rationale for respecting consent clear, since it involves such choice. But is what is wrong with insulting someone only that people (except under very odd circumstances) do not generally rationally consent to being insulted? Is it even true that never *in principle* would we rationally consent to such a thing? This special sense of using a person as a means does not fit entirely well with more ordinary considerations of what we mean when we say of someone that they are wronging another. There are a whole variety of ways to wrong persons that cannot be said to be using them as a means, except in an extended sense of the term. One can humiliate another, pay no attention to their needs, hurt their feelings, or (sometimes what is most devastating) just ignore them. This list is by no means exhaustive. The columns in the newspapers that give advice to the lovelorn are full of complaints from spouses about how their mates either do not listen to what they say or denigrate their opinions. In each of these cases, one is showing disrespect for a person, but one is not necessarily using them as a means. It is therefore certainly not self-evident that one may completely identify the two as Kant did. But is it even plausible? The key lies in the Kantian identification of respect for the dignity of individuals with respect for their autonomous choices.

Why would we value respect for autonomous choice at all? The Kantian answer is that what is valuable about persons is the capacity for autonomous choice. Without this capacity, presumably, persons are not valuable (or at least not valuable in the same way). Thus, not respecting autonomy is equivalent to not respecting people. Respect for the capacity for autonomous choice plays over into respect for the autonomous choices that are made.

Another answer involves an appeal to the inherent human *dignity* of individuals. Kantians argue that failure to respect autonomous choices of individuals does not respect their dignity, since the dignity of an individual consists in his or her capacity for autonomous choice. But why should we identify the dignity of individuals with their capacity for autonomous choice? Dignity is a feature of people as they *are*. It is a feature of them only in part because of what they do or *can* do.[24] A handicapped person may possess great dignity but be incapable of doing many things, physical or mental. Likewise, most cultures acknowledge that children up to a certain age are incapable of many things which much traditional philosophy regards as absolutely essential to the concept of human agency (or "rational" agency, or "moral" agency)—for example, fully autonomous choice, 'higher' feelings, responsibility for one's actions, and so on. It nonetheless makes sense to speak of treating children in dignified ways. Dignity is a quality of individual people; it expresses the kind of value that people have as being people. Likewise, treating with dignity is a type of behavior that is responsive to a person's value. I shall use "dignity" not as an explanation of why people have value but simply as denoting that feature of people that constitutes their value. (I am not presupposing that this feature consists of one item; it may be a set of items that together jointly constitute the value of persons.)

III. Respect for Persons and Respect for Choices

Even when persons fall completely out of the range of what much traditional philosophy thought to be essential to 'personhood' (when they are, for example, severely or profoundly retarded or in a coma), there remain ways in which one can treat them with the dignity commensurate to them or fail to do so. Using a comatose person as an object of public merriment, or as a public bulletin board for hanging notices would be, I take it, an unpardonable affront to their dignity, although only in a far-fetched way an affront to their capacity for choice. Consider the question of whether irretrievably comatose people should be used for medical research. Some would want to cast this in terms of a debate about autonomy or respect for choice. It is asked, "*Would* the person have consented—given what we know of their patterns of choice and values et cetera?" This would be a false turn in the debate. What if the person actually said at some time before going into the coma (and it was consistent with his patterns of choice and values), "It is all right with me if you experiment on me while I am irretrievably comatose; and it is also all right with me if you dress me in a clown suit and parade me around town, use me a punching bag for aspiring boxers, and pin notices about yard sales on me." Would we seriously say that we may pin notices on him, *simply* because the person gave consent? Even if we did, it would, I think, still seem much more problematic than experimenting on him. Bizarre examples like this do not, of course, prove anything; they do at least indicate, though, that appeal to choice or autonomy is not the basic thing that is at issue here; it is a matter of something deeper. There are a variety of things that perhaps ought not be allowed even if the person would have consented. Slavery, for example, is now believed to be so wrong that it is impermissible to allow a person to become a slave, whatever the status of their consent in the matter.

We can explain the different responses to the examples of children, mentally retarded adults, and comatose individuals by distinguishing respect for persons (or respect for "dignity") from respect for choice (or for "autonomy"). But what is this "dignity" that one respects (and why respect it)? I think that it has something to do with recognizing other persons as 'one of us.' Our own consciousness of self—and consequently our ability to form views of the world, and even to become autonomous beings—is constituted in the reciprocal awareness of others as self-conscious entities like ourselves. It is this capacity for self-consciousness and the inclusion of others as co-members of a common world that is the basis for recognizing the dignity of others. The dignity of a person is the value that this person has by virtue of being a self, an 'I,' which is a self formed in a social setting. The constitution of the self is accomplished in part by our organization of a world of values. It is as choosers of value that we come to recognize ourselves as also of value, and the acknowledgment of others as one of us is an acknowledgment of our shared value. In this respect, we see the comatose as remaining 'one of us,' even though they are no longer the active members of the moral world that we are; they must nonetheless be treated with the dignity commensurate to them. Their value comes not from their autonomy but from their being 'one of us,' even as they begin to slip away from us.[25]

A sense of personal dignity appears in the consciousness of individuals as a sense of self-respect. Self-respect is in large part the belief that one is worthy of respect from others—but not just any others. It must come from others who are themselves capable of respect for one (respect from one's loyal beagle does not therefore count). To be capable of respecting another is, however, to be capable of respecting oneself (to believe that one is also worthy of respect). Thus, the acknowledgment of others as worthy of respect is also implicitly an acknowledgment of one's own value as being the kind of entity that is capable of respecting others. To respect others is to believe that, because a person is 'one of us,' they are worthy of respect in terms of the value of being what they are, not necessarily in terms of what they do. The principle of respect for persons rests on the belief that entities capable of this type of mutual acknowledgment are of great—in Kantian terms, "immeasurable"—value. What is valuable about persons is the capacity to form the moral community of persons, which also implies the capacity to form ethical communities. This might seem to presuppose the capacity for choice, and thus to presuppose the Kantian view (that it is the capacity for autonomy that satisfies the conditions for being that valuable feature of people, possession of which deserves respect). However, the capacity for choice itself is possible only under the presupposition of the set of values that enables it; the capacity for choice, that is, presupposes the social unions that go to partially constitute an individual's sense of identity.

It is the character of self-consciousness that itself is possible only under the presupposition of a community of other similar self-conscious entities that explains how morality could be possible. The capacity to be

III. Respect for Persons and Respect for Choices 37

'one of us' (to be a self that is conscious of itself only in a community of others like itself) is the trait possessed by those entities that may stand in moral relationships with each other. It is also the capacity that elicits respect.[26] This ideal is part of abstract morality; it is something that is held in common by all people. But its concrete form is ethical; it depends on the types of social union in which it is embedded. In its concrete form, it assumes the idea of 'one of us' as belonging to a particular unity of people. It is noteworthy that much past and present rhetoric that would deny any moral status to another person or group of people tries to create the impression that they could not be one of us under any description. The rhetoric of hate almost always focuses on trying to depersonalize and dehumanize the object of the hate.[27]

The ideal of self-respect captures more than any other notion what is expressed in the common appeal to respect the dignity of others. Self-respect is the belief that one is *worthy* of respect from others. It is a belief in one's worthiness of certain kinds of treatment from others—a belief that some things ought not to be done to you because they are degrading or humiliating, or a belief that you have a right to certain things or to certain types of treatment that others must respect. It is not equivalent to self-esteem. The latter is a comparative idea vis-à-vis other people or vis-à-vis some ideal of one's own capacities. One may have low self-esteem in some areas—with regard to one's talents in playing the piano, for example, in comparison with Artur Schnabel's talents in the same area—but that need not affect one's self-respect, which is not a comparative notion. In social life there is often a struggle from those who have been deprived of self-respect for an acknowledgment from others that they too are equally worthy. This struggle over acknowledgment is a struggle over self-respect; this struggle can only reach equilibrium when equality of self-respect emerges as the outcome. The historical growth of belief in the ideal of equality is no doubt part of the inherent tendency (the 'dialectic,' as it were) of the ongoing claims to full acknowledgment that we make on each other.

What constitutes respect for the dignity of someone cannot be enumerated *a priori*; any enumeration of what constitutes respecting another person will depend on specific conceptions of what is an appropriate response to someone. We show respect for a person when our response is fitting to the value they have as persons. What will be fitting will, of course, depend on the social and cultural context in question. This idea of respect for dignity in the abstract, however, will help us sort out some ideas about distributive justice.

IV
Distributive Justice and Social Union

It is unclear what the demands of justice are. I shall take "justice" in its most generic sense as meaning "to each according to what is due them." Even in this most abstract formulation of it, it is unclear if this is all that justice requires. Does it, for example, not only demand that each *receive* his or her due but also that each *contribute* something (as evidenced in Marx's phrase "*From* each according to ability, *to* each according to need"; or is the element of contribution to be narrowed, as in Nozick's libertarian "From each as they choose, to each as they are chosen")? Nonetheless, I shall abide for the moment with the concept of justice as "each receiving his or her due" and return later to the issue of what the claims of justice may demand of people.

There are various types of justice, depending on what kind of thing is at stake. There is, for example, *distributive* justice, concerned with questions about who gets what in relation to certain social goods. By a "social good," I mean a good that it is in a society's power to distribute —this definition leaves open questions as to whether something that is in society's power to distribute ought in fact to be distributed at all. (Questions about the approaching possibilities of genetic manipulation make this an especially lively issue.) *Retributive* justice applies to those cases where some form of punishment is due a person because of crimes committed by that person. Finally, there are also matters of *compensatory* justice, where one must make good, must compensate a person for a violation of some other type of justice.[28]

I shall be concerned here, however, only with problems of distributive justice. These are basically problems about deciding who gets what and on what basis. Issues of distributive justice involve three elements: (1) persons; (2) their features (including not only natural ones such as their physical traits, but also socially acquired ones and even perhaps their intelligence and character); and (3) the benefits and burdens over whose distribution a society can if it chooses exercise some control. The

IV. Distributive Justice and Social Union

principles of distributive justice decide how in general we distribute which benefits and burdens to which people. Presumably this will have something to do with the various features that people have, although it need not necessarily be the case. A society might, for example, distribute all its basic burdens and benefits by some kind of huge lottery, ignoring whatever features people might happen to possess and making possession of any burden or benefit purely a matter of luck. This is not, however, an especially appealing criterion for what I take to be obvious reasons. In any event, it could hardly be called a *just* distribution. A more ordinary and appealing notion would be some general principle that linked persons to benefits or burdens by virtue of some feature or use of their features.

One plausible candidate for such a principle would be that of *desert*. Crucial to the concept of desert is the idea that to deserve something, one must be *worthy* of it. Morally to deserve something is to be morally worthy of it.[29] Desert is different from *entitlement*. To be entitled to something is to have some feature specified by an accepted rule or principle that gives one a claim to (or over) something. Desert is fundamentally tied up with the idea of worthiness, whereas entitlement is a matter of some socially determined rule. One can be entitled to something without deserving it, and one can deserve something without being entitled to it. Sam Rascal is an unsavory, unprincipled boozer who outbids you for the house that you wanted (and that he does not really appreciate). He does it with money left to him by a pious grandmother who never lived to see what a scalawag her grandson turned out to be, and who would surely have taken her riches with her to the grave had she known. Mr. Rascal certainly does not deserve the house, but he is entitled to it. A principled, clever, and honest political candidate might perhaps be said to be deserving of office but, by losing the election to his unscrupulous opponent, fail to be entitled to the office. Neither Catherine Deneuve nor Cary Grant deserve their good looks, but they are certainly entitled to them. Entitlement in general is a matter of luck; it consists in having those characteristics that society selects as giving one claims to social goods. Desert is never a matter of luck but of worthiness.

One possible principle of distributive justice might then be "To each as they deserve." This is certainly to many an appealing idea. It plays a major role, for example, in much Christian thought, where it is held

that, after the day of judgment, the deserving will receive the happiness that is their due. In more secular terms, the idea of desert may play a role in judging the justice of some kinds of social arrangements. Consider a type of politically conservative argument to the effect that the justice of a free market system with the proper safeguards consists in its tendency to reward the virtuous and, if not actually punish the wicked, at least deny them the goods that properly accrue to the virtuous. That argument links some considerations of capitalist virtues (such as industriousness, entrepreneurial bent, risk taking, thriftiness, and the like) with beliefs that the free market rewards precisely those virtues and withholds its blessings, as it were, from the lazy, the indolent, and the irredeemable goof-offs.

Despite the *prima facie* appeal of making desert the criterion of justice, on reflection it is not at all clear that it can in fact play this role. A powerful argument to this effect has been offered by John Rawls.[30] Rawls argues that only entitlements and not desert play an essential role in questions of distributive justice. In a just society, our entitlements boil down to our legitimate expectations of certain benefits and burdens that the rules of our society say that we may expect to receive through the use of our features. The legitimacy of the expectations is broadly determined for Rawls by his two principles of justice. His argument for replacing desert with entitlement is that many of our features are not themselves deserved (we acquire them by luck), and since we do not deserve these features, we cannot be said to deserve any benefits or burdens that follow from the exercise or possession of these features. Many of our features come to us by winning or losing in the various metaphorical lotteries of life. One can win or lose in three different lotteries of this type. First, there is the natural lottery. One can be born with handicaps or with advantageous traits; that is a matter of luck, certainly not of one's own choosing. One can win or lose in the social lottery by being born in fortunate or impoverished circumstances. And one can win or lose in the cultural lottery by being born and raised in an ethnic or cultural environment that encourages some traits that are valued highly or lowly in the world in which one lives.

Rawls's argument rests then on two points: (1) winning or losing in these metaphorical lotteries is only a matter of luck; (2) what counts as advantageous or disadvantageous will to a large extent be a matter of

IV. Distributive Justice and Social Union 41

social convention and therefore also of luck. A hunter-gatherer society may reward the fleet of foot while discouraging the loquacious. An industrial society such as the contemporary U.S.A. may not greatly reward the fleet of foot (unless they happen to be carrying a football under their arm) but may bestow great rewards upon the loquacious (witness the salaries that many lawyers get). Even a certain tenaciousness of character that enables one to develop one's capacities or make the most out of one's perhaps limited lot may also to an overwhelming extent be a matter of luck. Robert Coles in his series of books, *Children of Crisis*, details how children of certain kinds of impoverished backgrounds often internalize at a very early age a sense of defeat, a sense that there is no point in even trying, since they believe the odds to be stacked against them.[31] It is bad luck that put them there in the first place. They no more deserve to be there than those children of the fortunate who at an early stage internalize a sense of accomplishment, of limitless possibility. Of course, individuals may lose in some aspects of some lotteries and win in some aspects of the others. One may be born into ghastly circumstances but be fortunate enough to have a quick natural intelligence or supportive parents. Finally, there is the element of luck present in the opportunities one has; one does not deserve to find oneself in favorable or unfavorable circumstances in which to exercise one's talents.[32] Good hand-eye coordination is a marvelous gift and may indeed lead to great riches, provided one is lucky enough to live in a society that richly rewards athletes who have these skills. The kind of hand-eye coordination that allows Pete Rose to hit a curve ball consistently would be perhaps useless to Petrus Rosa living in the late Roman empire. An ability to throw wads of paper into the garbage can in the corner of the office (by tossing them behind your back!) may also express a great talent of sorts, but, alas, there is no market for it. Pete Rose does not deserve to have the game of baseball present in professional form; you, the great paper tosser, are not denied anything you deserve by having no professional sport in which to exercise your talent. Rose is lucky; you are not.

We cannot be said to deserve anything that depends on luck, and hence we do not deserve our features. Rawls extends this to the claim that, because we do not deserve our features, we do not deserve what follows from the use of them. Hence a society is violating no standards of desert when it interferes with a distribution of the burdens and benefits that without societal intervention would naturally result from their employment.³³ We may not and for the most part cannot interfere with the features (particularly the natural ones) of people, so Rawls thinks, but we can and may interfere with what happens as a result of those features or the use of them. The principles of distributive justice fix our concepts of what may be legitimately expected; they supply the rules and principles that link what we are and what we do with what we receive.

Rawls has been criticized in three major ways for this view. First, he has been criticized for inferring from his belief that people do not deserve their features to his claim that people do not deserve what follows from the exercise or possession of those features. Judgments of desert take the form "X deserves y because of some feature, C, of X that makes X worthy of y," but why must X deserve C in order to deserve what follows from C? The first men to go to the moon did not presumably deserve to go to the moon, but does it follow that whatever honor and recognition came to them because of it was also therefore undeserved? It seems false that X must deserve C in order to deserve y. (If so, then must X deserve some other feature, B, in order to deserve C? Surely the regress must end at some point in the possession of some property, Z, that is not itself deserved.)

Second, Rawls has been criticized for thinking that since one is only entitled to C, one cannot claim an entitlement to what naturally results from the possession of C. If someone chooses to marry you because of your undeserved good looks, does that mean that you are not entitled to that?³⁴ If you purchase the winning ticket in the New York lottery, you are entitled to the money. You are also entitled to what you purchase with the money you won. Does not deserving to win also undercut your entitlement to the new house that you bought with the winnings? Being "only" entitled to something may well give one entitlements to other things as well. This objection sees Rawls as being essentially in the right in denying desert as a basis for distributive justice. However, so the objection goes, just because we do not deserve our natural and environmentally determined features, it does not follow that we are not entitled to them (as the example of being entitled to one's good looks is supposed to show). We are entitled to our features and to what follows from those features, questions of desert aside. This view is closely bound up with

IV. Distributive Justice and Social Union

what I shall call the radical individualist ideal of liberty: that we ought, among other things, be left free to use our features as we choose, to develop them as we choose and to reap the gold stars (or demerits) as we succeed or fail.[35] I shall return later to this radical individualist ideal of liberty when I contrast it with the ideal of sharing.

Third, Rawls has been criticized for holding a view that is incompatible with the ideals of liberal individualism, for his view implies (so the criticism claims) a kind of determinism, a denial that we are self-choosers, which is clearly incompatible with the kind of Kantian liberal individualism that Rawls seems to profess.[36]

Can Rawls's general point be maintained in the face of such criticisms? To show how it would be possible, it is necessary to attend to two different things: (1) the idea of individuals' deserving treatment with respect; (2) the ideal of *sharing*, which, I would argue, is one of the major presuppositions of Rawls's point in this regard. Rawls might seem at first to leave no room for the concept of individual desert. In the words of one critic, Rawls's "principles of justice do not mention moral desert because, strictly speaking, no one can be said to deserve anything. . . . [O]n Rawls's view, people have no intrinsic *worth*, no worth that is intrinsic in the sense that it is theirs prior to or independent of or apart from what just institutions attribute to them."[37] Assigning this view to Rawls makes sense only if one takes Rawls to be completely rejecting all concepts of desert and replacing them with institutionally fixed legitimate expectations. The Rawlsian point can, however, be defended in the following way. We need to distinguish two levels of what is due to people. We can talk of an abstract sense of desert in that each individual deserves to have his or her dignity respected. People are deserving of having their dignity respected because of what they are, not necessarily because of what they do. (This harkens back to the point about respect for persons being different from respect for choice.) It is their value as persons, as selves, that gives them this desert. To claim this is, of course, to deny that desert is necessarily only applicable to things for which we are responsible. We can be worthy of certain treatment without being responsible for being the kind of entity that is worthy of that. Nor does this desert itself rest on any property that is itself deserved. Nobody deserves to be a person. (If one did, then could one argue that one deserved to be born? Would it have been a violation of anyone's just deserts if some possible parents had decided not to have any children at all?) But being a person gives one claims of desert to being treated with the respect commensurate with being a person.³⁸

This is an abstract principle that can be concretely specified only when a more specific background is provided. Rawls's point can be reconstructed in the following way. When one determines what would be the general features of a system that respected individual dignity, one arrives at a system of justice based not on desert but on legitimate expectations. This would give us a two-tiered view of the matter. At one level would be the abstract principle of respect for individual dignity, at the other level would be entitlements. Moreover, the abstract level would justify the more concrete level of entitlements. But why move to entitlements at all? Why not claim that also, on the concrete level, desert should be the operative notion? In order to support the idea that sometimes entitlements and not desert is the correct basis for distributive justice, one must be able to show that treating a person with respect does not entail society's always distributing social goods on the basis of desert. (It should be noted that the concept of a social good is a historically relative one. Developments in, for example, biotechnology may give us control over distribution of nose sizes, slim figures, height, and so on—in short, over a whole range of cases that formerly were left entirely to the natural lottery.)

The justification of this idea rests on the ideal of sharing that is expressed in a Rawlsian style of argument about desert and entitlements. Rawls says of his theory—what he calls justice as fairness—that in a social order structured according to it "men agree to share one another's fate."³⁹ The ideal of sharing our fate involves an ideal of a type of sharing that is best elucidated by what it is not. We can contrast this ideal of sharing with what we call the ideal of radical individualism. In this ideal, individuals view themselves and their features in terms of various metaphors of possession or ownership (similar to what C. B. Macpherson calls the ideal of possessive individualism).⁴⁰ Each is moreover ideally sufficient unto him or herself, and it is not considered wrong or amiss to put one's own interests ahead of those of others. For the radical individualist, the justifications of social and communal orderings involve claims about how these orders are of mutual advantage. The radical individualist is thus a possessive individualist. The possessive individu-

IV. Distributive Justice and Social Union

alist may share things with others, but this sharing is justified only to the extent that such sharing is of mutual advantage, or is an act of charity, or is something that the individual simply wants to do. The ideal of possession includes a belief that one has a right to enjoy the benefits of one's possessions without any special obligations to share those benefits with others.

The ideal of sharing, on the other hand, does not see it as *prima facie* right to put one's own interests ahead of others. The good of the individual is seen as bound up with the good of the community. One's features are to be used for a common good, not necessarily exclusively for a private one. The ideal of sharing includes a belief that one has special obligations to share one's benefits with others.

In Rawls's view, in a just system people *agree* to *share* their *fate*. It is important for Rawls that people *agree* to it; his theory is, after all, an ideal contractarian theory of justice. But as Rawls himself makes clear, it is not just any agreement that counts for establishing the principles of justice but an agreement made under certain conditions and constraints, which he calls the Original Position. Most striking for the present purposes is Rawls's imposition of the veil of ignorance (depriving people of self-knowledge and knowledge of their standing in society) and the principle of maximin as the principle of choice (maximize the minimum, pick the best worst outcome). Ignoring other formal aspects of the two features, one is struck by the fact that together they compel each person assuming the standpoint of the Original Position to put him or herself in the other person's shoes, to assume the standpoint of each representative individual.[41] Each is forced to weight equally the viewpoint of others with their own viewpoints. That there are separate lives or the distinctness of individuals is not denied. Nonetheless, a sense of the interests of others is incorporated into one's conception of one's own interests so that the only agreement that is feasible is one where one agrees to share the benefits of one's good fortune with those less fortunate. In contrast to the viewpoint taken by the possessive individualist, one understands that one is *entitled* to enjoy the fruits of one's good fortune only when one shares them with others.

This is one sense of "sharing"—but how is this sharing one's *fate*? One way of taking that would be to see us as sharing something over which we had no control. Another way would see us as viewing the outcomes of our free choices in terms of the recognition that those choices occur in a historical context and are constrained by the circumstances, opportunities, and good (or bad) fortune of one's situation. Part of our fate in both these senses is the people with whom we live and deal. In an obvious sense, we do not choose them any more than we choose to be born. It is true, of course, that we choose to associate with some people and not with others; nevertheless, we cannot choose what people there will be with whom we may associate. (Even parents who "create" their children find out, often to their chagrin, that they have brought forth independent people with their own ideas and goals.) We can take the idea that we share our fate with these others as meaning that there is a sense of identity that we share with them; we share with them who we are. For Rawls this sense of shared identity seems only to consist in being and acknowledging others as what he calls moral persons (entities capable of forming a conception of their own good and acting out of a sense of justice). If we see sharing our fate as sharing our identities, and our shared identity is only that of being moral persons, then it would seem that our shared fate is only one of having a certain abstract identity in common, one we share with all humanity. (If so, would the Rawlsian well-ordered society only be possible on a global scale?)

There is another objection to Rawls that is connected with this idea of sharing our fate with others. It has been objected against Rawls that his view of the primacy of justice—that justice is the first virtue of institutions (or at least of the ones that belong to what Rawls calls the "basic structure"), that it is like truth in theory, an uncompromising virtue—shows that Rawls either has or must assume a limited conception of moral personality or perhaps just an out and out untenable metaphysical concept of the person in this theory.[42] Justice in the sense of balancing competing claims of moderately self-interested individuals is not a *first* virtue of the family, of friendships, or of various kinds of communal institutions such as the fellowships of church and synagogue. If it were, then these institutions would have to change, to lose the very traits that make them what they are.

Rawls's views, however, need not be taken that way. (I shall ignore the fact that there are numerous passages in his book that suggest such a reading.) Rawls's basic view seems to be that justice is a first virtue of

IV. Distributive Justice and Social Union

dealing among citizens as *citizens*. People "share their fate" in their common identification as citizens of a given social and political order. It is *this* ideal of sharing that makes the Rawlsian program possible (but is not exclusively tied to the Rawlsian program, however powerfully that program may express it), and this sharing is possible only when each sees the other as 'one of us'; indeed, the Original Position is an elaborate way of structuring this view into deliberations about justice. Sharing a common identity means sharing certain responsibilities that may come about because of who one is, not what one has done. Rawlsian justice, construed in this way, not only includes an ideal of *distribution* ("*to* each according to ____") but also an ideal of *contribution* ("*from* each according to ____"). Rawlsian justice is possible only within a certain type of social union in which people share their fate with each other. It depends not just on each getting their fair share but also contributing their fair share. It depends, that is, on a certain democratic liberal sense of virtue, on shared understandings of the responsibilities of citizenship. These include the virtues of toleration, of civic courage (of standing up to injustices in the community), and of fairness (of being fair in one's personal dealings with others). These ideals of personality inform a democratic liberal social union and make that union possible.

The radical individualist ideal admits no responsibilities other than ones incurred freely by individuals; individuals are responsible only for their own fates and for what they freely assume. The ideal of sharing, however, acknowledges a kind of responsibility for things that are not necessarily freely incurred by individuals. Citizens may have special responsibilities, for example, to disadvantaged groups in their society because of the history of the social and political order to which they belong. Citizens have this responsibility by virtue of being citizens of the social and political order to which they belong; they have it because of *who* they are, independently of whether they had any part in the past erection of present inequities. By virtue of establishing that identity, they acquire that responsibility. It makes no difference if they themselves had no part in past injustice (or even if members of their families had no part—although it should be noted that the assumption of responsibility for family doings raises the same kinds of issues). Recent immigrants and the descendants of recent immigrants acquire this responsibility by virtue of assuming the identity of citizen.

More importantly, this sense of sharing presupposes some form of social union rather than establishing it. This is the reverse of the Rawlsian conception. We share our fate with others when we share some identity with those others. Speaking of an *agreement* to share one's fate in this sense of sharing is misleading. It is not so much an agreement on something that is at issue as it is an *acknowledgment* of who we are. The appropriate language is not one of choice but of knowledge and responsibility, of recognizing and owning up to who we are. The element of choice enters into the decision as to how that identity is to be sustained or modified, but it enters secondarily after one has acknowledged who one is, who *we* are. (I am not denying that some element of interpretation is present in this. Establishing this shared identity is not a simple, matter of fact affair.) The Rawlsian conception of sharing thus depends on there being a form of social union in which there are enough self-understandings common among the citizenry so that such sharing is possible.

The sense of sharing in terms of sharing one's good fortune with one's less fortunate fellow citizens receives expression in Rawls's difference principle.[43] This principle of justice calls for an equality of distribution of social goods unless an unequal distribution will work to the benefit of the least advantaged group in society. Once the 'decision' to share one's fate has been taken (which in Rawls's system is done by virtue of entering the Original Position), the *prima facie* justification of putting one's own interests prior to others vanishes.

It is this sense of sharing that justifies a partial system of entitlements rather than a system of desert as a basis of distributive justice. In a liberal social and political order, the worth, the dignity, of each person is to be respected, and our obligation to share our good fortune with those less fortunate would be based on some understanding of what is necessary to show respect for a person. It is by assuming the standpoint of other individuals that we get a sense of what is insulting, degrading, or humiliating to them, what counts as an affront to their sense of self-respect. This mediates our mutual acknowledgment of each other in a just order. We share what follows from the use of our features in the pursuit of a common good. We have a socially established set of rules linking our features with certain social benefits and burdens so that a common good is achieved. (For Rawls, this is the production of efficient

IV. Distributive Justice and Social Union

outcomes within the framework set by his two principles of justice, but we need not be restricted to Rawls's specific notion.) This view of sharing presupposes some form of social union, since it would be only from within such a union that any notion of a common good could ever be established. Because people deserve to be treated with respect and because of a common identity, we share the outcomes of the use of our features and distribute the social goods and the social burdens in terms of rules and principles derivative from an understanding of the common good.

Rawls thinks that we are entitled to certain social goods when they are the result of legitimate expectations, where the expectations are socially established and their legitimacy fixed by the principles of justice. But does justice have the primacy that Rawls imputes to it? Justice is a major virtue but not necessarily the *first* virtue of institutions that mediate between people in their identity as citizens. Unless one makes the most likely false assumption that people's identities are exhausted in their existence as citizens, it will be the case that, in many dealings with each other and with regard to many institutions that mediate between people, justice will not be the first virtue. Moreover, is it even true that, among citizens, justice in the Rawlsian entitlement sense is the first virtue of institutions? Justice is only one element of the common good, and its priority in it will depend on how that common good is to be conceived. Consider the following possible principles of distributive justice: need, desert, merit, social contribution, effort, or free exchange. Each of these is plausibly legitimate within some type of social relationship. Desert seems to apply to items like public recognition, as when we award medals to people. Effort makes sense in many types of organizations: successful corporations often reward employees for effort, not just for success; students are often rewarded for effort, not just for results. Which of these principles will be operative will depend on the particular type of social organization that is applying it. The ordering of these principles will depend on some more specific conception of the common good. More importantly, that will depend on some conception of our shared identity, which is articulated only from within various forms of social union.

We can see this more clearly if we put it in the context of issues concerning pluralism and distributive justice. Rawls claims that a conception of justice is necessary when: (1) there is a scarcity of desired social goods; (2) there is a plurality of individuals with a plurality of ends, of incommensurable values. Sharing no assumptions of value, the individuals must settle their disputed claims about scarce social goods by appeal to some principle of justice that for its acceptance does not depend on any one of the contested conceptions of individual value. This is illustrative of one of the problems of pluralism: to the extent that there is *only* a multiplicity of ends, there is no shared identity, no common good. There is therefore only the possibility of striking an equilibrium between competing interests. This would be pluralism at the extreme, and in it perhaps justice would be the first virtue of institutions, since there would be no other principle or value to adjudicate between competing claims. It is not clear, however, that Rawlsian justice would apply to such a society. In such a society, the individualist ideal of liberty would be paramount since there would be no other basis for regulating social interactions. (To be sure, reasons of prudence might lead to some limitations of liberty, but the ideal would remain intact.) Justice in terms of the ideal of sharing presupposes some common identity and is thus impossible in the limiting case of a completely pluralist society. Rawlsian justice is possible only when pluralism is not complete.

The importance that justice has—and which ideal of justice takes priority, the ideal of sharing or the radical individualist ideal of liberty—depends on the extent to which pluralism is a value and the place it has in a conception of the common good. To the extent that a shared identity exists—and to the extent of the richness of that shared identity—the radical individualist ideal of liberty will take second place to the ideal of sharing. Meeting the needs of one's fellow citizens will take precedence over self-interested pursuits or maximizing one's position in society. Social contribution will play a greater role in providing arguments for distributive justice in such conditions. Indeed, without a sense of shared identity and of a common good, the notion of social contribution could make no sense. Certain social goods, such as recognition or various official honors, which depend on desert as the basis for their distribution, would be senseless in a completely pluralist society with no notion of a common good to which one could contribute.

Rawlsian justice is not therefore opposed to a sense of community, as Rawls's critics have sometimes held. Rather, it specifies a *type* of community, which we can call the community of fairness. It may be both

IV. Distributive Justice and Social Union

distinguished from the complete lack of such community that would be found in the radical individualist ideal and distinguished from other forms of community, such as authoritarian community. The community of fairness receives its articulation in the form of the social union of democratic liberalism. People in a community of fairness come to share a sense of the ideals of character in that kind of community. Treatment of others with dignity (which is the fitting response to their having dignity) implies a certain kind of courtesy toward others and tolerance of alternative viewpoints that are appropriate to a liberal democratic culture. It also implies a willingness, as a virtue, to respect the autonomous choices of others, even when we find those choices to be tragically misguided. And it will be a social union in which ideals of mutual benefit play a role as expressions of the equality and dignity of its members, not as Hobbesian calculations to avoid civil war.

I now wish to see how these ideals might be weighed against each other in more concrete circumstances. In particular, I want to show that a democratic liberal social union need not be one in which there are only fragmented individuals and no possible conception of a common good. The oldest criticism of liberalism has been its supposed indifference to the values of community, of belonging, and its substitution instead of its ideology of liberty. I wish to show that this is a one-sided view of democratic liberalism, that it distorts what is enduring in the liberal vision as it has taken root in social practice. It both distorts our view of persons and distorts our view of the types of social relations in which democratic liberalism flourishes and that democratic liberalism encourages.

The goal is thus to provide an explanation of the basic principles and ideals of what I shall call a democratic liberal form of social union. My thesis will be that democratic liberal social union is possible only if certain principles and ideals of personality are acknowledged within it. I am not arguing for these principles or virtues independently but offering them as explanations of how a democratic liberal form of social union is possible. First, however, I wish to turn to questions of law and justice, since it is often in legal terms or the language of jurisprudence that people in the Anglo-American tradition understand claims of justice to be best expressed. These arguments set the stage for disputes about democratic liberal social union and bring to the forefront some of the issues to which I have been alluding.

CHAPTER
TWO

Moral and Legal Principles

I HAVE ARGUED that ethical principles have their role in the context of a kind of mutual acknowledgment from within forms of social union. But do not a whole variety of other things, such as politics and law, play similar roles? What then is the relation among principle, law, and politics? A provisory exploration of the relation between law and principle will be helpful in answering this question. This is because in the background of the debates about the relation between law and principle are certain key political ideas (in particular, I shall argue, the notion of sovereignty).

What follows is a proposal for a way of looking at the relation between law and principle that is to serve as a stepping stone to some of the more detailed ideas that follow. I shall argue that one can understand the relation between law, ethics, and politics only when one looks at the context in which each has a purpose. Understanding this purpose will help us understand the nature of a rule of law in a democratic liberal social union, which will be one of the major themes of Chapter Three. Instead of going directly to that issue, however, I shall first take a detour through the contemporary debate between legal positivism and what I shall call principle-based theories of law, represented in the English speaking world by Ronald Dworkin and in Germany by Josef Esser. The rationale for the detour concerns both what I take to be really going on in that debate, and what is important in it from the standpoint of the present inquiry. In particular, I want to argue that we should not understand the debate between the kinds of principle-based theories of law and positivism as a purely analytical debate about something like the "concept of law" but as alternative explanations and strategies for answering some problems that themselves can only be understood by looking at their historical origins. There is a general Hegelian thesis underlying this, that we understand the rational superiority of one theory to another in terms of its answering problems that emerge within other theories and that those other theories in their own terms are incapable of answering.

I
Sovereigns and Rules

Do principle and law have anything to do with one another? The position that argues that they do not is that of legal positivism. Two theses are characteristic of legal positivism: (1) law and ethics have no essential connection (sometimes expressed by saying that the two are analytically distinct);[1] (2) the criteria for determining what counts as a law depend on the purported law's origin, on how it came about. Outside of these two general traits, however, legal positivism can assume many different forms, and the differences among these forms are instructive. In particular, I would like to look briefly at the difference between two well known proponents of positivism, H. L. A. Hart and John Austin, to see just what that difference reveals.

Both Austin and Hart seem to be offering an *analysis* of something like the "concept" of law. Austin in particular professes an interest in law as it is, not as it necessarily ought to be—in, that is, positive law, the laws enacted by the relevant authorities.[2] A law, on Austin's model, is a rule for guidance of an intelligent being, laid down by an intelligent being who has power over him or her. The key words here are "rule" and "power." Rules are understood by Austin to be a species of command. To command people is to communicate a wish to them to do or forebear from doing something and to threaten them with a harm of some sort if they do not comply. (Hart enlighteningly calls this an "orders/threats" model of rules). Legal obligation then consists in being obliged to do something under the threat of harm if one fails to do it. What distinguishes, however, *legal* obligation from other forms of obligation is that legal orders come from a certain type of superior: not

I. Sovereigns and Rules

merely one who has the might to enforce his or her wishes but a *sovereign*, a person or body of people who receive habitual obedience from the bulk of society and who habitually obey nobody else. To be a *political* group at all, a group must have the bulk of its members habitually obeying some superior that is the sovereign. On Austin's model, then, a system of law is essentially a system of rules (orders backed up by threats) laid down by a sovereign.

H. L. A. Hart has strongly criticized Austin on these points, and his criticisms are so telling that they have practically become a piece of philosophical orthodoxy.[3] In Hart's view, Austin has crucially misanalyzed the *concept* of law. In particular, Hart disagrees with Austin's analysis of legal rules as orders backed up by threats issued by a sovereign. His objections to it are threefold. First, Austin's model fails because it cannot allow for the possibility of legislators applying the law to themselves. Orders are other-directed; one issues an order to another person, but one cannot order oneself, except metaphorically (as when one orders oneself in the morning to get out of bed). Yet in many legal systems—certainly the Anglo-American one—legislators enact laws that at least in principle also apply to themselves (for example, "The speed limit is fifty-five miles per hour"). Even in the most believable application of Austin's model—the criminal law, where laws might plausibly be seen as orders backed up by sanctions—the rules also apply in principle to the rule-giver.

Second, in Austin's model, the role of sanctions is crucial; without them, a rule cannot be said to be a law. Many laws, however, do not seem to involve sanctions in any meaningful sense. Examples are laws that bestow authority on people to do certain things or to make certain kinds of decisions (that is, which create certain types of capacities). A higher court's quashing of a lower court's ruling on the ground that the lower court lacked jurisdiction does not involve any sanction *per se*; the judge(s) of the lower court might have had no personal interest in the case at all, and it is hardly a sanction when the sanctioned party has no personal interest in the matter one way or another. Moreover, there are other varieties of law than straightforward injunctions to forbear from doing something or suffer a penalty. Many laws do not attempt to discourage or encourage behavior but only to help parties communicate with each other. The forms in which contracts or wills may be written are examples. Such types of laws need not influence the substantive choices of the parties (as to, for example, whether or not they actually contract for services); they merely state that unless the parties follow the prescribed mode of making their intentions known, they will not be said to have actually contracted, made a valid will, or whatnot.

Third (and perhaps the most important among Hart's criticisms), an "orders/threats/sovereignty" model cannot in any straightforward manner account for the continuity of a legal system. In any legal system, new actors appear and old ones disappear by electoral succession, death, appointment, and so on. The successors must be able to invoke some authority for claiming that they are in fact *legitimate* successors; any system must be able to distinguish, that is, between legitimate holders of an office and pretenders or usurpers. The order of a sovereign cannot decide the issue where there is a pretender, because the issue would precisely be *who* is the sovereign and *who* is the pretender.

Hart replaces Austin's orders/threats model with an analysis in terms of types of rules. The core of Austin's mistake lay in confusing the way in which a threat can *oblige* one with the way in which a rule can *obligate* one. To be obliged to do something is to believe that the benefits of doing it outweigh whatever harms may follow from not doing it. However, when one is obligated to do something, the obligation holds independently of one's belief about the advantages of doing it. Legal rules obligate one; they do not merely offer predictions of sanctions but function as reasons for doing something, even if no benefit or harm comes to one as a result. Rules, that is, are internal to behavior; a rule of behavior is not an inductive generalization about patterns of behavior but is a reason for behaving in one way rather than another.

Hart explains the possibility of a legal system by arguing that such systems are in fact composed of two types of such rules: primary rules and secondary rules. Primary rules tell us our rights and our duties; secondary rules either create capacities for people (for example, by stipulating who can perform marriages) or specify what rules are in fact the primary rules and what procedures must be followed in order for a primary rule to be adopted, amended, or voided. Both primary and secondary rules may be said to be either valid or invalid, meaning that they are derived or not in some appropriate fashion according to some accepted procedure. Ultimately, these lead back to what Hart calls a rule of recog-

I. Sovereigns and Rules

nition, namely, a supreme rule that rests only on acceptance, but that cannot be said to be either valid or invalid (because it is not derived from anything else.) In the context of the United States, this would perhaps be the complex rule of abiding by the Supreme Court's interpretation of the Constitution as the final voice in fundamental legal matters. Why the rule of recognition is accepted is, however, not a legal problem; it is at best a historical or social-psychological problem. (It is historians and psychologists who explain why a rule of recognition is accepted; it is lawyers who tell us what the primary and secondary rules are.)

What is at issue here? On the face of it, Austin's and Hart's models are strikingly similar. On Austin's model, we have a sovereign's issuing orders backed up by threats, and the sovereign is that person or body of persons to whom habitual obedience is given (or, in Hart's terms, whose orders the bulk of people *accept*). On Hart's model, there are primary and secondary rules that are valid or invalid (that is, derived from other rules). These rest ultimately on a rule of recognition that is either accepted or not. Both models culminate, that is, in the mere acceptance or non-acceptance of something. However, Hart and those who have accepted his criticism of Austin do not see it that way. They see the acceptance of the rule of recognition as significantly different from acceptance of Austin's sovereign. In the former we are internalizing a norm of sorts; our acceptance of the practice of appealing to the Constitution is not merely some habit of obedience but is acceptance of something that functions to give us obligations. But there is more than just a different account of acceptance at work here. As Hart sees it, unless some such acceptance of a norm is present, we cannot adequately account for the legitimacy of a sovereign at all. That we might take the king's word as law could not merely be a habit; there would have to be a be a norm for accepting the king's word for that word to be obligatory, to actually *be* law. The acceptance of the *legitimacy* of the practice of acceding to the sovereign's decrees as the final word is presupposed by Austin's so-called habit of obedience. Thus, Austin's account presupposes a notion of legitimacy rather than establishing the notion of legitimacy as it is supposed to do.

The debate thus might appear to be a purely conceptual one about the analysis of habits and rules. Hart is claiming that Austin has a faulty analysis of the concept of law based on his faulty analysis of rules. But is it just that? One way of understanding the difference between Hart and Austin would be to see the significance of Hart's replacement of Austin's notion of rules as simply one of Hart's picking up on Austin's achievements and correcting the analysis where it has gone awry. We can, however, look at it in a different way and get a much different answer. Hart is, after all, doing two things: he is throwing into question the very possibility of there even being such things as "sovereigns," and he is advising us to replace the idea of "sovereigns" with ideas more akin to those of authority and jurisdiction. This amounts to more than just a different analysis of the concept. It amounts to a different normative political theory.

The idea of sovereignty is crucial here. It originates as an answer to a political problem in the sixteenth century, specifically the religious wars in France between 1562 and 1598.[4] Although various edicts of toleration were issued by French rulers, they proved to be largely ineffective in curbing the civil warfare. In 1562 in response to the ongoing civil war, Michel de L'Hopital, the king's chancellor, offered a new formulation of the political problem: it was, he claimed, not a question of determining what was the true religion but of determining how the differing religions could peacefully coexist.[5] The solution to the problem of peaceful coexistence, given by theoreticians like Jean Bodin in his *De la Republique* in 1577, was the recognition of the idea of *sovereignty*. Each political society needs, Bodin and his followers argued, some pinnacle of power beyond which there is no worldly appeal. It seemed clear that competing communities (in this case, religious ones) could not agree on a set of substantive values that would mediate their conflict.

We can put Bodin's arguments in a more general perspective. One of the features of the modern Western world is the existence of a pluralistic culture. Where there can be no appeal to any commonly understood set of values, it would seem that one must make an appeal to something else, for example, a *summa potestas*, a sovereign power that wields its power independently of any basis in some shared set of values.[6] Appeal to a sovereign removes any necessity for finding a common set of values for competing communities; the sovereign can balance *interests* without having to endorse any particular community's values over another's. A sovereign may, of course, enforce one community's values over the pro-

I. Sovereigns and Rules 59

tests of other communities. This would, however, only be because the sovereign, a neutral figure, believed that this was the only way to keep the peace or was in some other way a correct balancing of interests.

The very notion of sovereignty arises therefore against the specific historical backdrop of the existence of a pluralistic society and the fierce civil wars that often resulted from this type of pluralism. Only against such a backdrop can it be understood. It is significant that the concept of a sovereign is fashioned to be as far as possible a value-neutral concept. What assumptions would underlie this? Perhaps one assumption is skepticism about finding any common ground in values between competing communities that would motivate an appeal to something that is not a community, namely, a sovereign. People, after all, *belong* to communities, but the sovereign wielding of power over them is not a function of this 'belonging.' Call this assumption one of value skepticism. A further assumption might be that only if power is wielded without being based on some particular assumptions of value can it effectively work to mediate (or suppress, as the case may be) competing communities. Call this a kind of practical assumption about effectiveness. Both assumptions help underpin the idea of sovereignty. In fact, the very rationale of the concept of sovereignty makes it impossible that it should be based on anything else than common acceptance or brute force; the legitimacy of the sovereign cannot be established by anything that might make it possible for some competing community to reject its legitimacy.

In this idea of the wielding of sovereign power, we can see the beginning of the idea of the liberal secular state: the concept of sovereignty has within itself the kernel of an idea of a sovereign's wielding its power independently of any religious basis. Outside of this historical and political context of a pluralistic society trying to make peace with itself, the notion of sovereignty is afloat, without the conditions for its intelligibility present. Seeing the beginning of the liberal secular state in this notion does not, however, mean that we see liberalism as exhausted by this notion. To see why, we must take the story a bit further.

Austin's invocation of the concept of a sovereign in his jurisprudence is not without historical resonance, for it also functions in his system as a way of legitimating legal directives. Austin's claim that a *political* group requires a sovereign is a shorthand for this historical tradition. Why then does Hart take such unqualified umbrage at it? Part of the original force of the idea of sovereignty was that only a sovereign could make the edicts of toleration stick, could give them a legitimacy that they would otherwise lack. (The practical assumption.) What is missing, however, in any account of sovereignty is a notion of *rights* as distinct from mere *tolerances* (or permissions). The sovereign may tolerate various kinds of behavior, but as the *summa potestas*, it also may not; any removal of a tolerance is legally as legitimate as letting it stay in place. It is easy to see how a doctrine of sovereignty would mesh nicely with a kind of positivistic insistence on the denial of any essential connection between law and morality. One may make moral appeals to the sovereign, but it is the sovereign's prerogative, by definition, to deny them. The sovereign's edicts remain legitimate independent of their consistency or inconsistency with any moral law, and to be able to say that a law is legitimate without its necessarily being just is to be able to make the central positivist claim about the relation of law and morality. Moreover, a strong doctrine of rights would be incompatible with a doctrine of sovereign power; if the sovereign is limited in its exercise of power, then it is not a sovereign at all.[7] It thus might seem than that any attack on the doctrine of sovereignty would be *eo ipso* an attack on positivism itself, since it would be an attack on one of the basic conceptual tools for keeping law and morality distinct.

I suggested earlier that one way of looking at Hart's attack on Austin's notion of sovereignty would be to see it as an attempt to replace the idea of sovereignty with something more akin to the idea of authority. It is, however, also more than that. Just as Austin's use of "sovereignty" resounds with a certain historical resonance, Hart's replacement of it is also an invocation of a particularly liberal concept of the state. This conception arises against the background of some of the more distasteful consequences that problems of pluralism have historically taken. Let us call the various solutions to these problems "strategies of pluralism." These strategies have typically been cast in different forms. Some strategies have looked to the creation of some 'higher' community that would somehow include or subsume all the others within it or to the emergence of some superior community that would replace the various competing communities and thereby unify the culture (either by revolution or by conversion).[8] Others, like the strategy of sovereignty, have looked to some neutral body to mediate the conflicts.

I. Sovereigns and Rules

The issue is a deep one and has to do in part with the change from classical to modern views of the proper objectives of the state. From at least Plato and Aristotle until modern times, the proper function of the state was seen in part to promote and to secure the virtue of its citizens. But this would be possible only if there were a unified culture with a single view of what the virtues are (or, more weakly, if there were indeed competing conceptions of virtue but no real threat of one group's actually challenging another). This view dominated Western theories of the political community more or less until the appearance of competing religious communities and the ensuing civil wars, such as occurred in France in the sixteenth century. One then had competing communities with different and incompatible conceptions of goodness. Each community's conception claimed to be absolute, and there seemed to be little prospect of finding any substantive considerations of value upon which both sides could agree. In these conditions, as Michel de L'Hopital put it, the point of the political community was not to determine the true religion but to see how the two competing factions could peacefully coexist. The purpose of the state becomes, if this view is accepted, not one primarily of securing the virtues of its citizens (that would require it to determine the "true religion") but to maintain an *order* that would allow people to coexist peacefully. The strategy that emerged in de L'Hopital's time sought to resolve the disputes between competing communities by an appeal to something that was not itself another community, but instead a sovereign: a person or body of persons that wielded unlimited power and whose legitimacy was not therefore based on its being a representative of one community or another.

Positivism, understood as a doctrine that separates the legitimacy of law from its justice, may be taken as a jurisprudential expression of this new view of the objectives of the state. This is not to say that positivism emerged immediately hand in hand with the doctrine of sovereignty. Indeed, the problems that were to beset positivism predated the construction of the positivist doctrine itself. The strategy for pluralism that turned to sovereignty as an answer soon ran into difficulty when it became perceived—as happened in the English civil war—that more than order was required; a doctrine of rights was also needed to check the abuses of the sovereign. This threw into question both the value skepticism and the practical assumptions about sovereignty as a strategy. Later developments led philosophers to see that the disputes between competing communities can only be resolved by appeal to something that does not indeed even resemble anything like a religious community. Hegel went so far as to claim that this was something categorically different, namely, a *state*.[9] In such a state, the "universal class" (the class whose own interests are identical with the interests of all) is the class of civil servants, the bureaucrats. It is they who implement procedures and laws without necessarily serving the interests of any one community.[10] It becomes a matter of contention if such a state would function not primarily to further the virtues of its citizens but to allow them to live peaceably with one another through a well-ordered system of laws. Thus, the liberal state will be separate from religion (indeed, from any particular community) and will naturally develop more procedural notions to safeguard the rights of individuals.[11] The construction of the liberal state thus serves the same general goal as the notion of sovereignty: keeping the peace among potentially warring factions by appeal to something neutral. Nonetheless, most philosophers of the liberal state have accepted it as an extension of the notion of sovereignty, not as a replacement of it.

Hart's radicalism consists in his implicit denial that sovereignty and the liberal state are compatible at all. In some of his writings, Hart has made it clear that he endorses some strong view of moral rights, arguing at one place that if there are any rights, then one of them must be the right to be free, since the ability to choose is a condition of exercising any other rights.[12] But in a society with a sovereign, no such strong view of rights is possible; rights are limitations on sovereign power and can only have a concrete existence in a constitutional state. A liberal form of the constitutional state will often rely on supposedly neutral procedures to resolve disputes between its citizens, and rights function as part of the procedure. But this can lead to an insistence on the idea that law and ethics *must* be separated. A legal system based on notions like legitimate *authority* (and not sovereignty) is the very soul of the existence of the liberal state. It thus appears plausible that only a state that is structured by such apparently neutral procedures can possibly protect the rights of its citizens, namely, by not favoring in principle the ideals of any one community over another.[13] This should at least lead us to suspect that the differences between Hart and Austin are more than merely "analyti-

II
Are Rules Enough?

There are three issues here in Hart's streamlined version of positivism. First, there is the issue of whether or not Hart has given an adequate analysis of the "concept" of law. Second, there are issues involving the nature of interpretation in judicial adjudication—what kinds of justifications a judge may legitimately employ in asserting that something is or is not the law in a given case. This could be called the "test for law" issue. Finally, there is the issue of the justification for the authority or legitimacy of the legal system as a whole. The first of these issues is not, I think, the major one at all, nor can a clear sense be given to it. The real point of contention lies in the second and third issues, particularly in Hart's notion of the legitimacy of the rule of recognition lying in its acceptance. Hart sees this basic form of legitimacy as resting in some general form of acceptance by the bulk of the population. But has Hart confused, as people accused Weber of doing, the *legitimacy* of a legal and political system with the *appearance* of legitimacy? If one focuses on this third issue, then one would approach Hart's positivism not in terms merely of legal theory but in terms of basic political theory, of the grounds of political authority in general. However, this is not an analytical issue but an explanatory one: how do we account for the possibility of liberal political and legal authority? Will acceptance be enough?

Imagine that you went on a camping trip in the wilderness and maintained no contact with the outside world during that time. Upon returning, you learned that a group of people unknown to you had met and drawn up a document that prescribed new rights and duties for everyone (including yourself) and claimed that this document would have legal force if certain procedures, themselves specified in the document, were followed. On the day that you return, you find that all the procedures have been followed, and the document now claims that it has full legal force. Everybody you know seems to like the idea. Does this document have legal authority? What is the structural difference between this fable and the actual ratification of the United States Constitution, involving as it did a bunch of people meeting in Philadelphia, drawing up a document that included the terms of its own ratification, and so on? What gives it its authority? In particular, one might ask: Why should mere *acceptance* by the bulk of the population bestow a legitimacy on this? One would want to know how it might be possible that acceptance could do this at all. Suppose one answered that such a procedure would be democratic (majority rule and the like) and hence deserved to be followed.[14] That would not take you very far, since it merely pushes the issue off to the question of why democratic procedure is valid. There seems to be no way out of raising very fundamental issues of valuative political theory in order even to understand why acceptance should be a plausible ground for the justification of a legal system at all.

Hart, like Max Weber before him, seems to identify legitimacy with acceptance (with *perceived* legitimacy). However, how could this be the case, unless one had a general justification for something like the claim that acceptance actually constitutes or confers legitimacy? The only way that one might be able to construct such a theory would be by focusing on the historical coming to be of a general acceptance of something like a rule of recognition and seeing how the history of a community could confer legitimacy on its legal setup. Something like that view is the one generally ascribed to the historical school of jurisprudence, associated with Friedrich Karl von Savigny. Von Savigny argued a thesis similar to one that the positivists hold dear, namely, that a legal system is to a degree to be analyzed as an autonomous system. It incorporates moral standards only, as it were, contingently. (Hart himself takes a similar view in his discussion of natural law.[15]) A legal system gains authority by being the expression of its culture, by incorporating and giving voice to its culture's standards (by expressing the *Volksgeist*, in von Savigny's words). The legal validity of a claim thus could be seen to rest on its place within a legal system (one determines the place of something in a legal system by doing what von Savigny would call the "systematic" study of the law), but the legal validity of the system depends on how it came to be, namely, as an authentic expression of the culture. Legal claims on von Savigny's views are a type of convention through which a culture expresses its (transient) beliefs.

Attractive as this idea might at first seem, it still does not answer the

II. Are Rules Enough?

basic question posed to Hart. Do the legal standards found in a legal system gain their legitimacy through their historical development, or do we see the legitimacy of the historical development in terms of its gradual realization of a valid principle (the debate, basically, between von Savigny and Hegel)?[16]

Let us enlarge the perspective in which the question of legitimacy is raised. There are those who believe that, in order to make judgments about what the law is, one must at least sometimes make judgments as to what the law should be. Let us call this the "principle-based" conception of legal authority. Not surprisingly, proponents of this conception have never been happy with the idea that acceptance alone constitutes legitimacy. But if something like Hart's view is true, where *could* a proponent of principle-based law possibly fit in such judgments about what ought to be the case? Where exactly would be the gap in the system of rules that such judgments could plug? Hart's view rigorously excludes questions of moral validity from legal validity; a principle-based conception of law insists on something close to the opposite of that view. One approach that the proponent of a principle-based conception of law might take is to find some interstitial space in Hart's theory where questions of moral validity would enter (some gap in the system of rules). This would presumably be either at the level of the rule of recognition or at the level of adjudication of particular cases.

Both Ronald Dworkin and Josef Esser (respectively, in the Anglo-American and the German traditions) have attempted to locate those interstitial points in the positivist's theory where moral principles would play a essential role. Seeing their theories in this way would be to see them as examples of how one might try to conceive the relation between history and principle in the issue of legal legitimacy. I shall for the most part stick with Dworkin's theory since it is the better known in the Anglo-American world.[17] Dworkin presents his theory as an alternative to the kind of positivist theory advocated by Hart, and I shall read him accordingly. I have interpreted Hart's criticism of Austin's idea of sovereignty as a way to open the door for rights. Dworkin's criticism of Hart is that his theory does not "take rights seriously," and the vehicle for his criticism is his view that Hart's theory offers a highly flawed account of legal interpretation. Among the major tenets of Hart's theory, according to Dworkin, are the claims that (1) law is a system of rules, (2) legal obligation exists only where there are such rules, and (3) where there are no such rules, there is no law and therefore no legal obligation. Anyone subscribing to these three tenets would be logically compelled to admit the existence of a strong form of judicial arbitrariness, what Dworkin calls judicial "discretion." If a judge is deciding a hard case—that is, a case for which there are no established legal rules, the application of existing rules is in doubt, or there are various and mutually inconsistent interpretations of the rule—then the judge can be under little or no legal obligation to decide the case one way or the other. To decide the case, the judge must therefore go outside the system of rules, that is, outside the law. The judge may decide the case on moral grounds, on grounds of cost to the community, on statesmanlike or foolish grounds, but he or she is under no legal obligation to decide it one way or the other. Moreover, given the open texture of language, cases where there are no rules or where the application of the rules is in doubt will be all too common; no set of rules can provide for all possible cases. The judge therefore has discretion in a strong sense of the word.[18]

Dworkin claims that such an account is flawed and offers as an alternative what he calls the "rights thesis," namely, that hard cases are about the rights of the parties involved and that, even where there is no established rule in the law or the rule is unclear, one of the parties actually has a *right* to a judgment in his or her favor. That is, even where there is no rule that dictates the outcome, there is nonetheless a right answer. If that is true, it would follow that judicial discretion in any strong sense could not exist. But what exactly is the flaw in Hart's theory?

Dworkin seems to find the flaw in the analysis of the concept of law in terms of rules. To support this claim, Dworkin distinguishes rules from principles. Judges typically invoke principles such as "no person shall benefit from their own wrongdoing," or "people have a right that others take reasonable care in their actions that might injure them," in deciding hard cases. A *principle* is some standard that is to be observed because it is a requirement of morality or justice that justifies political decisions by advancing or protecting some individual or group right.[19] Principles are distinguished from *rules* in three ways. First, rules apply in an all or nothing fashion, whereas principles merely *incline* a decision in one way or the other. Second, principles typically cannot be enumerated but change with changing social conditions; rules, on the other

II. Are Rules Enough? 67

hand, can be enumerated. Third, principles have weight, whereas rules do not; two principles can conflict without one's being false (for example, "do no harm" and "tell no lies" may in certain circumstances conflict with each other, but this does not entail that either "do no harm" or "tell no lies" is therefore false, only that one may be more weighty than another), but if two rules conflict, both of them cannot be valid. To the extent, then, that principles are part of the law, the law cannot be merely a system of rules.

Part of Dworkin's reason for thinking that the rights thesis is true is that it provides a better fit with actual Anglo-American judicial practice. First, it explains the phenomenology of the social practices called "law" better. Both attorneys and judges typically claim that they are after what the "law" says. In particular, rarely do judges say that they are just "making it up." Second, it better explains the binding force of precedent. The force of precedent itself rests on the principle "like cases should be treated alike." What is "alike" in various cases, however, depends on how one describes those cases, and an essential part of the description of a chain of cases as forming a precedent is a characterization of the underlying principles of the cases in question. This is not a non-controversial undertaking. In such cases, lawyers will try to argue for a decision in their client's favor by showing how earlier cases enforced a right that they are claiming for their client, and the opposing side will of course generally dispute that claim. Third, judges have the obligation to be articulately consistent; they must be able to justify their decisions in a way that is consistent with other decisions that are held to be right.[20]

What are we to make of the rights thesis? Statements about rights are objective to the extent that there is a human practice of moral and legal criticism of the government and social institutions with a more or less clear set of ground rules. What a judge must do then in hard cases is form a theory of what these social and legal practices are, and the "right" answer will be relative to the right theory.[21]

Not all moral principles may count as legal principles. For a principle to be a legal principle, it must (1) perhaps be found in prior cases or (2) be found in statutes. The origin of principles lies "in a sense of appropriateness developed in the profession and the public over time."[22] Dworkin is quite explicit on this point: "when a judge chooses between the rule established in precedent and some new rule thought to be fairer, he does not choose between history and justice. He rather makes a judgement that requires some compromise between considerations that ordinarily combine in any calculation of political right but here compete."[23] Or, as Esser says, principles are sources of the law "to the extent that they are institutionally embodied through legislative acts, jurisprudence or the life of the law."[24] In short, institutional history is essential to the establishment of principles as legally binding. This is because, as Dworkin puts it, the rule of law has two ideals within it. One is the "external ideal . . . of a perfectly just and effective system. This is the challenge that it offers to legislation . . . [I]t also stands in the shadow of a different, internal ideal . . . of itself made pure. This is the challenge it offers to adjudication: the challenge of making the standards that govern our collective lives articulate, coherent and effective."[25]

III
Principles and the State

What is the dispute between Hart and Dworkin? It is notable (and obvious, I think) that Dworkin's theory does not culminate in two things. First, it does not—it cannot—culminate in any theory of the relativity of morality. Second, it cannot culminate in any *theology*. It is worth raising as a question why the best theory should be one involving moral philosophy and not moral theology. The common sense answer is, of course, that the use of the latter would undermine the separation of church and state. In fact, it would undermine the very principle of the liberal state, namely, its supposed neutrality on things like religious matters that enables it to mediate between competing communities. I can see no other reason for Dworkin's not mentioning moral theology as a candidate for the "best theory." (This secular assumption, moreover, is—as events in our time have shown—no small assumption to make.) Both Dworkin and Hart, therefore, seem to be accepting the ground rules of the liberal state.

Consider moreover the exchange of arguments between the positivist and the kind of principle-based theory of law represented by Dworkin. Dworkin asks himself, How might positivists reply to his objections? They might reply that principles cannot be binding like rules. But why not?, Dworkin asks. That is no argument, merely a counterclaim. Prin-

III. Principles and the State 69

ciples, the positivist might say, do not determine results the way that rules do; but, Dworkin says, that simply points out that they are not rules, which was granted in the first place. Finally, a positivist might say that principles are controversial in ways that rules are not—but Dworkin replies that this only shows that judgment is involved, not that principles are not part of the law. But where do these argumentative gambits by Dworkin lead, except at best to shift the burden of proof back to the positivist? Dworkin's argument ends up merely saying that the positivists have not shown that principles *cannot* be part of the law. But why should one think that this gambit shows that they necessarily *are* part of the law? Why should any positivist be convinced by this? More importantly, how could one expect any kind of analysis of the concept of law to settle the dispute?

The upshot is that it will not answer the dispute. The issue between Hart and Dworkin is not a conceptual or definitional issue concerning the "concept of law"; it is an issue concerning strategies for the form of the liberal state. Any so-called conceptual analysis will at best reconstruct the norms governing the thought of a particular epoch but will be unable to give them the wider context in which they are embedded and that are the grounds for their intelligibility. One needs more than an 'analysis' for that; one requires a certain kind of reconstruction of the concepts involved that locates their intelligibility within a larger framework. The dispute is a political and philosophical dispute about what shape the law must take to best achieve the nature of the liberal state. On this view, the dispute between Hart and Dworkin would be one not simply between two competing 'analyses' of the concept of law or between one that offers a formal account of the law (Hart) and one that claims that the objectives of the law must be taken into account (Dworkin) but between either competing views of the liberal state or competing strategies for the realization of the principles of the liberal state.

Dworkin has argued that one of the basic rights that a legitimate state must protect is that of moral equality, specifically, equality of concern and respect from the relevant authorities. Because of this right to equal concern and respect, the government must as far as possible make its decisions on grounds that are independent of considerations about what constitutes the good life for man. But, of course, this is not itself a value-neutral position. It goes back to Michel de L'Hopital's insight that one of the new functions of political theory is to determine how competing factions in a pluralistic society can coexist, not necessarily what the best way to live is. It sees the underlying moral function of the state in one way as opposed to another. It could be said that the opposition between Hart and Dworkin is, as Hegel would say, mere appearance; the liberal state will always have what can be called the *appearance of positivism*, since it will attempt to cast its doings in important ways in as neutral a light as possible. Its legitimacy—which has the same basis as the legitimacy of the law—will be bound up with its supposed impartiality, its fairness.

Crucial to Dworkin's argument against Hart, however, is his assumption that the *impartiality* of the *liberal* state implies that it treat its citizens *fairly*. The move from impartiality to fairness legitimates Dworkin's theory as not just a theory of liberalism but also of *democratic* liberalism. Once both impartiality and respect for rights become integral parts of the legal system, it is a development of principle to claim that justice also be a part. Dworkin's theory is an expression of this kind of dialectic. The radical individualist ideal of which we spoke in Chapter One does not admit this. As I shall argue in Chapter Four, it permits a theory of impartial *limited* government but no theory of *democratic* government. For that, something more than just a theory of liberty rights is needed: namely, a theory of fairness as the principle of a type of political social union. It is this to which Dworkin is alluding. Just as Hart's theory recapitulates the move from non-liberal theories of sovereignty to the liberal state, Dworkin's theory recapitulates the development of liberalism from a doctrine of rights and limited government to democracy—that is, to a democratic doctrine of accountable government and equality among citizens. Dworkin's view rests on the assumption of the community of fairness as the social union that gives life to the practice of law.

Dworkin's so-called basic right to moral equality plays the same role in this regard as did Austin's notion of sovereignty and Hart's rule of recognition; it endorses a view of pluralism and makes sense within a particular conception of the state as providing the conditions of certain types of peaceful coexistence. It is worth noting that this conception also presupposes that, in a society structured around the principles of peaceful cooperation, there will be no fundamental interests that are irreconcilable; the presupposition is that some form of compromise can always be found. This is, however, no easy presupposition to make. Some theories, such as Marxism, would deny this, claiming that a class society will always have such irreconcilable interests within it, and that only a society purged of such classes could be truly one based on "peaceful cooperation." Underlying this position, then, are deep assumptions about the possibilities of social union.

This way of putting the issue might seem to some as not only a falsification of the debate but one that *ipso facto* gives the winning hand to some form of the school of principle-based conceptions of law. It might seem to be a falsification because it elevated the difference between Hart and Austin to a level where perhaps both would disagree. Hart is, after all, picking up and accepting much of Austin's work, improving on it and not explicitly basing his improvements at all on a theory of natural rights. The conceptual difference between Hart and Dworkin, on the other hand, is immense. To put the Hart/Austin dispute on the same level as the Hart/Dworkin debate is, so this criticism might run, severely to misread the positions involved. Is it also an underhanded way of tilting the debate in favor of the principle-based school? After all, it might be objected that I have framed the debate in terms of the moral objectives of the law, and it is precisely that way of framing it that positivists would like to reject.

Part of the hypothesis that I am advancing is, of course, that the difference between Hart and Dworkin is not an issue at all of conceptual analysis in any pure form. The debate is not primarily an analytical but a dialectical debate concerning how it is possible that we have certain kinds of legal and moral categories. It concerns the reconstruction of a form of life in terms of its basic categories, showing how some categories require certain types of links with others. Such arguments proceed by constructing alternative explanations of the possibility of these forms of life. Such explanations rely on certain descriptions about and interpretations of that form of life itself. Hart and Dworkin are offering alternative explanations of how various legal categories in a liberal social union are possible. They are not merely analyzing general concepts of law but attempting to explain how more determinate conceptions of law are possible. In particular, Dworkin is constructing the possibility of a legal system within a *democratic* liberal society.

Three features of this form of life are important for seeing how it is that questions of law at least *seem* to differ from questions of principle. First, one important way in which legal formulations will differ from moral ones relates in part to what Rudolf von Jhering called the "formal realizability" of the law, a precondition of its being uniformly applied.[26] Von Jhering's point is that some rules are more easily applied than others and (in his phrase) it was in the "spirit of the Roman law" that the importance of formalist approaches to legal draftsmanship came to be seen. A version of von Jhering's own example is instructive. One could draft a law about when a person should be able to vote, enter contractual arrangements and so on in two ways: one could define majority on the basis of when that person is mature and capable enough to manage their own affairs; or one could simply stipulate that a person must be eighteen years of age. The former is certainly a correct idea, but its formal realizability is small. It would require judges to develop capacities to decide these issues, it would burden administrative bodies with having to decide each case anew, and so on. Most likely, it would result not only in inefficiency but also in far greater injustice than the "formally realizable" rule stipulating an age limit.[27] Because of its need for "formal realizability," law will always take a different form from morality. There is no corresponding need to formulate principles of morality with the same attention to minute detail that the law requires.[28] Given one of the values of having a legal system (the value of uniformity), careful development of skills of draftsmanship for formally realizable rules would be appropriate. Von Jhering's point thus buttresses the claim that the "appearance of positivism" naturally emerges as a plausible strategy for securing a liberal state.

Second, there is also the fact that the common law judge familiar to Anglo-American jurists is not the same kind of official as the judge that is familiar to continental and South American jurists. The difference between the two points to a different understanding of how one is to understand the role of rules in a legal system. As Josef Esser has argued, the dominant conception of the continental jurist is more like that of a bureaucrat in his or her application of legal rules. The dominant conception of the common law judge, on the other hand, is not so much that of a bureaucrat as of an official who exercises what Max Weber would call traditional (as opposed to bureaucratic) authority. A bureaucrat is typically not seen to have any leeway with regard to the rules of the system

III. Principles and the State

in which he or she is operating; he or she merely applies the rules handed down to him or her by the relevant authorities. A common law judge, however, frequently brings in things like "public policy" (often a codeword for standards of justice) in deciding a case. What is proper to a common law judge is thus not proper to a bureaucrat, as that role is often understood. The role that principles play in our legal system depends to some degree on the *institutional* role that we wish our judges to play: the role of bureaucrat or of instrument of justice.[29]

Third, consider the idea of the "rule of law" itself, an essential component of this liberal form of life. Among the many components of this idea is the notion that the laws are not to be applied retroactively; that where they are applied, they are to be done so consistently with their spirit; that they are not to be impossible to understand and follow; that the system is to be stable and not change from day to day (it should provide a basis on which to make long-range plans), and so on. (We could enumerate the list of features further.[30]) In such a legal system of rule of law, one has implicit reference to certain principles of justice (justice as regularity and so on). In fact, it would be on grounds of justice, of principle, that one would adopt or argue for rule of law in the first place.

It would be useful to imagine an alternative legal system that might have something *like* a rule of law but would justify it on grounds that would undermine its really being a rule of law. Consider an absolutist system (like, say, seventeenth-century European absolutism). One would have supposedly a *summa potestas*, a sovereign who proclaims law. On grounds of efficiency and consolidation of its power, the sovereign might delegate some of its powers to local administrators; in order to promote efficiency and perhaps to dampen sentiment for rebellion, it might also issue clear laws written in easily available books, and it keeps these laws in place for long periods of time. It might also instruct its underlings to administer the law in a regular and consistent manner. (One might think in this regard of Frederick the Great of Prussia, the prototype of an "enlightened monarch.") To be sure, there would be many problems of interpretation for the administrators in this system, but would *principles* play any *intrinsic* role? It would seem not. They would play a role only to the extent that the sovereign included them in its edicts (for example, if the sovereign issued instructions to its deputies such as "Do not enforce unfair contracts"). But these would be only quasi-principles, since they would derive their sole authority from their being issued by the sovereign. If the sovereign included the principles as an intrinsic part of the system, it would cease to be a sovereign, for it would have then admitted other sources of legal authority into its system than merely those emanating from itself. This system would not, however, be a rule of law. Given an "enlightened" and benevolent *summa potestas*, it might look like one from the outside, but looks would be deceiving. It will *look* like one only to the extent that the sovereign has good ends in mind and issues its edicts accordingly. Since it all depends on the will and good faith of the sovereign, it is hardly a rule of law. Given a good-hearted sovereign, it might even become one; the sovereign could announce, "As supreme source of authority, I hereby proclaim that from now on, this constitution I am holding is the source of authority, and you will note that it contains principles as well as rules." But even in this case, we get the same old questions: Does the constitution gain its legitimacy only because the sovereign bestowed authority on it? Or because it is a fair rule of law?

Given Hart's criticism of Austin, we have reason to doubt the possibility of the fable in any case, for there is reason to doubt that there could ever be a sovereign. Is Hart's own system, however, intrinsically tied into the rule of law? Imagine a legal system in Hart's sense used only for pernicious purposes. The people who use it (I suppose that the Third Reich is something of an example) would have no intrinsic reason to use it. They might use it on grounds of efficiency (where it serves their purposes, fine; where it does not, out it goes), or they might use it to give themselves a mantle of legitimacy. However, they would have no reasons other than these kinds of extrinsic ones. But then we would have something that *looked like* a rule of law but was not the same thing at all.

Even in Hart's system combined with the idea of rule of law, problems of interpretation will arise that will make reference to principles as grounds for justifying decisions. Principles express the point of rule of law. They are part of the legal system in a different way than straightforward rules are. To employ a hierarchical metaphor, they operate on a different level. One cannot arrive at them by, say, beginning with specific rules and then by the process of abstraction reach them at the highest level of generality (as if one could construe the law as a sort of deductive

III. Principles and the State

system, with very general statements at the top and more specific rules at the bottom—for example, from "Contracts are seriously intended promises that are to be kept," to "Contracts consist of offer, acceptance and consideration," on down to more specific things such as "Consideration in commercial contracts of adhesion shall be construed to be . . ."). That would see the difference of principle and rule as one of gradations of generality. Principles are, however, more than general statements of specific rules. They provide directions in which to look to find the right rule, or they may serve to justify a judicial construction of a new rule. For that reason, a legal principle cannot be immediately applied but can serve to justify rules that can. It can serve, that is, to justify the adoption of rules without itself being a rule. There are, of course, rules that tell us if another rule is to be applied (for example, a rule that says that the rules about a contract's being accepted may come into force if the acceptance is done by telephone). But principles are more like guiding thoughts, first steps in constructing the right rule or constructing the right rule to find the right rule (such as counting acceptance of a contract by telephone as acceptance). If one of the reasons for having a rule of law is to secure justice, then it would seem that any explanation of how rule of law is possible would require principles to be part of the law to the extent that they are necessary in finding or constructing the right rule.

The force of arguments about the necessity of principle in law turn on the *form of life* being assumed. Principles will justify decisions about what rule to follow or construct in hard cases in a democratic liberal system devoted to rule of law. To put it more generally, principles play an intrinsic part in the legal system that is appropriate to a type of democratic liberal social union in which people think of themselves in a particular kind of way. "Rule of law" captures the *spirit* of a particular type of social union with its own history and traditions. The appeal to rule of law is an appeal to a very general set of concepts embedded in a general view of an ideal social and political order. Rule of law both evokes certain parts of this vision and is itself a part the vision. This view is not to be understood as merely one of various principles being aligned with one another in inferential patterns; it also includes a kind of dramatic view of the social order, of the types of characters in it, of types of relationships, and so on. One finds these views articulated in the art, common sense, and philosophy of a time. Out of the general view of types of relationships in an ideal social and political order, many different principles will emerge.

What kinds of legal arguments are arguments to principle and what is at stake in such arguments? Arguments of legal principle will be arguments about presuppositions, specifically, about what principles are presupposed by the legal system as a whole or by discriminable parts of the legal system (such as contract, tort, constitutional law, etc.) or even by 'parts of the parts' (such as labor contracts and so on). These presuppositional arguments will sometimes be philosophical arguments in the sense that judges and lawyers must from time to time construct explanations of how it would be possible that such and such rules are compatible either with each other or with more general precepts of the legal system as a whole. There can clearly be alternative explanations of this. It would not seem to follow, therefore, that principles justify only one right answer. Nor need a judge explicitly employ moral theory in any save a loose sense. There would be one right answer only if there were some way of uniquely specifying one theory as correct (which is, shall we say, highly improbable).[31] The principles would serve thus to show that (1) a given rule does not hold in this case because the justifying principle dictates another outcome; or (2) the construction of some new rule is justified because the principle presupposed dictates it; or (3) a given rule does hold in this case because the principle requires it.

This allows us to distinguish legal argument to principle from purely moral argument to principle (that is, to distinguish lawyers from moral philosophers, although admittedly that has not traditionally been much of a problem). Arguments to presupposition always begin with a given. Philosophical arguments of this sort are arguments as to how this given could be possible, assuming other things that seem to exclude this possibility. (This is the nature of a philosophical dilemma: it is not clear just how some X is even *possible*, given that we also believe Y to be the case.[32]) Lawyers and judges will typically be better than others at arguing to specific legal principles since they will understand the "given"—the intricacies of the legal system—better than others. And, of course, the scope of legal argument to principle will be much more limited than the scope of moral philosophy in general, since it must operate under the constraint of being consistent with the legal system at hand, whereas

III. Principles and the State 77

moral philosophy has a much wider scope and is not necessarily constrained to being completely consistent with any legal system.

Legal principles are historically dynamic. As embedded in a historical tradition, legal principles emerge and change as that tradition changes. New principles may, for example, emerge as new legislation emerges. A fable will perhaps illustrate the point. Imagine a democratic libertarian legal system and legal culture. (By "libertarian," I am here understanding a system where the only permissible limitation on liberty would be prevention of harm to others.) In this legal system, there would be no principle obligating one to provide benefits to others. (Let us call this for now the "principle of beneficence.") Now imagine that in this libertarian community, the ethos (about which we spoke in the first chapter) begins to change. As the new ethos emerges, new legislation begins to be passed, in accordance with procedures endorsed by those people. This new legislation, however, begins to acquire the look of being non-libertarian. After the appropriate passage of time (one generation? two?), jurists begin to claim that the existing legislation can only be explained by the principle of beneficence. The principle then could *become* a legal principle, giving rise to a new set of legal rights and duties, by virtue of the change in the system. As legislation creates new rights, principles that serve to explain this legislation give reasons to apply it in penumbral areas. *New* legal principles could legitimately come to be only *after* the legal system has changed. New *formulations* of principles—formulations not heretofore encountered—need not await new legislative development; they need only show that they capture what is already there. For all that, new formulations of principles may be highly creative; they may bring together a line of cases in a way nobody had ever before seen. But they must bring together what is in one sense already there. They are like brilliant new interpretations of philosophical or literary texts.[33] They will often be contested interpretations of what the spirit of the culture involves.

Two ingredients in the conception of a rule of law are the general idea of society as a pluralistic enterprise based on peaceful cooperation (Michel de L'Hopital's idea) and the ideals of justice (the emphasis on rights that emerged in the English civil war). Law is only part of the terms of cooperation in a society. (It is an occupational error of some jurists to think that the law *is* the terms of cooperation of a society.) Moral philosophy is one important element among many in this general conception. (And, of course, it can be dangerous; a well-argued piece of moral philosophy may well blind one to otherwise sound moral intuitions.) To the extent that we will want a rule of law, we will also be incorporating the principles of peaceful cooperation and justice into our legal system. The question of how principles enter into the law will then depend on other things, such as how we harmonize problems of the formal realizability of the law (which will include lots of capability problems of courts and judges) with problems of peaceful cooperation and justice. I cannot imagine any *a priori* method for resolving that.

The role of principle in law thus depends on the type of social union about which we are talking. It follows then that the role of democratic liberal principle depends on how we characterize that form of social union. I have tried to suggest that one cannot understand the form of democratic liberal social union and its concomitant principles outside of the tradition in which the type of not just liberal but democratic liberal social union has evolved. We are to see, I have suggested, the democratic liberal form of social union as evolving these principles out of itself as answers to problems that emerge within it. This rests on a kind of Hegelian way of reading history.[34] The conceptions of society found in new social forms emerge as answers to problems that occurred in the older forms but that were not answerable in the terms that constituted the self-understanding of those forms. In political theory we do not begin with certain characterizations, for example, of rights or general goals and then define the nature of democratic liberal social union from those. Rather we try to understand the nature of rights and goals as emerging strategies for both maintaining and defining the evolving form of democratic liberal social union.

The general issues involved in the jurisprudence of rules and principles emerge as answers to problems that arise within certain forms of social life. They are not merely analytical disputes about the nature of various concepts. However, not much in specific has yet been said about this form of democratic liberal social union. It is to a more specific characterization that I now wish to turn.

CHAPTER

THREE

Civil Obligation and Social Union

ONE OF THE basic ideas underlying all conceptions of liberal social union is the emphasis on individual liberty. The intuitive idea behind this is that there is a kind of natural moral boundary to be drawn around people that may be shrunk or expanded according to the individual's will.[1] But what are the principles that tell us which shrinkings and which expansions are legitimate? Allied with this question is the distinction between our duties and our obligations. This distinction, caught only imperfectly in ordinary language, expresses two different conceptions of our ethical requirements. Duties are those ethical requirements that we have without our voluntary or implied assumption of them; obligations are those ethical requirements that we have only by virtue of our voluntarily assuming them or that apply to us only by virtue of our voluntarily entering into some scheme of social cooperation that imposes the requirement on us. Thus, it is often said that we have *duties* to avoid harming others and *obligations* to abide by voluntary agreements or to give our fair share in mutually beneficial cooperative ventures. The kind of natural moral boundaries around people should then be captured by asking which express duties and which express obligations.

It would be neat and clean if we could divide up our legal requirements into duties and obligations; it would be even tidier if we could explain the distinctions between whole areas of law by the distinction between duties and obligations. If we could, then maybe something like the following would be true.[2] Tort would be that area of Anglo-American law that deals with the duties that we have to compensate people when we have harmed them or their property. Contract would concern itself with the obligations that we freely and mutually assume. It thus might seem merely another perversity of legal thought that legal scholars like Grant Gilmore could even suggest that contract is "dead," that it has merged with torts, or that first year law students should perhaps not have two courses, contracts and torts, but one merged course, suitably titled "contorts."[3] It might also seem like some kind of endemic continental confusion that what most of us think of as the law of torts and the law of contracts is handled by European law under the title of the law of obligations.

Is the distinction between the two basic at all to the conception of justice in a democratic liberal social union? Out of the myriad tangle of interactions that we have with one another, why, after all, should we sort some of them into duties and obligations or, for that matter, into "contracts" or "torts"? Let us call this the problem of civil obligation. I shall be interested here in explaining how civil obligation in a democratic liberal *society* is possible. I shall focus mostly on contractual obligation because of the crucial concept of consent that is present in it. What is it about a form of life that makes contract possible? A system that allows contracts must allow for the privilege or right to strike up contracts and must explain what happens if one breaches. The crucial desiderata here will be what justice requires in such cases. I shall argue that it is inextricably linked to the type of relationships that people bear to each other in relations of tort and contract within a form of social union that I shall call democratic liberal society. In this form of social union, one of the key links between members is choice; its driving force is the liberty to do with oneself what one thinks best and to associate with whom one pleases. What are the principles that make "democratic liberal society" in this sense possible? And what do they tell us about the nature of civil obligation? In order to answer these questions, I shall first look at some common strategies for answering them. I shall try to show that these strategies do not adequately measure up to the task. I shall then turn to the idea of social union to pick up where these failed strategies left off.

I
Contract and the Strategies of Distributive Justice

Contracts are legally enforceable agreements between people. If contract law has any real existence except as a name for a certain type of introductory course in law schools, it should tell us at least three things: first, it should tell us what kinds of agreements are legally enforceable; second, it should provide us with forms for stating our intentions so that we can know with some certainty what kinds of rights and duties we are creating; third, it should tell us what will happen if we breach.[4] How we approach all three issues will depend on how much we see individuals as having the latitude to impose burdens, risks, and harms on themselves and each other. In discussions of the basis of legitimacy of these kinds of distribution of benefits and burdens among parties, two types of strategies typically make an appearance. One is an outcome-oriented strategy of justification; the other is a process-oriented strategy.[5] These two strategies also are typically understood to be exclusive of each other: either one is basic or the other is basic, but not both.

What then are these strategies? An outcome-oriented view justifies the legitimacy of an interaction in terms of the kind of outcome in which it typically results. Other considerations, such as what goes on between the people in the interaction, are of secondary importance. Thus, on the outcome-oriented view, if the outcome of an interaction that follows a certain type of process is proper, then that process is itself proper. The process-oriented view, on the other hand, focuses on what goes on between the people in the interacting itself. On that view, if the process is proper, then the outcome is proper. The first strategy focuses on what *happens* as a result of the interaction and whether this result is proper; the second strategy focuses on what *goes on* in the interacting and accepts whatever outcome results.

Are these two strategies, however, really our only alternatives to looking at the legitimacy of enforcing certain sorts of agreements and not others? If they really are strategies, *for* what are they strategic? I do not think that ultimately these strategies prove to be helpful in resolving these issues. To show that, though, we need to look at how these strategies play off against each other. We can begin to get a hold on what is at issue in them by looking, at least briefly, at how they might apply to the three basic issues of contract law. In their application and in reflection on their application, we can begin to see what they amount to.

One common outcome-oriented approach would be classical utilitarianism. Let us understand by "classical utilitarianism" the idea that the right action or policy is determined by whether that action or policy produces the greatest amount of human well-being. Classical utilitarians would thus evaluate all the rules and rubrics of contract law in terms of their tendency to result in outcomes that embody some greater amount of well-being in comparison with other possible outcomes. The rules governing the making, interpretation, and enforcement of contract are then legitimate if the type of procedures based on those rules tend overall to result in better outcomes (those that involve more happiness) than any alternative set of procedures. This is by no means the only form that utilitarianism takes. Utilitarians of all stripes, however, ask of any interaction between people, Do the rules that permit or forbid these types of interaction tend to result in outcomes that promote or diminish overall goodness? (For example, do the rules enhance or detract from overall community welfare?) The utilitarian would thus assess the legitimacy of the rules of both contract and tort in the same way: Does this or that set of rules tend to promote the overall welfare of the community? This would not obliterate the conceptual distinction between tort and contract; it would just indicate that the rules for each would be assessed in the same way. What would be important is not that one involves promises or agreements while the other does not, but rather that certain harms and benefits result from both.

Utilitarianism is not the only form an outcome-oriented strategy of justification can take. One might also assess outcomes in terms of some notions of distributive justice. We might look at what kind of distribution of basic goods results from the following of a certain procedure. We would then examine the rules of contracts and assess the outcomes as to whether they result in some form of distributive justice with regard to some set of basic goods (such as income, wealth, or political power).

The three basic issues of contract law lend themselves to both kinds of outcome-oriented approaches. Consider the first of the issues: Which kinds of agreements should be enforceable? Suppose we constructed the rules of contract so that only those agreements were legally enforceable that tended to result in gains in overall community welfare or better approximations to distributive justice. We might thus rule out as legally enforceable a large number of agreements between individuals on the grounds that allowing those types of agreements would produce unwanted outcomes. In particular, we might be especially concerned with the kinds of harms that people might inflict on each other. Two such types of harms would be, for example, pains or losses inflicted on a person that are not offset by any benefit gained by inflicting the pain or loss—the utilitarian idea—or depriving somebody of his or her fair share of the basic goods. If so, we could imagine imposing duties on people not to harm individuals in specified ways and find it irrelevant that the harmed person agreed to it. For example, we might find it wrong both to force people against their will into indentured servitude or to allow people to sell themselves into it.[6] We could find this to be wrong because it resulted in some overall diminishing of community welfare, or because it involved some unacceptable distribution of political power.

We could apply these strategies to the third issue concerning the consequences of breach of agreement. Do we give people restitution (give back what is their own, thus nullifying another's wrongful gain) or reliance (compensate a person for harm incurred by virtue of his or her reliance on the agreement) or their expectation (give them what they would have received had the agreement been kept)? An outcome-oriented approach asks which of the three measures of damage produce the best results. Is it fair to award people the benefit of the bargain (expectation) or just repair the harm done (restitution or reliance)? Does it contribute to or detract from community welfare to award expectation damages? Should we simply demand specific performance (compelling the breaching party to do what he or she originally promised)? Will this make the community happier or promote justice?

Even in the abstract, there are basic problems with outcome-oriented strategies. Consider the utilitarian model. There are basic and well-known problems with any utilitarian theory.[7] First, there is the problem of comparing goods. In classical hedonic utilitarianism, this problem is acute, since "happiness" is not a univocal term, and there exists no way of measuring heterogeneous types of happiness against each other: there simply can be no neutral summing up of heterogeneous types of happiness. Second, if one moves away from classical hedonic utilitarianism to more modern variants such as preference-utilitarianism (in which one seeks to maximize the satisfaction of preferences), one is hard pressed to explain why satisfaction of preference is to count as the supreme good, since many preferences will be ones that have the wronging of another person or class of persons as their object (for example, the preference to exclude certain classes of people from the work force).

The third and most damaging objection is that the whole notion of summing goods according to some impersonal touchstone is just wrongheaded. It requires us to aggregate all the sufferings and enjoyments of individuals into one pot and to focus on the sum thereby attained, not (except derivatively) on who attains it. We treat all individuals as if they were only component parts of a large individual whose relationship to them is impersonal. As Hegel argued, this conception does not adequately take into account the differences among individuals.[8] It substitutes an abstraction that allows for the possibility of the sacrifice of individuals in the name of some impersonal good. Hegel saw this as the error involved in those theories that tried to account for all ethical categories by appeal either to utility or to Rousseau's "General Will." Indeed, in practice, Rousseau's idea resulted in a kind of terror, with individuals being eliminated in order to serve a 'higher good.' The executions of the French revolution, done in the name of an impersonal 'will,' resulted in "the coldest and meanest of all deaths, with no more significance than cutting off a head of cabbage, or swallowing a mouthful of water."[9] John Findlay and, following him, John Rawls have generalized Hegel's point into an overall objection against utilitarianism, claiming that it fails to realize the ethical significance of the differences among individuals.[10]

Some utilitarians have tried to avoid these problems by retreating to "ideal utilitarianism." On this view, we choose those actions that ideally maximize goodness, assigning all the while independent weights to various things held to be valuable on their own. Thus, we might deny that things have value only instrumentally, in terms of producing happiness (and thus deny classical utilitarianism) but still claim that we should sum goods. Among the candidates for things that are independently good are personal autonomy, personal commitments, perfectionist goals, some of the traditional virtues, general welfare, and so on. This form of utilitarianism is certainly "ideal," since admittedly no decisive weighting for these values can be given. But does it help? One problem with ideal utilitarianism is its abstractness, for it says little more than do that which is better. Another problem is that the injunction to sum goods is just an incoherent notion no matter what form it takes. There is no univocal meaning of "good" that would permit one to assign numbers or weights to various forms of goodness. If "good" actually univocally meant something like "whatever increases national wealth," then perhaps it might be possible; but, of course, it does not. Or if there was one good that clearly outweighed all other goods, then perhaps we could set up efficiency measurements as to the best ways to attain it. (I say "perhaps" because I do not think that even in these cases one could do it, but I do not wish to belabor the point.) To think of summing goods is, as John Finnis puts it, "senseless, in the way that it is senseless to try to sum up the quantity of the size of this page, the quantity of the number six, and the quantity of the mass of this book."[11] To be sure, you could indeed add up all the numbers, and you would even come up with a definite sum. Just what you would have thereby achieved, though, is difficult to make out.

There is, however, an underlying appeal to utilitarianism that is not really spoken to by any of these rather standard criticisms. Utilitarianism is a consequentialist doctrine, one that claims that our moral duties and obligations depend on the consequences of our pursuing certain actions or types of action. It is opposed to non-consequentialism, a doctrine that puts certain unconditional requirements on our actions independently of the consequences of doing so. Now, to many people, non-consequentialism seems false right from the start. The slogan "Though the heavens may fall, let justice be done," could be the anthem for a proper non-consequentialism (and, in fact, is often taken so, though usually by its opponents, not by its adherents). Some non-consequentialists have aided the task immeasurably. Kant's famous example of the strict immorality of lying even to save an innocent life from a killer has probably converted more people to utilitarianism than all the arguments offered by Bentham and Mill combined. Even John Rawls, a professed anti-utilitarian, says "all ethical doctrines worth our attention take consequences into account in judging rightness. One which did not would be simply irrational, crazy."[12] The appeal of utilitarianism is that it may seem like the only sound consequentialist theory, and since non-consequentialism is "irrational, crazy," one really has little other choice.

After all, to put it crudely, if one has to choose between two courses of action, one of which does more good than the other, isn't it logical to prefer morally the one that does more good? Or, to put it in a different way, if one has to choose between two courses of action, one of which made the world a better place than another, doesn't one prefer that one?

I put it in this crude form because I think that the deep appeal of utilitarian theories lies in the belief that two very general propositions are true: (1) the consequences are an important determinant of the moral quality of our actions; (2) the only rational way of measuring the consequences is in terms of *how much* overall good is thereby attained.[13] The appeal of utilitarianism lies in its *prima facie* plausible claim that *maximizing* goodness is the only rational course once one admits consequences into moral consideration.[14]

It is, however, this focus on maximization *per se* that is what is wrong with utilitarianism. To see why it is wrong, it is helpful to put it into a context where it at first seems right. Few actions are pure: a pure action would be one whose features were totally good or totally bad. Instead, many of our actions are impure; they have some good features and some bad features to them. Let us assume counterfactually that we could assign precise weights to the good and the bad parts of our actions, measuring the good and bad of each action by units that we can call bonums (goods) and mals (bads) of each action. Suppose that we had to choose between two alternative sets of actions, A and B, where each had the same number of bad features (let's say 2 mals), but A produced 10 bonums whereas B only produced 3. It would then seem that one should go with A, with what maximizes goodness. Consider, however, a different set of alternatives. Suppose that one could either (1) with action P do a lot of good, but necessarily produce a lot of evil in doing so, or (2) with action R do less good but produce little or no evil in doing so. In the mythical language of precise weighting, suppose P produces 10 bonums at a cost of 5 mals, leaving a surplus of +5 bonums, whereas R produces only 4 bonums with only 1 mal, leaving a surplus of +3 bonums. In order to maximize goodness, one must perform P; however, common sense morality, I would think, would opt for R.[15] Common sense tells us that doing good is not all that counts and that sometimes doing the most good is in fact not what one should be doing at all. Doing good at the cost of also doing evil is not preferable to doing less

I. Contract and the Strategies of Distributive Justice

good but with a lesser cost in evil. Doing good is only *part* of the moral calculus.

The crucial argument against utilitarianism is precisely that it is what it is, a maximizing theory. It instructs us to do P, whereas common sense morality instructs us to do R. The latter requires us to pick the best action with the smallest amount of evil. (This is a strong objection against utilitarianism, for it accepts what is surely a dubious premise in the first place, namely, that it makes sense at all to talk of maximizing goodness.) It does not tell us necessarily to prevent evil; rather, it puts prohibitions on certain types of action. We may well look to consequences in assessing the ethical validity of our actions, but we need not evaluate these consequences in a utilitarian manner, that is, in terms of the maximization of goodness. Once one sees that the link between taking the consequences seriously and utilitarian assessment can be broken, utilitarianism loses its deep appeal. Without its covert identification with respect for the consequences, utilitarianism is not the common sense doctrine that it might at first seem to be.

The utilitarian form of outcome-oriented strategy thus fails. Rather than try to employ a utilitarian maximization structure to assess outcomes, we might try instead to do it in terms of something like distributive justice. A theory of this type would be based on something like the following very general proposition: we have an obligation to abide by those general rules governing our private interactions if people's abiding by those rules would result in approximations to overall distributive justice. Torts involve boundary crossings of a certain type and the compensation for them; contracts would involve boundary crossings of another type and the compensation for that. Both would be part of a general theory that would focus on the moral space around individuals and the conditions under which boundary crossings would be permitted, with the special case of contracts being concerned with questions of consent. A complete theory of distributive justice would do that.

John Rawls's theory may be taken as an example of such a strategy. Rawls's argument goes roughly like this.[16] Justice applies to the basic structure of society in terms of how that basic structure distributes the primary goods (rights and opportunities, income and wealth, and the social bases of self-respect). A primary good is one that it is rational for any person to desire irrespective of their particular plan of life. A just distribution is a fair one, that is, one to which rational individuals could consent and that would take no morally arbitrary advantage of anyone. In Rawls's ideal choice situation (which he calls the Original Position), principles would be chosen that would give great latitude to individuals to transact with each other freely for their own ends. Rawls's view of civil obligation thus seems to bifurcate into two spheres: the daily sphere where we seem to have the widest possible latitude to pursue our own ends, provided only that we respect the liberty rights of others, and the so called background sphere (the basic structure) where we can manipulate tax laws and social programs (presumably things like welfare, job training, special education programs, and the like) in order to ensure distributive justice.[17] Because of the benefits each derives from the system of liberty, one has an obligation of fairness "to do one's part" by paying into a tax system that maintains "background" distributive justice. However, if the background institutions meet the requirements of justice (they are arranged so that everyone receives their fair share of the primary goods), then there is no more reason to interfere with the ongoing transactions between people. Thus on Rawls's view, we should leave well enough alone in the contractual sphere, focusing our efforts instead on the distributive effects of the background institutions.

Anthony Kronman has taken exception to Rawls's view that the rules of contract should not be manipulated in order to promote distributive justice.[18] He argues that this separation into two distinct spheres of obligation is arbitrary and not required by any theory of civil obligation that places fairness of distribution as paramount. It is arbitrary in that it almost seems as if what we take away on one level, we give back on the other (allow people to strike up whatever bargains they please, then later redistribute the wealth resulting from such bargains if the resulting distribution turns out to be unfair).

Kronman's point seems to amount to something like the following. First, the system of contract is surely part of the basic structure of liberal society. Hence, even though we might not want judges deciding particular cases on the basis of their distributive effects, this does not preclude us from designing the rules that govern such transactions to encourage outcomes that approximate distributive justice. If we persist in trying to avoid using contract law to supplement tax law for purposes of distributive justice, then it must for other reasons. What might they be? One

I. Contract and the Strategies of Distributive Justice

candidate is that contract law used in this way would require the state to single out some pursuits as worthy of either prohibition or strict regulation, and this would violate one of the principles of a liberal society, namely, that it make no policy based on judgments as to which pursuits of its citizens are more or less worthy. This reason fails. Any tax scheme will also fall into this category. Kronman notes, "A selective income tax (such as the one we actually have) that applies only to the income from certain types of transactions or a sales tax on specific items designed to finance a system of redistributive transfer payments are more obvious examples of discriminatory taxes."[19] Some tax schemes may be highly discriminatory, while some may not be. (Kronman: "But just as taxes vary in their neutrality, so do contractual regulations: a law requiring bakers to sell their bread at a fixed price spreads the burdens of redistribution less widely than a law requiring all employers to pay their workers a minimum wage."[20]) There is nothing inherent in contract or tax law that makes one preferable over the other for the liberal society.

Another candidate for a reason to prefer redistributive tax law to redistributive contract law is that the former is less intrusive than the latter and thus allows for greater individual freedom. But, again, some tax schemes may function exactly like contractual regulations in that they continuously apply to all transactions of a certain type (for example, sales tax). Besides, some periodic taxes like the income tax have the net effect of introducing a new rule into otherwise free contractual relations, namely, a rule that both must "share their income from the contract with the state."[21] Again, the difference is not one between inherent intrusiveness and laissez-faire attitudes to individual actions but one of degree that varies depending on the type of tax or contractual regulation. The upshot seems to be that an outcome-oriented strategy cannot avoid trying to manipulate the rules of contract if it also wants to avoid the charge of arbitrariness.

That is, however, not the end of the story. Things are not quite so rosy, however, for this non-utilitarian form of outcome-oriented assessment. Both Kronman and Rawls base their views on what is necessary to respect persons, not on what will produce the greatest amount of some form of goodness. Charles Fried has objected to proposals like Kronman's on the grounds that they violate a fundamental tenet of the principle of respect for persons. Contract, Fried argues, is based on promises that individuals make to each other. Any other basis for it would fail to show respect for individuals as moral beings. This objection leads to a process-oriented view that would reject at the outset any regulation of contract according to outcomes. The obligation to keep a contract is the same as the obligation to keep a promise—irrespective of the outcome. A promise (unlike a vow) is made to somebody who is willing to accept it and who does accept it. The moral basis of the obligation to keep a promise is that, in making a promise, one relies on a set of social conventions regarding speech forms intended to give moral grounds for another to expect the performance of the promise. In a liberal society that as much as possible allows people to pursue their individual projects as they see fit, the free arrangements of rational persons are to be respected—the implication of which is that the state may not take an interest in the fairness of the agreement.[22] Fried's argument thus tries to convict the proponents of distributive justice for contract law in terms of their own principles. The kinds of liberal principles (such as respect for persons) that would make one believe in the first place in assessing the rules of contract in terms of distributive justice exclude all outcome-oriented approaches to contract entirely.

Where the promise principle breaks down (due to ambiguities and the like), we must fill the gaps left open, and often tort principles for assessing damages will be the most useful ones to employ. Of course, Fried notes that not just any promise will count. The promise must be made freely and not be unfair; it must be made rationally and deliberately; and it may require regulation if the legitimate interests of third parties are adversely affected by it. Nonetheless, this does not obviate the moral force of contract or promise. For Fried, civil obligation comes in two packages: those duties we have to others that hold independently of our choices and those that we freely take upon ourselves. To regulate contract in the way in which Kronman *et al.* suggest is, for Fried, to undermine severely the principles of liberal autonomy; it is to focus on outcomes and not processes, which (if we respect the promise principle) is wrong.

It is certainly not clear, however, whether Fried's points in the end really dispute the kinds of outcome-oriented approach that people like Kronman take. For example, the promise must not be "unfair"; this seems to require some kind of outcome-oriented assessment. Moreover,

I. Contract and the Strategies of Distributive Justice

the parties must have a *right* to make the promise (offers and acceptance of indentured servitude are for Fried as for Kronman presumably out of the running). It is at least questionable whether any coherent notion of rights can be gleaned without looking at outcomes. And, of course, the offer cannot be a coercive threat ("your money or your life"). As a definition of coercion, Fried offers the following: "A proposal is . . . coercive if it proposes a wrong to the object of the proposal."[23] However, what is left unanswered by Fried is the nature of the wrong. If people have a right to distributive justice (or at least a right to have the basic institutions of their liberal society ordered along lines that would approximate distributive justice), then why is it not wrong to offer them terms that would violate the principles of distributive justice? (This is a shorthand way of asking why rules of contract—part of the basic structure—would be allowed to be formulated in ways that would not tend to approximations of distributive justice.) In any event, Fried leaves unexplained just why the will of someone necessarily must be respected. Fried claims that not to respect the will of the parties is not to treat the people involved as moral beings. (Fried says that not to respect the will of a person is to "infantilize" him.[24]) Why should this be so? It is just a *fact* that people will certain things. The question is what normative force this fact has. I argued in the first chapter that respect for persons is not equivalent to respect for choice. If that is true, then Fried's appeal to respect for persons as a reason for holding the will theory of contracts fails to work. But if the simple appeal to "respect for persons" will not work to justify the process-oriented strategy, what then will?

One might begin to suspect that these general strategies are in fact just too general. Instead of going any further down the path of tweedledee-outcome vs. tweedledum-process strategies of justification, let us change course a bit. Take another one of the basic questions of contract law: What form should our intentions take in order to make an agreement legally enforceable? (Note that this question is integrally tied into the first question, "Which agreements are legally enforceable?") In Anglo-American law, the textbook model for a valid contract is the triad of an offer to someone, his or her acceptance, and an exchange of something, called the consideration. It is not enough simply to make an offer and have the other party accept it; it is said that there must be something in addition that is exchanged. Consideration is understood as something either given or promised in exchange for a promise, that is, some benefit to the promisor or detriment to the promisee. (I offer a sum of money to you if you will perform some service, you accept, and I give you a smaller sum as downpayment; that smaller sum is the consideration.) The amount of the consideration is not relevant; it is only important that it be there. "The law is not interested in the adequacy of the consideration," as the saying goes.

There are many interesting and even amusing puzzles as to what counts as consideration in an agreement. A more basic question, however, is whether consideration is a legitimate part of contract law at all. Consideration is, after all, a validating concept; it promotes what would otherwise be a legally irrelevant interaction into a legally enforceable agreement. Is the idea of consideration to be justified by a process- or outcome-oriented approach? It is instructive to see just how the concept of consideration arose. Morton Horwitz has argued that, in the eighteenth century, the duties imposed by the common law were regarded as prior to any obligations incurred by private agreement and were seen to override or nullify the latter.[25] It might thus be tempting to suppose that an outcome-oriented approach then prevailed. However, in the nineteenth century, so Horwitz claims, the gap between contractual and noncontractual duties began to grow. Although contract law had existed prior to the nineteenth century, it had not existed in the form in which we now know it. It was subordinate to property law and functioned mainly to transfer title to the things for which the contract was made. In the eighteenth century, the fairness of the exchange was believed to put limits to contractual obligation: equity courts would refuse to enforce contracts in which what came to be called consideration was inadequate. These earlier doctrines tied the fairness of consideration into other doctrines of "fair price" and "customary price."

With the rise, however, of a market economy and a new type of social expectation, namely, that one may strive for material gain for material gain's sake, a new version of contract began to emerge, the will theory of contract.[26] This held that contractual obligation depended on a convergence of wills, on what the parties agreed upon. In a society that both sees goods as fungible and sees people as wanting to better their material lot (and thus speculating on goods), expectation interests come to play an increasingly prominent role. With this change in the notion of

I. Contract and the Strategies of Distributive Justice 93

what counts as a legitimate interest, contract began to be seen as something that creates an expected return, not merely something that transfers title to property or binds a person to the performance of some action. Expectation damages rather than merely specific performance came to play a greater role. It came to be seen that the market would only work if parties were allowed to enter freely into contracts simply because each believed the agreement to be to his or her advantage. The model of the social actor as a rational calculator of his or her own interests began to make its legal appearance.

As this new idea began to work itself out, however, certain problems inherent in it began to be seen. If the will theory of contracts was taken to its extreme conclusion, it would follow that individuals had the right to alter the legal rules that governed their transactions. For a period after 1830, according to Horwitz, one could even contract out of liability for one's negligence. But if this were so, then each contract would be a unique event, a *de novo* happening in the legal world, governed only by the individual wills of the parties. A well-functioning market system, however, cannot abide this. Markets require a certain amount of stability so that plans for future gain can be rationally made. The expectation interest, which played such a major role in shaping the new role of contract, also required some uniformity and standardization. For that reason, rules for the construction of the parties' intentions came into being, and the classical doctrine of contract as offer, acceptance, and consideration made its appearance. The doctrine of consideration arose thus as a way to hold to the idea of contract as an embodiment of the new social interests bound up with a market society and to stabilize that notion. It was a practical answer to a problem of possibility within a form of social order. It did not so much depend on an outcome- or process-based strategy of justification as it did on the idea of securing a workable conception of contract within a new type of social order.

According to Gilmore, the classical theory assumed its contemporarily recognizable form at this point. If people promise benefits to and accept benefits from each other, and some consideration is given, the agreement is enforceable, independent of all judgment as to the adequacy of the consideration. The outcome is irrelevant.[27] Gilmore summarizes the classical view in this way:[28] liability for breach was narrowed in that the existence of consideration needed to be shown; if one assumed a duty, then one had an obligation to fulfill it, even if one was rendered unable to do so by no fault of one's own, unless one had specified that in the initial agreement; and a negative approach was thereby taken toward recovery of large damage awards. The wills of the actors were respected, and the market was given a certain amount of stability.

As a matter of history, Gilmore says, this classical view has vanished and with it any meaningful notion of contract law. This is the sense of his claim that contract is "dead"; the old model of 'offer/acceptance/consideration' has turned out not to be of much use. The stumbling block in the classical theory, Gilmore argues, turned out to be the doctrine of consideration. It became impossible to pin it down either conceptually or historically. Historically, people could point to any number of cases that did not fit the classical model. Conceptually, consideration came to be seen as a concept that could be extended to anything.[29] It ends up in our times being a term "used merely to express the legal conclusion that a promise is enforceable."[30] Thus, it failed to do the practical and theoretical work for which it was intended. Even assuming that sense could be made of the doctrine of consideration, the most it can do is to restrict the class of enforceable agreements to those of bargains. Unfortunately, any quick perusal of modern American contract law will show that even this is not in fact the case. Many more agreements than those that are bargains (in any but the loosest sense) are found to fall under the rubric of contract.

Gilmore's only explanation for this is the switch from a laissez-faire economy to the welfare state. From a world that valued individualism and self-reliance and saw the market as a natural outgrowth of those, we have moved to a welfare state in which, Gilmore says, "We are now all cogs in a machine, each dependent on the other."[31] We now focus once again on outcomes of contractual agreement, and the test of contract is the type of harm that is produced. It might look as if we have returned to the rationale of pre-nineteenth-century contract law, in which our basic duties not to harm others preempts or nullifies whatever obligations we incur through contractual agreement. However, it is also true that, in a lot of modern thought, the market itself is no longer seen as a natural outgrowth of natural human desires, but as an institution that at best grows naturally out of highly socialized desires (for example, the desire to better oneself, to work hard to do so, and so on).³² Gilmore's point seems to be that, in the modern social setting, damages have come to be assessed both in tort and in contract on reliance, that is, on the principle that where another relies on you to do your duty (not to go through the red light, to deliver the goods that you promised, and so on) and is harmed by your failure to do your duty, then you must compensate for his or her reliance. This would have as a corollary the idea that those agreements are enforceable that would result (or do result) in people's being harmed by their reliance on them when they are broken. Likewise, on the flip side, where there is no harm done, no enforceable agreement is present. This functions as the contemporary strategy for underwriting the market oriented society in which we live.

Where are we? The original issue seemed to be determining in the abstract what is to count as a crossing of a moral boundary and what it might mean to compensate someone for such a crossing. To compensate a person for a harm would seem to be leaving the person harmed as well or better off than he or she would be had the harm never occurred. Is this restitution, reliance, or expectation? One cannot answer that in the abstract. To favor one type of compensation over another is to make some assumptions, obviously, about what is legitimately due a person, and this depends on the conception one has of the interests at stake. Gilmore's historicist point is that, as the United States passed from a pre-market to a market society, the idea of what was due someone, what was legitimately their own, changed.

Where have we ended up? The alternative of outcome-oriented and process-oriented strategies of justification does not satisfactorily answer the basic questions with which we began. The strategies themselves need to be located within a larger context, namely, the kind of democratic liberal society for which they claim to be the best principles. It is not as if we construct the ideal of liberal society out of some kind of outcome- or process-oriented strategy; it is rather that these strategies are strategies for realizing the (multifarious) ideals of a liberal society. Are we just left then with nothing more than the ideal of liberal society in whatever manner it happens to take? Or may we explain the possibility of liberal society as a form of social union by appeal to some basic principles that are embedded in it?³³

II
Sharing and Fairness

Let us start again. We are asking how civil obligation is possible. There are different stances one might take to this. One might, for example, identify law and morality and hold that our moral duties are our legal duties, pure and simple (and by implication that moral rights are legal rights). Civil obligation would then be explained by moral obligation, leaving aside how one would explain the possibility of moral obligation itself. If one opted for a straightforward explanation of civil obligation by moral obligation, then one could refine the legal questions of compensation to questions of violation of moral rights: when a moral right is violated, the wrongdoer must compensate accordingly. Now, there is nothing *per se* incoherent about this view. If it is incoherent, it is such only from within some more specific context. We considered part of that context in Chapter Two. There we looked at some reasons why this immediate identification of law and morality was, from the standpoint of a liberal form of social union, difficult to make.

There is a general point about the connection between law and morality here. To understand the valuations made in legal or moral systems, one must understand the point of the evaluation, the interest behind it. People do not make valuations totally disinterestedly; there must be some point in it, even if that is buried deep in history. Both law and morality serve very similar purposes, namely, to mediate in the peaceful resolution of disputes; without them things would tend to go badly. Each rests on our mutual acknowledgments of the kinds of claims that others make on us, on our recognizing the status of other people within our moral worlds. How or whether we see the two (law and morality) as diverging depends on how we see these purposes as being fulfilled. The determination of the relation between law and morality is thus not something to be made in the abstract but depends on the structure of a particular moral world, of the forms of social union in which we find ourselves and that we can justifiably hold to be proper.

In a democratic liberal society, the relations between law and morality are bound up with the more basic idea of full acknowledgment of the other's status as equally worthy of respect, of giving full weight to the other's point of view. This more basic idea is difficult to formulate, but it

II. Sharing and Fairness

involves a full acknowledgment of the selfhood of the other as a being like oneself with whom one can converse and reason and who is capable of both rational conversation and acting on it (as distinct from a view of others as, say, corrupt and requiring remaking or as intrinsically lesser beings than oneself). To ask about civil obligation within a liberal society is therefore to ask about what the proper types of relationships between individuals in a liberal society should be. What concatenation of enforceable rights and duties gives proper expression to the ideal that the legal resolution of conflict is to show respect for persons?

It would be a mistake to look for some unitary principle from which we could deductively elaborate principles that would answer these questions. These principles must be elaborated against the background of the kind of interests that motivate ethical evaluation. The general principles that one finds in such a manner will be those that are constitutive of an ethical life. As I have argued, this kind of procedure is a close relative of the kinds of arguments offered by Hegel: one seeks to elaborate the conditions under which some domain of human life or experience is possible. Now, one point of ethical evaluation is to facilitate our interactions with each other so that things do not go so badly as they would without it. Another important point to ethics is that it embody the kind of acknowledgment we have of each other as self-conscious, rational beings. Ethical evaluations thus serve two distinct interests. One is a practical interest in having a world that runs more smoothly than it otherwise would; the other is a practical interest in the people we are (in our self-understandings) and the kinds of lives we lead. Neither interest is more basic than the other.

Some caveats need to be mentioned again here. The ethical principles are formed against a complex background of human needs, of limited sympathies, of individual and communal searches for the good life, of wants, desires, and the like. One would therefore expect a number of independent ethical principles to be developed, not all of which necessarily are consistent or coherent with each other. Moreover, one would expect that different types of principles would be devised in different types of circumstances and cultures. As new possibilities open up, new principles emerge; the countering of limited sympathies and the expression of our mutual acknowledgments will lead to different strategies as the historical context changes. One can expect, however, similar principles to emerge in different contexts to the extent that life remains the same. To understand the rationality of ethical conversation, debate, and argument, one must understand it as set within this larger context of human life lived among others in a common world. What makes any rational argument possible is commitment by the community to certain modes of settling disputes. Moreover, the *variety* of ethical arguments is part of the nature of ethical argument. Ethical debate alternately attempts a variety of things: to provide maps of the ethical world (through the construction of philosophical and theological systems of ethics or through the construction of rule-of-thumb maxims), to edify us into acknowledging features of the subjective life of others, to disclose (as in some literary depictions) alternative ways of living, to hint at what could be the more fulfilling form of life, or to provide imaginative renderings of the failure of certain ideals and ways of life and adumbrations of new achievements of certain basic human goods. Philosophical ethics is an important but by no means the only component in such debate.

Connected with these kinds of arguments are different models of society and correspondingly different principles for the allocation of goods. We can distinguish three such models. First, there is the utilitarian model itself. This sees the goal of all moral decision as based on some kind of calculation of what would overall promote a greater aggregate happiness. The ideal utilitarian society is one in which all the social goods have been parceled out so as to produce the greatest amount of human happiness (or satisfy the greatest number of preferences) possible. Second, there is the familiar model of a society based on some overarching neutral framework of rights. The ideal rights-based society is one in which individuals choose their own individual goods within a system of basic rights that only put constraints on those individual choices—for example, one may not be permitted to choose a good that involves violating somebody else's right. These two models of society also contain two different models of what is morally important about individuals. The utilitarian model sees the morally important self as basically a bundle of desires and sees society as a kind of quasi-individual, a vast system of desires as the sum of all individual desires. The rights-based model sees society as a rule guided framework within which individuals go about choosing their own values.

A third model can be called a "social ethics" model of society. It sees

II. Sharing and Fairness

individuals neither as bundles of desires nor as choosers independent of any particular aims but as beings whose identities and autonomy are constituted by their being members of different types of communities with different histories. Moral choices and social decisions about rights cannot be made independently of some idea about the proper values and goals of the social and political order in which they are situated. On this model, the good for an individual cannot be even identified outside of a common good. The ideal "social ethics" society is one in which there is a workable consensus about what values are constitutive of the good life, in which individuals find a point to living, and in which individuals find their fulfillment as communal beings of a sort. Although this view is a bit more difficult to articulate—for one reason, it does not offer the clear-cut set of alternatives that the rights-based or utilitarian theories do—it does offer nonetheless a third alternative view of an ideal social and political order.[34] It is this third model that I will be trying to articulate here in terms of a theory of democratic liberal social union.

What would make one think that such a theory of the principles of a democratic liberal social union is even possible? There is a view associated with the school of critical legal studies that holds that this kind of reconstruction must of necessity fail. Duncan Kennedy has presented a particularly forceful version of this criticism.[35] Kennedy's points are especially instructive, in that he too sets the debate in terms of the larger question of the kind of society involved, but he rejects any theoretical solution to the problems. I wish to look at Kennedy's reasons for doing this and then to contrast them with the view presented by John Finnis. Finnis too sets the debate in terms of the type of society, but reaches a fairly traditionalist solution concerning civil obligation. Both Kennedy's and Finnis's arguments turn on the role that the principles of sharing and fairness play in a liberal society.

Kennedy couches his argument in terms of the debate about 'rules' versus 'principles' that we went through in the second chapter. He argues that there is no way to resolve that issue since there will always be equally valid but incommensurable claims about what the correct principles are or about whether principles or rules are called for. The real argument is thus, on his account, not one about 'rules' or 'principles' at all. It is a practical, political argument about which legal settings keep some group in power and at the same time keep some groups out of power. In particular, the arguments between outcome- and process-oriented strategies of justification reflect this incommensurability. Kennedy's explanation for why these strategies are unsatisfactory is that they are just appearances of a deeper issue concerning basic but incompatible views of the world.

He characterizes these views as those of individualism and altruism. An individualist view of the world consists (1) in a distinction of one's own interests from those of others, (2) a belief that it is legitimate to have a preference for one's own interests, and (3) a willingness of each to abide by the rules that make peaceful coexistence with other individualists possible. It is a view of the world grounded in a vision of people as autonomous agents, of self-reliant individuals choosing, pursuing, and achieving their own goals without being dependent on others and without demanding that others make sacrifices for them. (It is, incidentally, not equivalent to an egoistic view of the world, since such an individualist view puts a strong emphasis on respecting the liberty-rights of others.) On this view, the fundamental form of social interaction is exchange (at "arm's length"). The altruist (one might also call it the strongly communitarian) view is one that sees people as inextricably dependent on each other, that sees our interactions with each other as based on sharing and sacrifice; it does not see as legitimate a preference for one's own interests over another's. The fundamental form of social interaction on the altruist view is not exchange but the kind of sharing and sacrifice that makes us vulnerable to the failure of others to reciprocate.

Kennedy argues that it is not the case that one of these views is 'false' and the other 'true.' It is as if the human world was one of those optical illusions, such as the one consisting of two human profiles facing each other that, from another point of view, appear to be a vase against a background; one can see the picture as faces or a vase, but not both at the same time, and each is equally a true way of looking at the object. Both the individualist and the altruist viewpoints are equally valid components of a view of the human world, but, on Kennedy's view, both are incompatible with each other. One cannot be both self-reliant and dependent.[36]

The argument for rules or principles, so Kennedy argues, is just this argument for individualism or altruism. Rules are inherently non-

II. Sharing and Fairness

interventionist; they simply give the parties means for communicating their intentions to others, or for regulating their interactions with each other (putting people on notice as to the consequences of their actions if they do something forbidden by the rules). Rules give the actors a kind of certainty about the possible consequences of their actions so that they can make their self-interested plans accordingly. An insistence on rules is therefore really an assertion of the truth of the individualist world view. Principles, on the other hand, require judges to refer to some objective of the legal order and to assess the facts of individual cases to see if there is a fit between fact and objective. Much more than rules, they are outcome-oriented. A regime of rules, however, is process-oriented: if the actors have followed the rules in their interactions, then the outcome will be (from the legal standpoint) irrelevant. Principles, on the other hand, are generally invoked to mitigate the harshness of a regime of pure rules; where the strong, who are capable of manipulating the rules to their own advantage (or can find or purchase the services of someone who can), manage in a system of rules to triumph over the weak, principles are employed to show that this was not, for example, the point of the rule. A system of rules lets the wily among us know that, if they can figure out a way to exploit the rule to their own purposes (with the more trusting falling by the wayside in the process), then they will be allowed to do so. An appeal to principles is a brake on the wily among us.

Kennedy's position is thus that liberal society involves a kind of fundamental contradiction in it. On his view, no compatibilist explanation of its principles is possible, and hence no general theory of civil obligation is possible. At best, there can be competing theories, and the choice between them is a practical, political choice, not one of better or worse explanations.

John Finnis approaches these questions of civil obligation from the standpoint of what justice requires under natural law.[37] In his view, the natural law tradition views justice as a matter relating to our dealings with each other where there are moral duties present and where some sense of equality is to be maintained among people. He distinguishes two senses of justice embedded in this tradition. First, there is distributive justice, where the problem is how to distribute a common stock of resources or burdens and benefits of a common enterprise, in order to promote the common good. Second, there is commutative justice, which concerns proper dealings among individuals where allocations of common stock or burdens and benefits of common enterprise are not in question. The former notion is concerned with the justice of who gets what (and how much) of something common; the latter notion is concerned with the justice of dealings among individuals. Commutative justice does not concern itself with the parceling out of some quantity of burdens or benefits but with determining what one party 'owes' another (what is 'due' them). For example, a judge has a duty of commutative justice to the parties in question to faithfully apply the law and apply only the relevant rules, independent of the questions of distributive justice at hand, and, Finnis claims, the act of adjudication is always one of distributive justice, since the judge always has to distribute gains and losses in a case.

Finnis thinks that this is the key to understanding issues involving civil obligation. The common law of torts in its classical period was, says Finnis, a doctrine of commutative justice. It invoked a standard of fault to determine if legal liability for some harm was to be established. It established a general duty of care (a duty owed by all to all the world) and asked not merely if harm was done but if it was wrongful harm. It concerned itself, that is, with the duties owed by one individual to another. The more recent law of torts has departed from this view toward a doctrine of distributive justice. A tort theorist with concerns for the latter is apt to ask not about the proper standards of conduct that we owe to our neighbors but about the proper distribution of harms, benefits, and risks. Strict liability (that based only on harm or loss caused, not on the harm or loss being the result of faulty action) is a doctrine that answers to these distributive concerns. The move in torts has been from questions about proper standards of due care and compensation for those wrongfully harmed to questions about distributing the risks of common life. It has, that is, moved away from questions of commutative to questions of distributive justice.

One finds, says Finnis, a similar situation in contracts. We have a duty of commutative justice to keep our promises to each other; thus, if one breaches a contract (an enforceable promise), then one has an obligation to restore the other party to where they would be except for the breach. Thus, one has a duty of commutative justice to perform that

II. Sharing and Fairness 103

which one originally promised, and if one does not, an obligation to pay the equivalent in damages. If one looks at contract in terms of distributive justice, however, one will be looking at some parceling out of gains and losses in the contractual situation. If the contract is viewed as a joint enterprise, a partnership of sorts, then one can see failure of performance as a risk undertaken by both. (Finnis thinks, in fact, that this view is the one taken in much modern contract law.)

The fundamental question for Finnis in matters concerning civil obligation is thus whether it is reasonable to regard the people whose activities are in question as participating in a common enterprise. Finnis seems to think that the answer is negative with regard to a wide range of cases. In contract, for example, one's duty is not "do X that you promised *or* pay damages." It is simply a duty to do X. (One might say: it is not a duty to do X *or* Y, but only to do X). If one violates this duty of commutative justice, to keep one's promises, one has wrongfully harmed another and must compensate. Only in that way can the common good be promoted; the institution of promising is justified because it offers people a means for coordinating activities while allowing for autonomy, and promising means doing what you said you were going to do—*not* doing it *or* deciding to pay (unless, of course, the promise itself was couched in the form of "do X or pay").

From the standpoint of Kennedy's view, the question that Finnis thinks is one of choosing between two different types of justice is rather one of two equal and competing world views. Finnis sees the problem as one of deciding if it is true that the enterprises in question are shared or not; Kennedy sees it as rooted in equally valid competing visions of the world, such that one cannot say that one is true and the other is false. Both are, as it were, 'true.'

Kennedy's point of view can be seen as an alternative explanation of the possibility of how principles could be part of the legal order. There are, however, problems with this view (considered in this way, as an explanation of the possibility). Why cannot a strong libertarian (an individualist in Kennedy's terms) argue for principles and not merely rules in an individualist, libertarian legal order? For example, the principle of respect for choice (giving rise to doctrines like "freedom of contract") would be such. Where a person had managed to manipulate the rules of a legal system so as to void effectively someone's freedom of contract, could not—quite consistently—a libertarian judge invoke the principle of respect for choice (making reference to the objective of that legal order, namely, to protect liberty-rights) to block that move? Indeed, in the same way an altruist judge might block enforcement of a contract that called for an unfair sharing of risks?

A more complete explanation would be one that made room for both Kennedy's and Finnis's views. This would involve seeing the relevant principles as embedded in different types of relationships. Some contracts may indeed be best seen as partnerships; others may not. Both Kennedy and Finnis think that it is an either/or situation: one thinks that it involves competing visions of the world; the other thinks that it involves competing visions of justice. However, both Kennedy's and Finnis's views rest on some understanding of the nature of the social unions in which justice plays a role. What Kennedy presents as an either/or situation is really two different versions of the social union: one in which there is no shared identity (individualism) and another in which we identify our interests with others in some version of a common good, where we share our fate with others (altruism). By setting the issue as one between commutative and distributive justice, Finnis implicitly construes it as an issue concerning the type of relationship that the individuals have to each other; whether commutative or distributive justice is at issue depends on how we see the common stock of goods as being allocated.

The basic idea behind this is that society is best seen as a cooperative enterprise. What then are the *terms of cooperation* of a democratic liberal society? How can people legitimately expect, ask, and demand of others that they cooperate with them? That is, what are the legitimate terms that would ensure that justice is secured and the 'peace is kept?' Early strategies of liberalism, as we have seen, focused on the protection of certain basic human interests, in particular, those of security of the person. Michel de L'Hopital's proposal was aimed at that. The system of sovereignty that grew out of his proposal, however, generated problems that it could not in its own terms resolve. To resolve them, the modern liberal theory of rights as protections of fundamental interests came to be. The justification of rights lies in their explanatory power. The claim that people have rights is based on the claim that positing such rights best explains why it is, for example, wrong to do certain things to people.

II. Sharing and Fairness

By a right, I shall understand a "valid claim" where by "valid" I shall mean "derivable from some basic set of rules and/or principles." This, however, does not by any measure tell us all there is to know about rights. A suggestion by Mill is helpful here. Rights are a certain type of valid claim, namely, those such that society ought to protect us in our possession of them.[38] A right, that is, is a valid claim against others that the state ought to enforce. This means that rights are not merely a function of moral considerations concerning the possessor of the right but also of moral considerations concerning the person (or body of people) against whom the right is asserted. It may be wrong on certain grounds to treat a person in such and such a way, but it may also be wrong on the same or other grounds for the state to compel somebody to abstain from doing that. Particularly in a liberal society, one will expect that the domain of ways in which one can wrong another and the domain of ways in which the state may compel one not to do so will be different; the latter domain will be smaller. It may be wrong to break dinner dates without notice; it is surely not right for the state to compel the guilty parties to show up. Mill had a general reason for believing this to be so. Invoking an outcome-oriented theory where outcomes are measured by their utility (itself measured by how much human well-being is achieved), Mill could determine that rights existed only where the costs (in utility for the society overall) did not exceed the benefits (again measured in utility for the society overall). Many wrongs done (so a Millian can argue) are of such a nature that preventing them would cause more harm than the wrongs themselves. We can hold something very much like this to be true, even if we cannot accept the theory of utilitarianism for reasons like the ones mentioned earlier. That is, we can accept the general principle that we view those moral duties that we owe to others as correlated with (or perhaps implying) rights in terms of which ones will be properly enforceable by the state, that is, which ones do not incur greater moral costs (measured in some other way than utilitarian).

The determination of what counts as a basic interest is thus of crucial importance here. A basic interest would be one that it is believed individuals will take seriously, such that failure to respect it will undermine the conditions required for a stable pluralistic democratic liberal society. However, what interests we will count as basic will depend on what kind of society we wish to create and sustain. It is not so much that we begin with an abstract account of the interests and then structure our ideals of social union around those; rather, we form our ideas of the basic interests around the various ideals of character and of flourishing that we find either present or possible in particular kinds of historical situations. The basic interests will be those that individuals will think are important enough so that injury to them will undermine their willingness to cooperate, or they will be those that individuals take seriously enough to demand a mutual acknowledgment of them within a given social and political order. Conceptions of what constitutes our basic interests are based on some understanding of our shared identity, of a common good. Determination of this common good requires us to interpret what this identity is. But no amount of analysis of the "concept of a rational agent" or an appeal to the "terms of cooperation" in the abstract is going to do that for us.

What is required in constructing any theory of rights is therefore a determination of the types of relationships that we are to bear to each other. Only by determining this can we have any real idea of the moral costs that are incurred by state intrusions into the lives of its citizens. In a democratic liberal society, there will be an initial presumption in favor of individual liberty. An incursion into that will count as a moral cost of some magnitude. By no means does this rule out *a priori* all such incursions; it will merely state that they should be of great weight. A purely liberal society would put great stress on individual rights to liberty; in it the radical individualist ideal would be paramount. A *democratic* liberal society, on the other hand, is one in which the ideal of fairness and of sharing enters into the sense of who the members of that society are. Or, as we might put it, in a democratic liberal society, not merely liberty but also equality of a sort plays an essential role. (I shall have more to say about the role of equality in Chapter Four.)

Kennedy's contrast between altruism and individualism captures two aspects of the liberal tradition. Individualism corresponds to that element of the tradition that stems from classical liberalism, with its stress on the 'natural' rights of individuals and limited government. Altruism accords well with the democratic tradition in liberalism, with its emphasis on equality and fraternity. Kennedy's argument may be taken as an expression of the fragmentation of the tradition, of there being potentially competing elements within the tradition. He, of course, thinks that these

II. Sharing and Fairness

elements are simply incommensurable with each other and thus are necessarily, not accidentally, competitive. The goal of the kind of explanation being offered here is that they need not be seen as incommensurable but as compatible with each other when seen in terms of the social unions that make them possible.

What is required is then to look at the general types of relationship that can flourish within a democratic liberal society. This is the same as asking: How is it possible that one could have a democratic liberal legal order whose chief principles are respect for persons (the basic one) and the two principles of rule of law (justice and peaceful coexistence)? The notion of justice being used here, it will be remembered, is that of giving people what is due to them; in particular, we will be asking what rights individuals would have, where we are taking rights to be those duties that we have that ought to be enforceable (that is, those duties for which the 'cost' of enforcement does not outweigh the 'benefits').

What other principles, if any, would be intrinsic to a democratic liberal legal order? One basic principle would be that of reliance (or of trust, as it might equally well be put). The principle of reliance can be understood as holding that people may legitimately expect that others will abide by their duties and obligations. If nothing else, this principle is a condition of peaceful coexistence in communities. The reliance principle is bound up with the idea that people have a right not to have their legitimate expectations disappointed. The trust we place in others to fulfill their duties and obligations renders us vulnerable to them in a way that is only barely recognizable within the radical individualist ideal of social union. Trust can be called an enabling principle. For the other ideals of liberal society to function, there must be trust among its members. Without such trust, the other principles—such as respect for choice—lose their rationale. The importance of trust may be seen in the almost universal repulsion of its violation in its starkest form: betrayal, commonly and widely held as among the worst vices.[39] Trust injects an element of the personal into the otherwise impersonal world of the marketplace; we rely on others to do what is right. An impersonal world would be one in which the value of trust would not be as high; it would be the world of Machiavelli's court, where, for "reasons of state," betrayal was the result simply of calculations one made about how better to further certain ends, much as a shrewd merchant might calculate when to breach a contract.[40] But without some shared identity, there can be nothing to which to be loyal; trust has no place in the radically impersonal world of the radical individualist. But where great latitude is given to individual choice (as is the case in a democratic liberal society), trust must play an important role.

The principle of reliance is thus fundamentally connected with the principle of respect for choice. Within a democratic liberal society, there is also the ideal of individual autonomy, of people developing and maintaining a critical reflective independence from mere authority. It is often asserted that such autonomy undermines any hope of shared self-understandings or of community. Yet a society that would be populated by such autonomous individuals (a kind of limiting case ideal) would be one in which the virtue of trustworthiness played a large role, and in which therefore this ideal of character development as a good would be shared. Blind trust can obviously play a role in other forms of society; perhaps medieval serfs blindly trusted their masters. In a democratic liberal society, blind trust of this sort is out of place. Trust is autonomously given and bestowed; it is earned trust.

This goes further than merely the fact that a liberal society that respects autonomy is one that demands trust. Consider promising. A society that values autonomy will be one in which many relations between individuals will be associative ones based on mutual agreement or promises. The very act of promising itself can produce legitimate expectations by others. A promise is morally binding not because it creates reliance on the part of another but for the opposite reason: the other may legitimately rely on the promise because the promise is morally binding. A promise is a speech-act based on certain social conventions that elicits a reliance on the part of the other. Part of what would explain what is binding about a promise is that a person who breaks it exploits the other by violating a principle that both accept as mediating their acknowledgment of each other. And part of what excuses one when one breaks a promise are other principles that are equally accepted. A phenomenology of the concrete ethical life would no doubt disclose many different types of excuses based on principles anchored in certain types of relationships. Such excuses offer a way out of the charge of betrayal. It is interesting, for example, in this regard how many people in business often see what legally is a breach of contract not as a breach of contract or promise at all but as an excusable "withdrawal of acceptance" or "withdrawal of an offer." They quite often see the lawyer's perspective on this as downright harmful to good commerce in general and their own interests in particular—even when they are the victims of the breach. They do not, that is, view all breach as betrayal but as excusable (even if not laudatory) behavior.

In concrete human practice, which includes far more than merely the ethical life, principles such as reliance are interwoven with non-moral values (such as security of commerce), which leads to overall greater benefits for the society at large and for the participants in that daily piece of theater. Security of commerce is one component of stability, an essential part of a peacefully coexisting liberal society. Since the legal order has as one of its key objectives the preservation and maintenance of stability, the principle of reliance will be an essential principle in any such legal system.

More importantly for our purposes, it is also interwoven with other moral principles that would also be part of the legal order, if only by virtue of their connection with the principle of reliance. Take the case of what one might call "missed connections" in contract: one person, X, promises something to another person, Y; X understood that she was promising ϕ to Y, but Y, alas, quite legitimately understood that X promised θ.[41] Given the principle of autonomy, it would seem that X could not be bound by something she did not promise (if she promised, how can she be morally bound to θ?). Yet the principle of reliance would seem to imply that Y, who quite legitimately relied on the promise being to θ, has a right to that. It would seem that one would have to balance somehow the two principles in the interests of both justice and peaceful community. But the balancing would not be merely between two principles. It would also seem that this balancing would involve yet another principle to assist in determining whether the reliance was itself justified. These would be something like the principles of conscientiousness and good faith. These are requirements not merely to *do* one's duty but to *be* a certain way. Each must strive to take note of the other in an 'honest' way. In the American Uniform Commercial Code and some labor law concerning union-management bargaining, reference is made to the necessity of "good faith" on the part of the parties who are bargaining.

A contract must on this view be interpreted in terms of its rational purpose within the social union that is democratic liberal society, in terms of what honest people in these circumstances would expect according to the customs of commerce. The reliance induced by the contract must be one that a "reasonable person" could expect—that is, one based on the "good faith" and "conscientiousness" of the parties. One relies on the other to be a good person, to bargain in "good faith."[42] Even in the marketplace, character in the form of trustworthiness plays an ethically significant role.

Likewise, in non-consensual cases, one must be able to rely on the other to take "due care" (a principle of tort). The good faith principle in bargaining is the mirror image of the "due care" principle in tort; each is a development from the overall reliance principle in a just legal order in a democratic liberal society. Moreover, it is clear that these would be principles in our sense. "Good faith" and "due care" do not specify any particular decision but can serve to justify one decision over another. To be sure, any system that incorporates these principles will develop sets of rules to assist judges in determining when, for example, "good faith" is present. This will be particularly true when great value is placed on individual autonomy, for this leads quite naturally to a great value being placed on formal realizability, something that a principle will always be lacking in any strong fashion.

This principle of reliance on the other person shows up elsewhere: the duty in contract to mitigate damages and the duty in tort to avoid contributory negligence. Both are duties that the harmed person has to the other to be a conscientious person. It is not enough that the other person has violated a duty or obligation (failed to take due care, or broken his or her promise): the injured party must also be conscientious, must attend to his or her duties or obligations as well. (This is not to pretend, of course, that the impact of the principle will be the same in tort and contract; considerations peculiar to each will lead from similar principles to rules that will look quite different.)

The role that these principles should play in this law is thus not well explained by a postulation of a sharp distinction between individualism and altruism nor by an abstract distinction between principles of commutative and distributive justice. It is based on a kind of implicit understanding of the background order of types of relationships that people have and the role of law in this. There is no one type of relation, but

II. Sharing and Fairness

many; and the role of law in this will be, of course, complex. What I have tried to do here is reduce part of the complexity to a few central principles in order to show how they could function in a general way in the area of private agreement and in civil obligation in general. This is a "speculative" answer in the Hegelian sense; we have tried to reconstruct the principles of a form of life (a democratic liberal legal order) by asking how we might best explain the possibility of that form of life.

A democratic liberal form of social union is thus different from a purely liberal point view. Libertarianism is the expression of the purely liberal view of society. The libertarian weights the principle of respect for choice above all others in his or her theory; he or she allows people to set their own terms of cooperation within a wide range of cases. The libertarian stress on respect for choice as equivalent to respect for dignity will be justified to the extent that we also see people as capable of such autonomous choice, as capable, as it were, of choosing their own course of action and assuming responsibility for their own decisions and actions. This is a view of persons central to the liberal tradition. (The liberal view need not always see people as capable of doing this. Liberals typically do not, for example, see small children as capable of full autonomy and allowances are made for the insane.) Indeed, the reliance principle is so basic because it partly rests on this view; reliance on others to do their duty and hold to their obligations (keep their agreements, take due care, mitigate damages, and so on) is justified by appeal to the idea that people are capable of assuming responsibility for their lives. But libertarianism would be the complete explanation only: (1) if people had no shared identity (if social life consisted of associations and not social unions or only associations of various unions); (2) if people were always fully autonomous; and (3) if respect for free choice were of such great weight that it could never be overruled. All three conditions are unlikely to be met. Respect for persons is not equivalent to respect for choice nor does it entail giving it the strong weight that the libertarian requires. Nor is autonomy an all or nothing affair; there are gradations of autonomy, depending on a person's level of understanding of the situation before him or her and the level of voluntariness present (measured by what kinds of constraints are present).[43] Full autonomy is an ideal to which probably none of us attain.

But is democratic liberal society really a form of social union? This requires a closer look. The focus on the structure of mutual acknowledgment is tied in with the view of the legitimacy of moral principles as resting on a kind of sharing between the agents; part of what is shared are the principles that mediate this acknowledgment. The abstract principle of respect for persons as structuring our mutual acknowledgment takes more concrete form in societal duties and obligations as the principles of good faith, toleration, and reliance on others to act responsibly, to do their duties and keep their obligations. We rely on others to treat us with respect, to be conscientious, to act in good faith, and so on. Overall, these principles are taken to be articulations or specifications of a general idea of a type of ethical world: specifically, one that incorporates a democratic liberal legal order, and one of peaceful cooperation and justice in a social order in which wide latitude is given to choice and in which trust is an essential element. Each principle is justified as being required in explaining the possibility of such an order. The ideal of fairness is an essential part of this. One treats another fairly when one does one's part—fulfills one's duties, keeps one's obligations—acts conscientiously, with a sense of respect, in good faith, when one acts in accordance with the principle of reliance. A system of principles is fair when it is or could be a system that people could share and in which each respects the dignity of another. In games, one acts fairly when one plays by the rules consistent with the common understanding of how the rules are to be understood. But not all of life is a sporting event, with clear rules along with winners and losers. One could of course see things like that (it is not logically impossible): one might see, for example, the market as a vast social game with winners and losers. On that view, if the winners play by the rules, then their gains are legitimate, and it is "unfortunate, not unjust," that the losers end up so badly off. However, the ideal of the market includes much more: the right of people to make their own choices, the demand that people take responsibility for their actions and modes of living, and so on. Moreover, the market is not a single thing, with rational individuals always making arm's length bargains for mutual benefit. Consider contracts of adhesion (those written exclusively by a dominant party with the weaker—the "adhering"—party having to accept them without negotiation). These are common in an advanced, industrial capitalist society, but they hardly fit the model of parties bargaining at arm's length with one another for mutually ad-

II. Sharing and Fairness

vantageous results. Not being a single thing, the market does not give us a single principle (such as "respect for choice").

These abstract principles offer only general guidelines for policy making and adjudication without requiring any particular decision. (They fulfill in part negative functions: it is much easier to list things that would violate the principle of dignity than it is to determine what exactly promotes it.) To go from the abstract to the concrete also requires some reference to the practices, mores, and standards of the society and of institutions within that society. It is to make the passage as Hegel understood it from what he called the abstract principles of morality to the practices, customs, and usages of ethical institutions, *Sittlichkeit*. For example, the principle of good faith in bargaining requires, first, an understanding of what a "reasonable person" would consider to be good faith, then an understanding of the prevailing customs of commerce. It requires us to ask what the one party (or parties) expects under the prevailing customs and ethos of an institution from others, that is, on what they are legitimately relying. More than a reference to mores is required. One must see these mores in terms of the social unions in which they are anchored and have their life. The mores are part of the ethos of the union, and they thus require explanation by its spirit.

The American Uniform Commercial Code displays some awareness of this need to go from principles to the types of relationship. For example, section 2-609 (2) states: "Between merchants the reasonableness of grounds of insecurity and the adequacy of any assurance offered shall be determined according to commercial standards." This might look as if it is saying that, if the prevailing standards of the market are low, then those low standards provide the principles for assessing the reasonableness of the terms. But in fact, the Code is cluttered with terms such as "reasonable time," "reasonable grounds," "good faith," and so on, offering "custom and usage" as guides to decision making. "Good faith," for example, is measured by "reasonable commercial standards of fair dealing in the trade." This imposes certain ideals inherent in the social union that is liberal society; it claims, in the terms used here, that its ethos must match up to its spirit.

One of the essential components of a liberal social order is then the element of trust, which can only be explicated by looking at the types of actual relationships that people bear to each other. The full measure of the extent of reliance and the focus on the nature of the relationship as giving concrete form to the abstract principles of autonomy, fairness, and the like is wonderfully illustrated by Justice Cardozo's opinion in *Meinhard v. Salmon*,[44] a contract case that brings out the element of joint partnership that Finnis dismissed as proper to contract. Salmon leased a building in New York City for twenty years and changed it over from a hotel to shops and offices. He procured the necessary funds from Meinhard in a joint venture. Meinhard provided half the funds; Salmon was to "manage, lease, underlet and operate the building" and share profits with Meinhard; losses, if any, were to be borne by the parties equally. As the lease drew to an end, Salmon joined with a new owner of the building to lease it for an additional number of years in what looked like a possibly very profitable venture. Salmon did not tell his partner, Meinhard, anything about this new plan. Meinhard discovered it only after finding that the new lease had been signed and that he had not been included or even informed that such negotiations were being undertaken. Meinhard sued. To be sure, the lease was in Salmon's name and the duration of his agreement with Meinhard was coming to an end. A strict application of the principle of respect for choice without reference to any ideal of fairness would perhaps leave us only shrugging off Salmon's underhandedness vis-à-vis his former partner. Cardozo felt otherwise: "Joint adventurers, like copartners, owe to one another, while the enterprise continues, the duty of the finest loyalty. Many forms of conduct permissible in a workaday world for those acting at arm's length, are forbidden to those bound by fiduciary ties. . . . Not honesty alone, but the punctilio of an honor the most sensitive, is then the standard of behavior. . . . Only thus has the level of conduct for fiduciaries been kept at a level higher than that trodden by the crowd. It will not consciously be lowered by any judgment of this court."[45]

Having claimed that special duties (what I have been calling obligations) arise from the nature of this type of contractual arrangement — not an "arm's length" but a "fiduciary" agreement — Cardozo argued that Salmon had a "duty of disclosure" to his "coadventurer," Meinhard, for the "trouble about his conduct is that he excluded his coadventurer from any chance to compete, from any chance to enjoy the opportunity for benefit that had come to him by virtue of his agency."[46] Or, as we may read this, a principle of fairness must be considered. Salmon had

II. Sharing and Fairness 115

elicited a certain reliance or trust on Meinhard's part, making his later acts unfair; his "duty of disclosure" to Meinhard derived from this. If it was only an arm's length bargain—if that was the nature of the relationship between the two—then there would be no duty of disclosure. This duty can only come about if the nature of the relationship is such that one relies on the other to be "conscientious," to act and bargain in "good faith" and to be "fair." None of the terms appear in Cardozo's decision, but they seem to be the underlying principles of what is at issue. Meinhard provided money; he shared losses. (Cardozo: "For each, the venture had its phases of fair weather and of foul."[47]) Salmon's attempt to pull out of what must be understood as a shared undertaking without disclosing any of this to his partner was thus unfair—unfair, not because of the application of some more abstract pattern of equality of burdens and benefits, but because of Salmon's violation of the reliance on the part of Meinhard that he would at least be told of any such plans. It was Salmon's refusal to give his partner a meaningful choice that made the transaction unfair.

Cardozo restricted Salmon's liberty in the name of certain ideals that make a liberal democratic social union the kind that it is. This type of conclusion worries libertarians. They would argue that the principle of fairness is incompatible with a vigorous understanding of the importance of liberty. Robert Nozick has offered an excellent version of this objection.[48] He takes the principle of fairness to be something like "if one receives something of value willingly and not as a gift, one has an obligation to give something in return." Nozick offers the following counterexample (shortened and slightly altered, naturally, here). In your neighborhood, people discover an intricate broadcasting system and in a group meeting without your being present (without, that is, your consent) they decide upon the following plan: each of them (364 of them, 365 if you were to be included) will take charge of it one day per year, broadcasting what they please (jokes, records, whatnot). This begins, and you find that you thoroughly enjoy it (you derive benefits from it). Your day comes; the others are relying on you to do your part. Do you have an obligation to do so? Nozick says that you do not, even though you derived great benefits from it. Nice if you do, not wrong if you do not. You have, after all, not consented to it.

Nozick is probably right with regard to this fable. Benefits that are imposed on one need not necessarily generate any corresponding obligation to return the payment. If I plant flowering trees in my yard next to yours, thereby increasing the value of your house just as you were getting ready to sell it, you incur no obligation to share your extra profits with me. But note how little we know about the "real" circumstances of Nozick's fable. (These are questions we might ask in a longer discussion with you about why you did not serve your turn.) First of all, it is important to know whether or not you have elicited their reliance. If they come to you after the meeting and tell you the plan and you say, "OK . . . Sure . . . I'll do it," you have consented. Suppose that you only nod your head. Suppose as each day's broadcast ends, your neighbors greet you with phrases like, "Well, two months from today—your broadcast day—is the day, eh?" or "Well, Thursday's the day, right?," and each time you nod and say, "That's right." You mean that perhaps you know that it will be your turn, but you do not as yet in your own mind take responsibility for it, or take it as implying that you have consented or will broadcast. (You may be merely acknowledging the fact that you know that Thursday has been set aside for you.) We can of course imagine a whole range of cases going from direct consent to outright denial. What makes the 'in between' cases sometimes hard is that it is a debatable proposition whether or not you gave indication of your consent, gave others legitimate grounds to rely on you. Not doing your part is unfair if you elicit the reliance, if you act in such a way that the others legitimately take you to be consenting. Where others have been given grounds to trust you to do X, your not doing X without good excuse is betrayal. Where the imposition of a benefit is made from an honest mistake, or you somehow gave encouragement to it, the case for the applicability of the principle of fairness strengthens. If you come over to paint my house by mistake (you are supposed to do the one next door), and I realize that it is a mistake but I give you no indication that you are making a mistake (I simply sit inside and grin at what I take to be my good fortune), then I have unfairly elicited a benefit. Fairness requires some sort of compensation on my part. Nozick's counterargument against the principle of fairness applies only to cases of imposed benefits where there is no elicited reliance on your part. The principle of fairness, however, should not be taken as covering *all* imposition of benefits but

II. Sharing and Fairness

only those that have in some sense been elicited. (Let us call this "private fairness." Later in Chapter Four, I will distinguish it from public fairness. The latter has to do with the central concept of citizenship.)

The principle of fairness will also apply in what are called quasi-contract cases. These are cases where a benefit is bestowed on someone without their consent because the person was incapable of giving consent and the provider of the benefit had a duty to provide the benefit. The most common example is that of a doctor treating an unconscious patient, although this has—or should have—some restrictions relating to the *possible* consent of the patient. One would want to say that not only is a benefit conferred, there is also a duty to confer the benefit, and the person would consent to it, would "elicit" it if they could.

In American law, some contracts are deemed to be unenforceable because of factors like unconscionability. This would at least *prima facie* seem to be a concept of distributive justice. Or, if not, it might seem at first to be something that only a theory of distributive justice would adequately explain. After all, unconscionability seems to be a property of the terms of agreement, not of the choice itself; and to hold a contract void because of unconscionability seems to be equivalent to saying that, whatever the character of the choice that was made, such radically unfair bargains will not be held to have been enforceable.

I would like to consider an instructive case in this light, *Williams v. Walker-Thomas Furniture Company*.[49] An indigent woman on relief, Ora Lee Williams, purchased a stereo record player on credit from Walker-Thomas Furniture Company. She had purchased things from Walker-Thomas before (on credit) and had always paid her bills. The contract that she signed had a provision in it that stated, in effect, that if she had any other items on credit from the company, all items were to be considered as having a balance due until the whole balance was paid off. In other words, if one bought on credit, for example, a sofa for six hundred dollars from the company, paid five hundred and ninety dollars of the bill, then purchased a television set from them on credit for two hundred dollars, and kept on paying the bills until one owed only ten dollars, both the sofa and the television set were considered to be unpaid. Thus, if one defaulted on the last payment, the company could reclaim ("replevin") both the sofa and the television. If one had done this over a period of years, buying all of one's furniture from them, then by defaulting on payment of the final bill, one could lose all of the items. That in fact happened, and the court found the contract to be unconscionable.

Why? One way would be to say that the terms of the contract are radically unfair, that it involves an unfair exploitation of poor people who must buy on credit. What is unfair, however, about it? Surely it cannot be unfair in the way that striking a binding bargain with a child or with a mentally handicapped person would be. Why should we treat poor people as having somehow less control over their decisions? Why should we treat them, that is, more paternalistically? Surely, this would be an affront to the principle of respect for persons. It would mean that difference of income or class marked a moral difference, such that treatment proper to one set of individuals (upper income, upper class) would be permissibly different from treatment given to others (lower income, lower class).

The terms of the contract that gave Walker-Thomas this right are worth looking at:

> If I am now indebted to the Company on any prior leases, bills or accounts, it is agreed that the amount of each periodical installment payment to be made by me to the Company under this present lease shall be inclusive of and not in addition to the amount of each installment payment to be made by me under such prior leases, bills or accounts: and all payments now and hereafter made by me shall be credited pro rata on all outstanding leases, bills and accounts due the Company by me at the time such payment is made.[50]

The court rightly goes on to describe this as an "obscure provision."[51] It then goes on to say that in its understanding, what makes a contract unconscionable is the absence of meaningful choice. What is being said here? What "negates" the "meaningfulness" of the choice? Because one party simply has more or less bargaining power than the other? The court notes:

> Whether a meaningful choice is present in a particular case can only be determined by consideration of all the circumstances surrounding the transaction. In many cases the meaningfulness of the choice is negated by a gross inequality of bargaining power. The manner in which the contract

II. Sharing and Fairness

was entered is also relevant to this consideration. Did each party to the contract, considering his obvious education or lack of it, have a reasonable opportunity to understand the terms of the contract, or were the important terms hidden in a maze of fine print and minimized by deceptive sales practices? Ordinarily, one who signs an agreement without full knowledge of its terms might be held to assume the risk that he has entered a one-sided bargain. But when a party of little bargaining power, and hence little real choice, signs a commercially unreasonable contract with little or no knowledge of its terms, it is hardly likely that his consent, or even an objective manifestation of his consent, was ever given to all the terms. In such a case the usual rule that the terms of the agreement are not to be questioned should be abandoned and the court should consider whether the terms of the contract are so unfair that enforcement should be withheld.[52]

Two different concerns are being voiced here, one dealing with the relative inequality between the parties, the other with a concern as to whether informed consent was given. Nonetheless, the court goes on to apply a kind of fairness test to the terms of the contract:

In determining reasonableness or fairness, the primary concern must be with the terms of the contract considered in light of the circumstances existing when the contract was made. The test is not simple, nor can it be mechanically applied. The terms are to be considered "in the light of the general commercial background and the commercial needs of the particular trade or case." Corbin suggests the test as being whether the terms are "so extreme as to appear unconscionable according to the mores and business practices of the time and place." . . . We think this formulation correctly states the test to be applied in those cases where no meaningful choice was exercised upon entering the contract.[53]

There seems to be a set of different rationales at work here. One deals with problems of distributive justice between the parties; the unspoken principle there seems to be that grossly unfair contracts may not be enforced, and the fairness of the terms changes according to the bargaining power of the parties. If so, however, why are not almost all "bargains" in modern liberal society suspect? Almost anyone buying gasoline from any of the major energy companies will find themselves in an enormously weaker bargaining position. Why, moreover, should people who sell furniture to the indigent be forced to maintain distributive justice, whereas those who sell to the better-off do not? Is not that also unfair? And what if the adoption of such a view leads to a state of affairs where nobody will sell furniture to the poor on credit? Is that fair to the poor as a class? Moreover, the claim that the test of unconscionability depends on the "mores and business practices of the time and place" has as an implication that wildly unfair or exploitative practices would be permissible provided only that such practices were typical. This would make the test for fairness or unconscionability a function of how corrupt or uncorrupt the prevailing climate of the marketplace was.

The other rationale is that of informed consent, and it provides a better way into understanding what is troubling in this case. Anyone reading that contract provision will realize that it is very difficult to comprehend. Part of the intuitive repugnance of the contract is that it almost seems designed to gain consent without its being an informed one. Thus, we could formulate a test for unconscionability as being lack of informed consent. On this reading, one would not be holding the view that one must treat the poor paternalistically; one should treat them and their trading partners with the same respect with which one treats all other citizens of a democratic liberal society. In this case, we have a bargain for mutual gain (not a sharing relationship) but one that one of the parties did not understand (and that the other party most likely had reason to know that the other did not or would not understand). At best, the fairness test in looking at the relative inequality between the parties should only be a clue to the claim that the contract was unconscionable; that is, it could give one reason to suspect that the person may not have given informed consent. But it could not be conclusive evidence for it.

The concept of "meaningful choice" used in the opinion is best elucidated by the idea of informed consent. A choice is not meaningless only if the range of choices for one person is less than somebody else's. (Even the middle-class automobile purchaser has no meaningful choice in that sense; he or she cannot purchase the Lamborghini, Ferrari, or Vector that he or she wants and must settle instead for a Chevrolet on credit.) It is the lack of informed consent that is really what is objectionable in the *Williams* case. It is not as if being poor made one incapable of choice or reasoning. Unconscionability is not a separate principle to be balanced with a respect for autonomy but is a development of the principle of respecting autonomy itself. We respect people (in part) when we allow them to make their own choices (that is, where they make more or less autonomous choices). But we must rely on others to give us reasonable information, not to exploit us.

Autonomy comes in degrees and depends at least on the elements of comprehension and of voluntariness in the situation. These are determinable only from within the context of the situation. This is not a matter of sorting people out for different treatment depending on income or class, but of looking at the type of relationship present and determining what degree of comprehension of the terms of agreement is there and what kinds of constraints are present in it. If pushed to the limit, of course, this would make each proposed case of unconscionability specific to the individuals involved; unconscionability as a legal principle would be wanting in what von Jhering called the formal realizability of rules. (Whereas the former types of considerations may be proper to moral principles for dealings between individuals, questions of formal realizability are equally valuable considerations for legal rules and principles.) Formal realizability implies that we come up with certain tests, but these tests are tests for informed consent; they do not define it or replace it.

III
Risks and the Balancing of Principles

There are of course other concerns than just harms caused by failures to live up to contractual duties. In particular, one can harm another by an action of one's own without any contractual relation being present. This comprises part of the Anglo-American system of torts. Torts involve illegitimate harms to persons and property that are to be compensated. We have already spoken briefly about this. We must now ask, What kinds of principles would make this possible?

Reliance would be an obvious explanatory principle here. What is it that one relies upon? One relies on the other to be conscientious, to take due care not to harm one. One is relying on the other not to cause harm intentionally or by some faulty action. An action may be faulty when the following conditions are met: (1) the actor either knew or reasonably could have known that some duty existed; (2) by failing to meet his or her duties, the actor harmed the person through his or her action; (3) a reasonable person could know that such an action would or probably could result in such harm. The actor is negligent if he or she did not cause the harm intentionally and/or did not intentionally violate his or her duty, but nonetheless is guilty of not taking sufficient care in his or her action (he or she was careless, reckless, or whatnot). This could happen in two ways: he or she could have recognized a duty but through thoughtlessness did not; or he could have seen that this action would lead to harmful results but proceeded in a thoughtless or reckless manner. The fault principle is an expression of the liberal view of autonomy —that people are capable of making their own choices and assuming responsibility for them. The basing of liability on faulty harmful action is also an expression of putting a high value on respect for individual liberty. If we were all responsible for all harm, the range of our real choices would be restricted.[54] How far, though, does this simple idea take us?

Others have a right that we not harm them through faulty action; they also have a right that we not submit them to certain risks of harm. The concept of risk is important here, for when we talk of negligent (faulty, although non-intentionally so) behavior, we are bringing in a concept of exposing others to risks. Driving one's Maserati through the school zone at 110 mph is negligent behavior because it submits the school children to great risk. The importance of the concept of risk goes further, however, than merely delimiting a range of faulty actions. We are exposed to risks every day through people's driving automobiles, running electrical plants, and the like. It cannot be that people have a right not to be subjected to any risk; it must be that they have a right not to be subjected to some risks. Surely considerations of efficiency must enter into the calculation of risk somewhere. Is there any principle or set of principles that would help us pick our way through this?

Robert Nozick has offered a libertarian theory of risk imposition, as a part of his general theory of impermissible violation of rights.[55] For Nozick, as for most libertarians, consent always functions to justify what would otherwise be an illegitimate violation of rights. But he also allows what would otherwise be illegitimate boundary crossing without consent when the person can be compensated. A person is properly compensated when he or she is brought up to a standard that leaves him or her better off than he or she would be without the boundary crossing. (In addition,

III. Risks and the Balancing of Principles

this implies that the risk imposition would also be efficient, in a particular sense to which we shall come shortly.) He puts several important conditions on this. The harms that might result from the risk must be compensable (death, for example, is not). It must be either impossible or impractical to obtain the affected people's consent. It would be impractical to obtain consent if it would cost too much to do so, that is, more than it would if the transactions were done face to face—the idea being that each would sell it for X amount of money if asked, but it will cost X + n to find everyone and ask them. The payment to them must be fair—more than enough for them to be left as well off as before. And the risk must be such that the people affected by it do not fear the joint event of being harmed and being compensated for it.

This last condition requires explication. Nozick introduces the non-fear condition in response to puzzles about why people cannot knowingly inflict harms on others provided that they compensate them. The reason, Nozick conjectures, is that many harms—for example, broken limbs—would be such that people would fear the event even if they knew that they were going to be compensated for it. And since such fear is a harm, they would deserve to be compensated both for the fear and for the broken limb. But how would people who fear the breaking of their limbs—but who do not get them broken—be compensated for their fear? By whom? Moreover, if D knowingly breaks P's arm and happily compensates P for the broken limb, why should D also compensate P for P's fear, since it was not D specifically who caused the fear. Thus a system that allowed people to intentionally inflict harms provided that they compensate would be one in which almost everyone was never compensated for one harm, namely, the resulting fear of the other harms.

Some people will want to engage in activities that submit others to risks, but these same people will be financially unable to purchase the right to do so from those affected. Some of these activities will, moreover, be very important to these people since it will concern their ability to make a living (operating, for example, a plant that produces somewhat dangerous pollutants). To say that they cannot do this is to prohibit them from engaging in an activity important to their lives. Nozick claims that since a libertarian must give pride of place to freedom of action, we must compensate people for prohibiting them from engaging in such activity. The upshot is, of course, that the people have a right to engage in these risk-imposing activities unless they are 'bought off' by the people affected. Thus, people will be forced to accept having risks imposed on them unless they are willing to pay for protection. Two rights clash: people have a right to impose some risks (those relating to important activities for them), and people have a right not to have some risks imposed. Nozick's view seems to be that the person wanting to impose the risk should be allowed to do so unless the victims purchase the right.

Risks may be imposed without consent, then, under two options. *Option A*: you may impose the risk if the imposition leaves the victim better off and the above four conditions are met (the victim would have consented to the imposition, the harm is compensable, transaction costs do not make it inefficient, and the victim does not fear the joint event of harm and compensation). *Option B*: if you cannot buy off the victim (due to lack of resources on your part), and the activity is important to you, then the victim must buy you off; if the victim does not (if the protection is not worth the price), then although he or she is not better off, he or she has 'consented' (by not buying off the risk imposer). Option A and Option B thus boil down to two things. Either the risk imposer buys off the victim (if he can), or the victim buys off the risk imposer. Which option, A or B, comes into play where?

Option B, as opposed to option A, is not one in which the victim is left better off. Thus, we cannot imagine the victim giving even hypothetical consent. Option B involves something more like a threat, where the victim would be better off if the other person had never made the offer in the first place. ("My job is making explosives, next to your house; they go off all the time. Either pay me enough money so that it is not worth my while to stay in business—by the way, I make a lot of profit on this, but not nearly enough to buy you off—or run the risk of finding yourself inside a fireball.") It thus seems strange that this solution would interest a libertarian.

Moreover, the condition that states that people not fear the joint event of being harmed and being compensated for it would seem to rule out a whole range of cases in option A. Consider somebody who is terribly afraid of ordinary things, such as automobiles or electricity or whatnot. This person fears the entire modern world and is not comforted by knowing that he will be compensated if, for example, he is struck down by an errant Oldsmobile. Note also that Nozick's idea that

III. Risks and the Balancing of Principles

the harm must be compensable; death is non-compensable, and it is this that the person scared of Oldsmobiles on the loose fears (not without reason). Option A may end up covering only a very minor range of cases, if any at all. Of course, driving automobiles is an important—maybe necessary—part of many people's lives, so option B will come into play. In fact, since option A will probably cover almost nothing, option B will be the effective theory of legitimate risk imposition (in Nozick's scheme). Under option B, the people terrified of automobiles will most likely find it impossible to buy off all of the automobile drivers.

Nozick's theory thus seems to come down to the claim that one must bear all risks imposed on one by others unless one is willing to buy them off (if the risky activity is an important part of their lives—presumably on Nozick's libertarian theory, the risk imposers will be the ones who get to decide this). The victim must compensate the risk imposer for not imposing the risk. What happens, though, to the right not to have risks imposed on one? It seems to vanish, or to become merely an idle notion, the wheel that turns with nothing else turning with it. Nozick's view thus would seem to rest on some kind of principle such as, "Rights to activities deemed important by those who undertake them always take *prima facie* priority over claims not to have risks imposed." (Moreover, if the onus is on you to buy the risk imposer off, it is tempting to say that you really have no right at all not to have risks imposed.) At best, this only prevents risk imposition by activities deemed frivolous by those who do them. Of course, option B does allow *some* intuitive results; it allows the automobile drivers to continue driving unless the inveterate pedestrians convince them otherwise. Unfortunately, it also allows almost any other type of risk imposition. For Nozick, efficient risk imposition turns out, on libertarian grounds, to have a moral justification. (An allocation of rights is efficient in this sense when the right is given to that person or body of persons who would be willing to pay the most for the right.[56])

Nozick's theory allows in option A consideration of hypothetical and not merely actual consent; although actual consent cannot be gained, hypothetical consent serves to justify the imposition. This of course involves a counterfactual imputation to people of what they would say were they to be confronted with the choice. And, as Hegel long ago argued, this kind of imputation can only be done by appeal to the customs and usages, the mores, of a society or social grouping. Various versions of, for example, "reasonable person" tests are applications of this Hegelian idea. The question then would be: would a reasonable person accept this kind of risk? Are the benefits enough to make the risk worthwhile? This would seem to require in principle two kinds of overall compensation: one for people prohibited from engaging in important activities, the other for people exposed to risks. That there would be only one such scheme of compensation is unlikely. The scheme, moreover, will be institutional in character; we will be required to arrange institutions in such a way as to allow for both types of compensation. We can put the matter like this. People should be allowed to live the lives that they choose, to make their own choices. But this also requires a principle of responsibility: they must as an abstract requirement bear the costs of that life, and they must compensate others for the costs that they impose on them. The idea of democratic liberal society as a cooperative enterprise with wide latitude given to individual choice requires a balancing of the two rights (the right of free action and the right not to have risks imposed). This requires some kind of institutional framework to provide the moral space for both these notions to operate. This is part of the justification of the appeal to mores, to what a "reasonable person" would accept.

An ideal arrangement perhaps would be one in which those who wish to take risks are permitted to do so and those who do not are protected from having risks imposed or even from taking certain risks. Food and drug regulations would be an example of prohibiting people from taking certain risks. It is not irrational for risk-averse people—or simply those who dislike acquiring enough information to make their risk taking informed—to want some official body to prohibit risky choices. In any real sense, however, allowing some people to take risks means that some risks will be imposed on others. A utilitarian theory would justify the imposition of risks on others if the overall gains would outweigh the losses, but we have seen that a maximizing theory such as utilitarianism is inadequate. Any institutional arrangement for risk imposition and compensation must be one that does not necessarily produce *more* good but produces as much good as possible while not producing any *extra* evil (to return to the results of our earlier argument).

One way of realizing this would be an institutional arrangement in which all benefit by the arrangement. This appeals again to the ideal of

III. Risks and the Balancing of Principles

sharing and stands in contrast to Nozick's overly individualistic views. Rawls's "difference principle" (no inequality unless to the benefit of the worst-off group) is one way of thinking about the manner in which these benefits and burdens may be distributed. No risks will be allowed to be imposed unless such risk imposition works to the benefit of the worst-off group. (Note that this differs from a more rigorously egalitarian distribution of rights of risk imposition, such as that offered by Charles Fried.[57] His view is that a person, X, may impose a risk of nth-magnitude upon another person, Y, only if X is willing to have an equal risk imposed on him or her by Y. A Rawlsian view—although Rawls himself has never offered a theory of risk imposition—would have to be that extra benefits overall to the worst-off group would justify some unequal risk imposition. Justice in risk imposition would not require the rigorously egalitarian standard that Fried's view requires.)

To see where this leads, let us consider the rights of a minority who fear something that the rest of us do not, for example, the manufacturing of televisions. How do we respect these people's rights? This already falls outside the scope of option A, since these people fear not only the risk of harm by the manufacturing process but also fear the joint event of harm and compensation. By hypothesis, living free of such fear is also an important part of their lives.

We should distinguish two types of risk imposition. One is risks that are imposed on most of us by virtue of the way in which our society is ordered (for example, the risk of death by automobile accident, diseases caused by pollutants, and so on); let us call this *normal risk*. The other is risks imposed by individuals or groups that exceed this normal level (such as the risk of disease or death posed by unsanitary conditions at the local meat packer, the blasting operation next door to my office, my neighbor's reckless driving); let us call this *extraordinary risk*. It might be tempting to opt for a conceptual division of labor by using an individualistic model for justifying risk imposition in cases of extraordinary risk, and using the institutional model for cases of ordinary risk. That is, we would decide institutionally what risks all of us would run (this would concern the requirements that must be built into the basic structure of society) and then use various tort and insurance schemes to compensate for risks imposed on specific individuals and groups.

However tempting such a division of labor would be, it would be a mistake. Consider the point of findings of negligence in tort and various insurance schemes. Negligence is used to adjust the balance of risk taking and risk imposition among individuals and groups, and those who negligently cause harms must compensate those harmed. Insurance schemes offer individuals yet another means for adjusting the balance; in such schemes individuals pool their resources to avoid an unlikely but large loss for a smaller but certain cost. (That distinguishes it from gambling, where at a small cost people acquire a small chance at a huge gain.) Both schemes are inadequate for covering all the risks of the type that they are supposed to cover. Tort remedies may not, for example, be enough if the offending party does not have the means to compensate. (This kind of situation leads to the earlier mentioned dilemmas in Nozick's theory.) Moreover, when the negligence standard is used, tort remedies must presuppose what kinds of risks it is reasonable (that is, not negligent) to impose—hence, it relies on the background system of normal risk imposition. When the probability of a harm is low, then it will most likely not be negligent to run the risk of causing such a harm, and the person who is (improbably) harmed will find no succor in any system where liability is based on negligence. Insurance schemes can plug some of the gaps left by a regime of liability based on negligence but not all of them. In insurance schemes, people pool their resources to avoid large losses; they will understandably be unwilling to pool with those who are high-risk cases. Indeed, the people who form the pool of high-risk cases will most likely find nobody with whom to pool, except others who are high-risk cases, and it will not make much insurance sense to pool with those. (Insurance schemes suffer from the same defect as social contract theories of the state, as we shall see in the next chapter: they tend to exclude certain non-beneficial groups.) Tort and insurance schemes, although fitting the radical individualist model, will not cover all the cases of people having risks imposed on them. Further institutional measures are necessary.

How then do we deal with the reluctant minority? One possible way might be compensation in a twofold sense: that the system of private interaction (economic, federalistic, and so on) is to their advantage and that just compensation is available in the event of harm. The individualist principle of responsibility for damages caused would hold those who cause the damage or who allow the risks to stay in existence (par-

III. Risks and the Balancing of Principles

ticularly if they benefit from it) to bear the costs of compensation. A legal rule of strict liability is one partial systemic answer to this. Strict liability for some harms caused is liability without the fault condition being present; if one causes the damage, then one is responsible for compensation, even if one is not at fault. In American law, this is the rule for defective products and for abnormally dangerous activities. Those who expose people to such risks presumably benefit from these activities (and presumably there are benefits for others and for society at large). The dropping of a fault condition would be a means of compensating those exposed to the risks, since it reduces in one way at least the fear of not being compensated. It allows a person to single out easily the cause of the injury, not merely the negligent party. That the manufacturer of defective products is liable for such harms even without fault is a way of compensating those whom he or she endangers; it imputes a responsibility to the manufacturer that is stricter than a normal sense of responsibility because the manufacturer derives benefits from a process that exposes others to non-negligible risks. For the right to impose risks, the manufacturer "trades" another right, namely, the right to avoid responsibility where there is no fault on his or her part. A system of strict liability is one institutional setup for compensating those on whom we allow risks to be imposed by those who benefit from such risk impositions.

But the idea that compensation will be forthcoming will not be enough for some of our imagined minority. They will still believe that their rights not to be exposed to risks are being violated. The principle of responsibility tells us that each party (in this case, the manufacturers and the complaining minority) must in an abstract sense bear the cost of their choice of their lives, but this abstract principle can point in two exclusive directions: the complaining people must compensate (buy off) the manufacturers, or the manufacturers must purchase the rights from the complaining people. A balance must be struck, and it cannot be a simple weighing of harms and benefits, for harms count for more than benefits. That kind of balance cannot be struck simply within the ambit of the principles of private interaction. Another possible balance is institutional and political, involving regulation of the manufacturers by the state. The state could compel manufacturers to lower the risk by installing, for example, anti-pollutant devices. A supplementation to this would be a system of compensation to those harmed when full compensation from the offending parties is not forthcoming. This requires all of us to share in the losses that some of us endure. But this at least seems to take us out of the sphere of private interaction and involves us in the problems of state/society interactions. In more Hegelian terms, it requires for the purposes of completing the explanation a move to a different categorial level than merely that of liberal society. Some conception of the political state must be developed. Before we do that, however, let us look at least briefly at the very conception of balancing itself.

IV
Balancing and Cost/Benefit Analysis

We have spoken of balancing principles and how, when we begin to balance two competing principles, it seems that we need to bring in not only empirical considerations but other principles to make the balance. How is it possible, though, to balance principles at all?

Consider an interpretation of what might be included in the idea that we have a duty not only not to harm others or subject them to certain risks of harm but also to "do good." This duty to do good has sometimes been called the "principle of beneficence." It can be taken in two ways: (1) as expressing a duty to provide benefits to others; (2) as expressing a duty to *balance* benefits and harms so as to maximize benefits.[58] It is not hard to see how the latter interpretation of the principle may seem to follow from the first. The duty of beneficence is in its first formulation a duty to do good, and this requires us, where we must, to balance good over bad. (There are too few opportunities in life that are simple opportunities only to do good without having to consider possible bad effects.) One way of taking the principle would be as a formulation of the principle of utility: do that which overall produces a greater amount of good than bad. One can accept the principle of beneficence as being equivalent to the principle of *utility* without, however, being committed to *utilitarianism*. It is merely one principle among others; it is not a principle that overrides all others, as utilitarianism would have it. In utilitarianism, one has a maximizing principle—do the greatest good, for example, balance harms with benefits so that the greatest amount of good is produced. But as one principle among others,

IV. Balancing and Cost/Benefit Analysis

the principle of utility should be not be identified with utilitarianism at all. It merely expresses that one desideratum for ethical judgment is the goodness of the consequences of one's actions; it does not claim that this is the only or even the most important consideration for ethical judgment.

Nonetheless, do the earlier arguments against utilitarianism rule out any appeal to this "principle of utility"? If they do, then they might seem to rule out any kind of cost/benefit analysis as a way of resolving social problems with moral components. Or at least those arguments would require that any cost/benefit analysis weight costs more than benefits. That would most assuredly be a wrong conclusion to draw, and it is worthwhile to see why.[59] In such analysis, a cost may be anything of negative value to human welfare; a benefit may be anything that is of positive value to human welfare. One of the primary costs to taken into account are risks, that is, possible future harms. Risks may be measured in two ways, either by the probability of their occurrence or by the magnitude of the harm. (Nuclear reactors, for example, present little risk when measured by the likelihood of a nuclear accident, but they perhaps present enormous risks when measured by the magnitude of a possible nuclear accident.) Total risk can be something like probability of harm multiplied by magnitude of harm, adding in factors like uncertainty. The goal of cost/benefit analysis (or risk/benefit analysis, if we think in terms of the probability times magnitude of a risk compared with the probability times magnitude of a benefit) would be the conversion of all these things into some neutral equivalent, for example, money. For example, one might talk of the monetary costs of expected legal battles, the monetary costs of medical coverage when non-pollution measures are introduced, and so on. To be sure, not all of these things will be easily quantifiable, and all but the most rabid proponents of this type of analysis easily admit to that. Many, however, will be quantifiable, and cost/benefit analysis will show those costs—and even where it will not, it will at least give us a better idea of what kinds of trades we are making.

The reason why cost/benefit analysis may seem to be inconsistent with some of the considerations raised here is that it might be too easily confused with either utilitarianism *per se* or with something much like it, namely, wealth maximization (analyzing things in term of whether or not they maximize overall social wealth).[60] But it is neither. Ronald Dworkin has made a convincing point in this regard.[61] He distinguishes two different models of balancing, which he calls "compromise" and "recipe" views. We can take his distinctions to be a general answer to questions as to how balancing would be possible at all. A compromise balance occurs when we have two or more things, each of which is valuable on its own, but where having more of one means having less of the other; one must compromise and accept less of both A and B than one would want. If Smith has, for example, only a finite amount of money to spend, and would like to have a fast, expensive auto and a well-appointed Georgian townhouse but cannot have both, then Smith must compromise; he must accept a less elegant townhouse, or pinch pennies on the appointments, or buy a VW, or economize in some other way. Ideally, Smith would want both, but he cannot have all of both. The right balance on this view is a compromise; some of one thing is given up in order to get more of another. The recipe view of balancing is different; here the goal is to balance ingredients to achieve the correct end result. The items in the balance have their value not independently of the balance but only in terms of the contribution they make overall to the balance. It is not as if the chef would like ideally to have as much butter as possible; he wants to have everything in the right proportions (butter, flour, eggs, and so on). Here one does not give up butter in order to have more flour, as Smith does when he gives up on buying the sleek sportscar in order maintain the Georgian townhouse. If he could, Smith would have both: a faster auto, a more plush townhouse. The chef, if offered more butter, would not necessarily accept it, realizing that too much butter ruins the sauce. (Even Smith, in his ongoing pursuit of more and sleeker, will, when it comes to appointing the Georgian townhouse perhaps switch over to the recipe view, realizing that the object is not to have as many Persian carpets as possible but to achieve the "right mix" of Persian carpets, antique furniture, and Old Master paintings.)

Cost/benefit analysis shows us what kinds of compromises we must make in many areas of social life, but it would not (could not) give us the correct recipe for a well-ordered society (to use Rawls's term). Cost/benefit analysis would be one component of a "balancing" overall in the recipe for a well-ordered society. It is helpful, however, in pursuing efficiency (a perhaps non-moral but nonetheless important value—I say "perhaps" because it seems to me, for example, that when representatives using money gained by taxation use it in inefficient ways, they are

IV. Balancing and Cost/Benefit Analysis

violating a basic trust, and trust is one of the crucial elements of a democratic liberal social union). The more basic principle of weighting moral wrongs more than moral rightness shows that cost/benefit analysis must be integrated into a larger picture. We have already mentioned efficiency. It can serve, for example, to provide informational requirements based on the principles of respect and autonomy so that people know what risks they are running and what possible benefits might accrue to them, to others, or to society at large before they give their consent to some undertaking.

The recipe view of balancing requires some view of what the end result should be. In abstract terms, this would be a democratic liberal society in which the principle of human dignity is respected, and which was stable and just. Of course, as a matter of practical common sense, there will be no single clear recipe for a well-ordered society, any more than there is a single clear recipe for, say, something general like a well prepared, tasty vegetarian dish. That is not to say that there are not better and worse recipes. The goal of philosophical theory is in part to construct such recipes by constructing various alternative theories that would explain how it is possible that we can rank principles and so on. We should thus be suspicious of any one single recipe for democratic liberal society.

A final point needs to be made in this regard about balancing competing principles. It concerns the relation between principles and the conditions of their realization. There is a practical inconsistency in willing something that if one attempted to realize it would undercut either its own realization or the realization of other principles that one holds to be equally strong (and one had reason to know that). To take an example adapted from Kant and put it to different use: one might believe that one should not lie, but what happens (Kant's example) when a would-be murderer tells you that he wants to and will kill X, and asks you if X lives next door (and you know that X lives next door)? Kant apparently thought that you should tell the truth in this situation. It is certainly not clear, even on Kantian grounds, that this conclusion would follow. But other considerations make it also implausible, and it is useful to try to say why. If one also held that we should strive for human cooperation, and one knew that, in a world where people betrayed their neighbors to almost certain death because one "could not tell a lie," cooperation and trust would be at a minimum (and if the obligatoriness of truth telling rests on both accepting a certain set of background social conditions that each relies upon in making assertions), then in willing the principle "never lie" one would be contributing to creating a world in which inevitably truth telling came to be seen as an optional duty at best. One would be holding a practically inconsistent set of beliefs, since one's actions would undercut the realization of the principle that supposedly animated them. In the Kantian example, the choice should be between two recipes or parts of a recipe: "Always tell the truth even if it means sometimes sending innocent people to death" or "Do not send innocent people to death even if it means sometimes lying." Another example: "Never interfere with personal choice even it means that some people will have no effective choice in their lives" or "Give people some effective choice even if it means that one must put limits on personal choice." Each of the propositions on the left or the right of the "or" are recipe proposals. If one had reason to believe that a world in which people never told lies even if it meant that innocent people were sent to death would be a world where people came to put no stock in truth telling (seeing it, say, only as a piece of moral hypocrisy practiced by fanatics), then in insisting on truth telling in all circumstances, one would be willing a world in which truth telling would come to be seen as of little or no value. Or, if one knew that in a world where only personal choice counted, the strong would, after a while, come to dominate the weak completely, and that in such a world liberty in general would come to be seen as only a piece of "ideology" whereby the dominant group maintained power over the weaker, then in willing free choice in the face of everything, one would be willing a world in which respect for the autonomy of individuals would vanish. No baker would knowingly add so much flour to the bread that it tasted too bad to eat; no rational person would will a principle that would lead to a state of affairs in which the principle became unrealizable.

The so-called problem of "theory" and "practice" is not one of compromising the lofty goals of moral philosophy with the hard facts of the world (as if one might have to trade the goals of justice for the hard facts of economic efficiency) but of adjusting the mix of principles so that the good society is achieved. This is the core idea behind the notion that our duties and our obligations are, as many philosophers have argued, only

IV. Balancing and Cost/Benefit Analysis

prima facie; a *prima facie* duty or obligation to do X requires us to do X in all situations unless it is outweighed by another *prima facie* duty or obligation to do Y. To say that our duties and our obligations are only *prima facie* is to say that none of them are absolute, although some may be so weighty as to be unlikely ever to be outweighed (such as the restriction on the intentional taking of innocent human life). They must all be weighed in terms of the larger picture of social union in which they operate. An action that taken alone would be impermissible might be permissible as a necessary part of a larger course of action that is itself permissible. This larger course of action must itself be located within a larger framework of possibilities for action.

This larger framework is the social union in which these considerations arise. Consider in this light the libertarian principle that the state has no *prima facie* right to interfere coercively with the voluntary transactions between consenting adults, and the burden of proof is on those who wish to justify such coercive interference. *Even if* one accepted the libertarian principle, one would not be morally compelled to say that such interference may never occur or is always unjust when it does occur (the idea behind the claim that we must sometimes sacrifice a little justice for something else), only that the greater weight is on the side of those who wish to follow their own lights. Even on libertarian terms, although limiting someone's autonomy is *prima facie* wrong, it could be justified when it occurs as part of a larger framework of policy and action that is right in the larger sense. The initial plausibility of the libertarian principle is derivative from the larger goals of the liberal social union from which it comes. As *the* basic principle of such a union, however, it loses this initial plausibility.

In a liberal democratic rule of law, I have argued that the guiding principle of this general map of the well-ordered society is the principle of respect for the dignity of all. Rights are enforceable claims, but not all ethical duties are enforceable or ought to be—thus, not all ethical duties will be correlative to rights. We can now see that this is part of the argument about theory and practice, and we can see the force behind the common sense claim that the state should not try to enforce all ethical claims; this gives the state too much power and will ultimately lead not to a better realization of our ethical duties but rather to a tyranny opposed to that. (Overall, such considerations seem to me to be only further specifications of the Hegelian idea that the true moral life is always the concrete ethical life.)

These are very general considerations about how it would be possible to balance principles with an emphasis on those principles involved in private agreement and civil obligation in general. In reflecting on how it would be possible to have a coherent understanding of civil obligation, we will be implicitly operating within a general view of liberal society, a picture of the structure of possible types of mutual acknowledgments. An explication of the principles at work here is, in Hegelian terms, an explication of the "moments" of a category; one justifies such an explication by showing that it is an adequate explanation of how a social category is possible. A social category gives us a general delineation of a possible social order; the explanation and explication of the category shows how this possibility would be itself possible. But we reach impasses in explicating principles found in only one set of categories. These impasses—contradictions, incoherences, and the like—require us to supplement our explanation with new categories. This kind of explanatory movement, to use a Hegelian metaphor, is what Hegel called dialectic. The stage is thus set for an examination of what the dialectic of state and society involves.

CHAPTER
FOUR

Basic Principles, Basic Rights, and the State

THERE IS A general type of justification for the state that appears over and over again in the philosophical and political literature. It is a kind of pragmatic justification, and it goes roughly like this. In society, there are X, Y, and Z interests that society merely on its own cannot satisfy. A variety of different reasons are generally given: intrinsic bad will on the part of human beings, coordination problems, prisoner's dilemma situations, and so on. In order to satisfy these interests, an extra body is constructed, namely, the state. With its acquired monopoly on force, the state then goes about securing what society on its own could not (keeping the peace, protecting property rights, or whatnot). One of the most attractive models for this kind of conception is, of course, social contract theory. There one imagines a "society" (of sorts) in which the people jointly agree to set up a body that will further certain important goals and interests that they have. What is basic to this strategy for justifying the state is the following picture: a number of individuals interacting with each other in a *private* way make a set of *private* agreements with one another to create a *public* body. This public body, however, is justified only to the extent that it furthers some common (but nonetheless private) interests.

This image and the terms "private" and "public" need some unpacking. In order to do this, I want initially to pursue this basic model a bit further. In particular, I would like to view it in terms of some classical criticisms of the view, because I believe that there is a basic point to the criticisms that the more recent exponents of the view have not quite addressed. Hegel, for example, distinguished two different conceptions of the state. He called one the *Notstaat*, the "state based on need."[1] This "state based on need" is a conception of a minimal state devoted exclusively to the enforcement and furtherance of private interests. Such a conception nicely fits the picture of a body constructed to secure private interests such as enforcement of contracts. Hegel's view was that the "state based on need" is only a part of the full conception of the state. The full conception of the state, Hegel argued, involves more than the satisfaction of private interests. It also involves certain political elements that cannot be adequately understood in the terms of the "state based on need." I wish to argue that Hegel's distinction of the two aspects of the full conception of the state is substantially correct, even if not in quite the way Hegel made it. This distinction of these two aspects and how they relate to one another will help us to see what is flawed with a social contract model of the justification of the state. Hegel's distinction amounts to a denial that anything like the "state based on need" is sufficient to explain the kind of social unions that make up a democratic liberal society and state. I shall defend that denial. To do so, I shall look first at what kinds of reasons would legitimate the "state based on need" and then consider as working hypotheses other kinds of reasons that might take us further. I would like then to see what implications this has for our understanding of political rights.

I
The Minimal State as a Social State

Robert Nozick offers a model of a state that has similar features to Hegel's "state based on need."[2] Both are bodies constructed to secure private interests that could not otherwise be secured. Moreover, like Hegel's, Nozick's model does not depend on generating any kind of "contract" between people; people do not set out to create a state. Rather, Nozick's explanation (again, like Hegel's) is one that shows that it would be possible for such a body to arise in such a way that it would violate nobody's rights and yet not be the direct object of anyone's choice. If such a derivation works, then it would show the compatibility

I. The Minimal State as a Social State 139

—perhaps stronger, the congeniality—of the existence of a state and individual freedom. Rather than being seen merely as a body that restricts an individual's choice in the interests of something else, the state can be seen to be the unintended but justified result of a series of free choices that would be made by individuals to protect their rights. Nozick's view bears a look, since it is an attempt to stop at exactly the point where Hegel thought one had to move on.

Nozick's derivation goes something like this. We imagine individuals in a state of nature having certain natural rights, namely, life, liberty, property, and (importantly) the right to enforce their rights. Unfortunately, where people would have to rely on their own efforts to enforce their rights, there would be constant feuding: people tend to overestimate the harms done to them, they overpunish, they make mistakes that encourage vendettas to become established, and so on. Some people (the weaker) would lack the power to enforce their rights, and sometimes the rights violators would simply be quicker and would thus get away with it. There is also just the sheer expense of tracking down the wrongdoers. For these types of reasons, individuals would find it worth their while to band together into various *protective associations*; these would acquire the right to enforce members' rights against others and against the members themselves. Through an "invisible hand process," these associations will come to unite. (Either one always loses disputes, and thus its clients tend to defect to the other side; or the respective associations realize how costly it is to engage in such skirmishes, and thus they unite.) Out of the union of various smaller protective associations, therefore, a dominant protective agency would arise. Since individuals in it transfer to the agency their rights to enforce their rights, any further self-enforcement becomes prohibited. The agency will also prevent those people who are not clients of the agency (the independents) from enforcing their rights against clients because of the high risk of unjust enforcement. But this disadvantages the independents, who now lose a right that properly belongs to them. The agency must therefore compensate them, since it is the agency and its clients who benefit from this prohibition. The cheapest and most effective way of doing this is also to provide the independents with protection—to enforce their rights equally with the rights of the clients.

Once this step is taken, the dominant protective agency becomes a minimal state: it acquires a monopoly over the use of force in a territory, and it protects the rights of everyone in the territory. Moreover, given the arguments made in Chapter Three relating to imposition of risk, this minimal state might (although Nozick does go this far) also acquire certain regulatory functions, ensuring, for example, that manufacturers of products do not impose unnecessary risks on people (or are made to compensate them if they do).[3]

I shall not question whether or not Nozick's derivation is correct; for the present, I shall simply assume that it is. The more important question for our purposes is whether or not we need go further. Is the minimal state all that we need? Nozick's answer is that it is, that anything that is more than the minimal state would violate individual rights. The state arises as an organization to secure the "natural" rights of life, liberty, property, and the right to enforce our rights. Any more powers that it might have would need to come from the actual consent of those governed by it. Without this consent, it cannot legitimately gain any more power, and, so Nozick thinks, gaining such consent would be highly unlikely (although he does discuss how such an unlikely state of affairs could possibly appear).[4]

The independents are compensated for the loss of their right to enforce their rights by being given protection by the dominant protective agency. (This is required and justified by the principle of compensation.) Do the independents, however, have any political rights—such as a vote —in the minimal state? The question of voting rights is crucial. The right to vote is not one of the rights that one has in the state of nature because as yet there is nothing to vote *for*. Voting is a political activity that presupposes a political background. It does not have a place in Nozick's list of basic rights because it *cannot* have a place. One cannot have a right to vote for a government or organization that does not yet carry with it the authority of being a (at least possible) government. One may not complain that the government that you and your friends would like to see established but does not yet exist (say, the joint federal government of Texas, Thailand, and Ghana) has deprived you of your right to vote for it or to select its officers. Nor is a vote the same thing as consent to a contract or to transferring one's rights to a protective agency. Nor is voting "within" the state (for representatives, for laws, and so on) the same as ratification of a government or state; the process of ratification presupposes some political unity or organizational form already existing. (Otherwise, how would one be able to decide who gets to vote for ratification?) Suppose that the minimal state simply tells the independents that it will enforce their contracts but not allow them to vote. Is any *harm* done such that they must be compensated? (Is voting an important activity such that any prohibition of it must be compensated, and the only viable compensation would be giving the people the vote? If voting is such a valuable activity, why is the turnout for election in the United States so low?) If in fact compensation is required, why is efficient protection not compensation enough?

In any event, whatever type of harm is being done to the independents, it is clear that no "state of nature" right is being violated. The minimal state need not worry too much about this, for it is, after all, not primarily a *political* institution. It is a *social* institution for the protection and enforcement of *private* rights. Political rights, to the extent that they exist in the minimal state, are fancified versions of or derivations from the more basic private rights. Indeed, since the minimal state is basically just a corporation compensating the non-shareholders (the independents), any political rights that people would have would be shareholder's rights, that is, a type of *property* right. If the corporation compensates the non-shareholders for limiting their rights, need it go further and also give them stock in the corporation? (For that matter, would not a "one person–one vote" principle be a difficult position to defend? Is not the preferred solution "one share–one vote," with the obvious conclusion that those having more shares also receive more votes?) Nozick's minimal state *can* have political rights in it *only* as a species of property rights. Is this enough? It is this distinction of private (social) rights and public (political) rights that I take Hegel to be making when he moves from the "state based on need" to the state proper. This requires us, however, to back up and look at the rationale of this distinction itself.

II
The Political State and Basic Rights

To what exactly does this distinction between the "private" and the "public" amount? As Hegel argued, society is the sphere of the private. In it, the 'glue' that holds the system together is that of personal interest;

one is bonded to another by beliefs that such bonding is in one's own interest. ("Interest" in this sense can have either altruistic or non-altruistic content.) The legitimacy of the "state based on need" is founded on this collection of personal interests; this *social state*, as I shall henceforth call it, is required to protect or enable the satisfaction of those interests that could not be satisfied without it (because of things like free-rider problems and the like). But this personal interest is still the only glue that can legitimately hold "society" together.

We might ask then why this view of society should be seen as legitimate. If we reject any utilitarian justification (that the overall welfare in some sense is higher in such a society), then it would seem that this would be the case only because such a society would be the best embodiment of a recognition of the right of individuals to make their own choices. Each is allowed to associate with whom he or she pleases, to decide on his or her own manner of life, and so on. Those who wish to live in, say, religious communes may do so; those who do not want to may not be compelled to do so. Nonetheless, "society" in this sense is only an outgrowth of personal interest and empirical dependencies. To the extent that I cannot produce everything myself, I "need" others (being unable to make all my own furniture, grow all my own food, and so on). My relation with the other person(s) remains, however, a matter of *private* choice. This much would be justified by respect for autonomy. The libertarian model is a model of such a society, and the libertarian state is a function of that society.[5]

The principle of respect for autonomy, however, is itself justified by the more fundamental principle of respect for the dignity of individuals, coupled with beliefs about how individuals are capable of making their own choices and what is a proper ideal of personal development. The principle of respect for human dignity is a principle involving a type of acknowledgment between people. The values inherent in the social union of democratic liberal society are realizations and embodiments of this basic principle of respect for the dignity of individuals. Yet society is that realm where individual choice is paramount. As a being capable of choice, a person seeks to become an autonomous person, making reflective independent choices expressive of their character. It is this element of independence that is misinterpreted by the libertarian as being *the* principle of society (perhaps it lies at the root of the identification of

II. The Political State and Basic Rights 143

respect for persons with respect for choice). But even if it were the principle of society, it is not the principle of the state.

Hegel's interesting thought experiment as to what this would entail in the absence of any kind of social union is instructive. (This occurs in his discussion of the dialectic of "Master and Slave" in his *Phenomenology of Spirit*.[6]) The radical individualist conception of society fits Hegel's model of the dialectic of master and slave: each individual seeks to become independent, and this naturally leads to a struggle on the part of each. The struggle involves both a competition for goods and a struggle to get others to do what one wants them to do. Each is, as it were, demanding acknowledgment by the others as an independent person. Absent any jointly accepted mediating principles, as Hegel argued, this struggle leads either to death or to the subordination of one of the combatants to the other. Yet each has an equally valid claim to acknowledgment; there is nothing intrinsic to one or the other that classifies one as the "master," the other as the "slave." On this model, we would think of society as a constant struggle to push through one's own "interests," to maintain our independence vis-à-vis others, and this personal independence involves making the others dependent on us. The principle of this form of society, so we can put it, is personal interest. On its own, this society would remain a sphere of struggle and subordination. (Note too for the "masters," those who have managed by skill, luck or both to arrange the conditions of their lives so that both their independence is secured and the others—the "slaves"—remain subordinate to them, there will be little reason to extend the vote to the independents; it is enough to protect their rights to life, liberty, and property, since they will remain subordinate so long as they have not accumulated enough to be able to pursue their own interests.[7]) "Masters" might accept limited government; they could never accept democratic government.

The solution to the "master-slave" dialectic is, as Hegel saw it to be, a conceptual move to a different plane. In the abstract, it is a move to a mutual acknowledgment, the expression of which is a mutual respect for the dignity of each, the perception of the other as 'one of us.' This abstract principle yields other abstract rights (life, liberty, property), and also yields the ideal of private society, where each interacts with the others on the basis of private choice. However, this form of society is by its nature incapable of fully embodying the principle of respect for persons, for it is a sphere of subordination, competition, and the like. Another step is needed, and that is the step to the *political* state (not merely the *social* state). It is, moreover, this step that makes possible the conception of "society" as a form of liberal *democratic* social union rather than merely *liberal* social union.

This is a categorial difference, for we have here two different types of concepts of social union, of unities of a plurality of individuals.[8] In society the unity of the plurality of individuals is produced by the free choices of individuals and the protective (and perhaps regulatory) functions of the social state; the 'glue' that holds the unity together is personal interest. Even in the social union of democratic liberal society, the element of personal interest is paramount. In the political state, however, the unity is not that of interest but of *citizenship*. The 'glue' that holds this unity together is the set of rules and principles that both define and command the conditions under which each is a citizen of the state. One is a *social* unity; the other is a *political* unity. In distinction from social groups in which ideally one is a member by choice, one is a citizen of a political state not by virtue of choice but by virtue of the laws of the state. As such, this unity seems to require *prima facie* a special justification for its legitimacy, for it is not based in individual choice or interest as the social state is.[9]

The same abstract principles that justified society as a type of unity require one to move on to the political state. The argument for this is that if the category of 'society' explains how it would be possible to realize or embody the principle of respect for persons, but only explains it in part (something is left out), then one must introduce a new category to explain how the principle would be more fully realized. This also leads to a particular way of construing the state (in a democratic liberal and not authoritarian fashion). The same abstract principles that generated the idea of liberal society also generate not only a new category, the political state, but a determinate form that the political state must take. The intuitive idea here is that society realizes part of the principle of respect for dignity by giving each a sphere of maximal liberty of choice, whereas the state ensures that each individual's full dignity will be protected. The principle of respecting the dignity of individuals forms liberal society into a particular type of social union, with constraints on individual choice emerging within it. It becomes democratic liberal society.

II. The Political State and Basic Rights

Liberal society is an association of individuals, each possessing certain basic rights of liberty and property. *Democratic* liberal society is a social union in which a community of *fairness* is established. As we saw, however, even the democratic liberal social union of 'society' is unable to resolve all its own problems. We might put it like this: if the principle of society is *interest*, then the principle of the democratic political state would be *political equality*.[10]

A crucial distinction between these two forms of social union consists in the different models of rights present in each. We can call these the economic and the political models of rights. The point of society (the values that it realizes) consists in its realization of the individual liberty of each to pursue his or her own interests; the point of the state is its realization and securing of the concrete conditions under which individual dignity and liberty may be achieved. On its own, society is a sphere of economically modeled rights; they are pieces of property over which individuals have disposition. The state, on the other hand, is a sphere of politically modeled rights; these are not tradeable any more than one's dignity is tradeable. The determinations of these political rights will depend on what conditions are necessary for individuals to participate as political equals.

The set of rules and principles that define and command these conditions is the *constitution* of a state. The 'glue' of the unity of the political state is the constitution, just as interest is the 'glue' of the unity of society. The authority of the constitution is its ethical force. It is the constitution (written or unwritten) that unites the components of the society and the social state into a unity that we can call *civic community* (as the unity of state and society): it defines the non-negotiable conditions under which people participate as political equals. It is a public sphere, unlike the private sphere of society where people to a great degree negotiate the terms of their cooperation and interaction with each other. A constitution is thus the overall draft of the form of the civic community; it inherently includes certain moral ideals and cannot be understood outside of these ideals. Democratic liberal society is a union for mutual benefit; the democratic liberal state is a political union protecting the dignity of each individual. Together they define a type of shared identity, the community of fairness.

Any constitution structured around the principles of respect for persons, justice, and peaceful cooperation will have some kind of statement of *civil* rights as claims that people can bring against others and the state. These claims are justified by their being necessary for each to participate as a political equal. Rawls may be read as offering something like this, although not quite in these terms.[11] Rawls distinguishes two principles of justice, the first of which entitles people to equal maximal basic liberties, and the second of which entitles people to fair equality of opportunity and, most importantly, equality of social goods (with inequalities being justifiably introduced when they would work to the benefit of the least advantaged). Rawls gives the basic liberties what he calls a lexical priority over the other principles of justice; this has the effect, as Rawls notes, of prohibiting any trade of the basic liberties for gains in welfare. But what are the *basic* liberties? We might interpret these as just the rights and liberties necessary to participate as a political equal. But Rawls does not say so, and it is important to note why, for it reveals, I think, a basic flaw in any social contract theory. First, Rawls has no theory of the state, so it would be difficult for him to read the basic liberties in this way. But this is a weak objection; perhaps a Rawlsian theory of the state is either on the way or could be satisfactorily constructed and thus could handle this objection. More important, though, is the fact that Rawls's contract model is only another way of trying to generate the state out of private interests, even if those interests can be shown to be common (that is, would be chosen by all under conditions specified by the Original Position). In order to generate a set of interests that, in the conditions of the Original Position, individuals would regard as issuing forth in non-negotiable rights, Rawls must make some far-reaching assumptions. We can see this by taking some examples. Consider the right to freedom of speech. It is not clear, for example, that it is always in the interest of each individual not to trade such a right for something else. One might, for example, trade the specific right to espouse certain neo-Nazi (or plain, old-fashioned Nazi) ideas for some gain in welfare because one never had nor likely ever will have the slightest inclination to espouse such ideas at all. In order to avoid this, Rawls has his individuals make their choices behind the veil of ignorance using maximin (choose the most favorable worst outcome) as a principle. But it is extremely unclear if that will work. Let us imagine that some person takes it to be a divine commandment that there should be

II. The Political State and Basic Rights

no one-way streets. Since people do not know if they will end up being that person (they are behind the veil of ignorance and use maximin), the result will be a non-negotiable constitutional right to two-way streets. (A United States judge did once prohibit traffic lights as interfering with the constitutional rights of U.S. citizens; his decision was, needless to say, quickly overturned.)

Rawls must assume that the participants in the Original Position do not have any such non-negotiable interests that in principle could find no political solution. Indeed, any liberal theory must assume that. One way to do this would be a form of pragmatic common sense (the kind of objection that one sometimes gets from undergraduates when one is offering them the typical array of philosophical counterexamples). There just aren't any such people who take one-way streets to be a non-negotiable religious right, so there is no need to worry about them in the Original Position. As it stands, this objection is not a bad one. Rawls's theory is, after all, not intended to answer such hypothetical objections. Common sense, however, is the common sense of a particular culture in a particular time. It is dependent on the form of social union of which it is the common sense. The Rawlsian theory—as a theory of the Original Position—must therefore presume a type of social union that precedes the deliberations that go on in the Original Position: it must presume a type of social union that structures the interests of the parties so that such non-negotiable conflicts do not arise.

Rawls's theory is another answer to Michel de L'Hopital's argument that the point of politics is not to find the true religion but to find how the different religions can peacefully coexist. There is of course another element of Rawls's theory that is different from the doctrine of the Original Position. This is his conception of reflective equilibrium. According to this doctrine, one reflectively tests one's considered judgments against one's moral theory, altering each until the two finally come into a state of equilibrium with each other. But for reflective equilibrium to be possible, a democratic liberal form of social union must exist in which the presence of non-negotiable interests is avoided. The Rawlsian doctrine of reflective equilibrium highlights the kind of assumptions that must be made for Rawlsian justice to be possible.

The Rawlsian scheme will provide an understanding of civil rights only with the supplementation of a theory of social unions. Such a theory would provide the arguments concerning the conditions under which people could be said to be political equals. Of course, any argument to establish civil rights will involve more than *a priori* speculation about them: it will also involve sets of empirical assumptions and historical argument, both set against the background of ethical principles that are essential to a democratic liberal constitution. Certain rights such as freedom of speech seem easiest to identify. Others such as "one person–one vote" are perhaps harder but nonetheless equally fundamental.

How might we then construe the idea of basic rights in a democratic liberal social union? I argued earlier (Chapter Two) that the idea of a right is an explanatory notion that may be justified as an answer to problems raised by the idea of sovereignty. What kind of explanation is offered? Martin Kriele has suggested that the basic model for construing civil rights is found both historically and conceptually in the right of *habeas corpus*, which in Edward Coke's original formulation of it states, "No man can be taken, arrested, attached, or imprisoned, but by due process of law and according to the law of the land."[12] The importance of this is in part its recognition of the principle of moral equality, for it speaks of all people, rather than, for example, as the comparable part of the Magna Charta speaks, of all "*free* men." (Restricting it to all free men meant restricting it to a certain propertied class within the society.) It is the acceptance of this principle of moral equality that allows for a justified historical movement from privileges of the "estates" to the rights of all free citizens, to the rights of all members of the state, and finally to the idea of human rights. Moreover, the principle protects a sphere of independence; it shields the individual against arbitrary punishment, arrest, and the like by the state. Of course, one may specify what counts as arbitrary and non-arbitrary treatment in purely juridical terms, such that gross violations of rights can occur in procedurally justified ways. (Hannah Arendt talks, for example, about the Third Reich's fetish for procedure in its pursuit of some of its more murderous policies.) But in a legal order that has justice as one of its basic principles, "arbitrary" will have to take on more substantive colorations. It will require a more elaborate statement of the *basic* rights that individuals have. One condition of a procedure's being fair is that it does not violate any rights that an individual has. Hence, if it is to have any more than a kind of "abstract" force, *habeas corpus* requires supplementation by a "bill of

II. The Political State and Basic Rights

rights." The important point, however, is that it is an answer to problems that emerge within a state in which the idea of sovereignty is being undermined. It is a solution to a dilemma found in the early outlines of liberal social union.

It is better to speak here of *basic* rights rather than natural rights in order to avoid the possible confusion of basic rights with rights found in a state of nature (which then get carried over into society and the state). Some rights may be basic (like voting) but not "natural" in this sense. The way of generating principles that would assist in deciding which rights are basic is the kind of dialectical argument used so far. Moving from some kind of explanation of the possibility of moral principles by appeal to the need for a structure of mutual acknowledgment, one justifies various principles as explanations of the possibility of certain kinds of social and political categories. The argument moves then from abstract principles like respect for individual dignity to respect for autonomy as a basic principle. A concrete realization of a due respect for another's autonomy is that the person be vouchsafed a wide sphere of private rights (property, contract, the right to choose with whom one will associate). Such rights would be side effects of the same principle of respect for persons that moves one from the category of the social state to the category of the political state. The political state would be justified to the extent that society and the social state are incapable of realizing the principles that serve to justify them as categories (basic types of social union). In each case, the basic rights will be those claims that individuals ought to have as enforceable claims. (Thus, an individual can argue from within the standpoint of the civic community that his or her status as a moral and political equal is impaired by lack of a right to vote.)

The kernel of the argument for the move to the political state is the necessity to distinguish private rights (which are like property rights — they can be freely redefined and traded) from public rights (which are specified by the constitution and cannot be freely redefined and traded). Society has a feature to it that can only be solved by this move to public rights; in society, rights are like pieces of property and individuals should be allowed to trade them freely. But this has or can have the tendency to result in some people's having much control over others, to the point where slavery or indentured servitude can come to be in the interest of those not so well off. Such arrangements are, however, affronts to human dignity. Whereas society and the social state cannot prevent this and remain consistent with their principle (that of interest), the constitutional order puts these affronts to dignity outside the bounds of individual choice. The constitutional order is justified as the draft of the political order in which each person is guaranteed a respect for their dignity. Since this right cannot be freely traded like a normal property right, those rights intrinsic to a just liberal constitutional order also cannot be bartered. To reiterate: the principle of the political state is not "interest"; it is moral and hence political equality, derived from the principle of respect for persons.[13]

Much of this may seem like just so much kvetching with social contract theory over exactly where one places one's principles and in what order. Is the basic argument against social contract theory only its confusion of the social state with the political state? There is a deeper reason for rejecting any form of social contract theory. This deeper reason lies, moreover, in what also gives social contract theory its strong underlying appeal, namely, the Kantian identification of respect for persons with respect for autonomy or free choice. Once this identification is made, respect for the choices of individuals becomes equivalent to respect for them as persons. This view gives credence to a theory that would see the state as the result of some kind of contract or set of choices that individuals make. Respecting choices certainly is an important element of respecting persons, but this identification of the two has an unattractive side to it: if the state is the result of a contract (and we think of contracts as bargains between individuals for mutual self-interest), then presumably people will want to include those in the contract who in some sense either provide some kind of benefit to them or are simply too dangerous to keep out. The state then becomes conceived as a kind of voluntary association, a club that has the power to exclude undesirable people from membership. This leaves the powerless, the handicapped—in short, those who neither provide benefit nor pose a threat—without protection. At best one would end up with a state based on mutual protection, a form of social state. As an agency erected by individuals in society, however, the social state must of necessity be a particular thing, most likely an organ by which some group can press its own interests on to others who are too weak to resist.[14] The point of a democratic liberal constitution, however, is to protect the dignity of each person, especially where they are powerless to protect themselves. Such a constitution is not well construed by a contractarian theory. And thus, despite its initial plausibility, a contractarian theory does not provide the best model for understanding basic rights.[15]

III
Welfare Rights and Property Rights

What is the relation between the "social" state and the "political" state? The social state is constituted by the principle of interest; the social state provides for those common interests that society by relying on its own mechanisms could not provide. The political state is an organ in society that unites itself with the social state to form *the* state proper; it constructs and preserves a *union*—what we have also called a *civic community*. Both the social state and the political state are parts (in Hegelian terms, moments) of the union. The constitution in part specifies the relation between the two (although it is, in the imagery used here, a part that unites itself with another to form a whole greater than itself). The civic community overall forms what we have called the community of fairness.

The relation between the social and the political state is, however, not free of conflict. There is the danger that the social state can corrupt the political state. If society is a sphere of interest—a kind of mitigated struggle for "mastery" and "slavery"—with each person seeking to preserve his or her independence (and in advanced capitalist countries with many trying to extend their range of power as far as possible), there is always the practical danger of the state's being taken over by an interest group to be exploited for its own particular interests. In such cases, where this is successful, the ideal of the state stands in opposition to its actuality. (Marx raised this danger to a level of necessity; for him, the state was always a particular organ in society that was used by the dominant interest group—which he also held to be always the social class that owned the means of production—to further its own goals. This tension was for him an ever present *fait accompli*.[16]) This would be the democratic liberal state in its corrupted form. One of the ideals of the democratic liberal state is thus to prevent its own corruption. (It does this through freedom of information acts, legal aid programs, regulation of elections, and the like; other things like the practical necessity of a division of power, an independent judiciary, and the like would follow. These would not—to stay with our Hegelian terminology—be part of the concept of the democratic liberal state but practically necessary parts of its actuality.[17]) To the extent that the democratic liberal state is to keep its citizens as political equals, it must avoid becoming the province of any particular interest group.

If so, then it would also seem that the democratic liberal state has an obligation to effect distributive justice at least in so far as that is necessary to protect the political equality of its citizens (although this is only an abstract obligation). A democratic liberal social and political order is open to arguments about the relative goodness of various egalitarian schemes (which can vary quite obviously with the amount of social wealth at hand). Such an argument can turn on the preservation of the union, the civic community itself. Or, "solidarity" (or perhaps the more francophonic "fraternity") among the members of the civic community can be one such good that might serve to justify some more or less egalitarian redistributive schemes. The civic community can promote a solidarity among its members through a kind of sharing of burdens and benefits. Or, to take another example, the adoption of more rigorously egalitarian schemes remains a question of the relative goodness of freeing people from types of what has been called economic coercion.

Of course, it is conceivable that a society would refuse to do any of these things. Libertarians endorse such a state of affairs, claiming that it might be "Unfortunate, but not unjust." This slogan is a bit too weak, however, for a society that had the means to alleviate some rather humiliating conditions for some of its more disadvantaged members and chose not to do so. For that society, the preferable slogan instead might be "Not unjust, but nonetheless bad."

The actual *goodness* of things like "civic solidarity" is a matter of public debate, of consensus building. Just how good it is would be something that is only disclosed in participation in social and communal activity. This element of solidarity among the members of the civic community also appears in arguments about the basic rights. For example, in the claim to a basic right to free speech, there are two arguments at work, each of which strengthens the other. One is an argument to the

III. Welfare Rights and Property Rights 153

effect that one's standing as a political equal is adversely affected if one's views are not allowed to be expressed. The other is an argument about goodness: a public debate is required for consensus building about a whole range of important issues, and a wide-ranging right to freedom of speech is a condition for a genuine consensus to be formed and for there to be a genuine debate. This latter condition refers to the virtues of citizenship and common activity in building and sustaining the political community. On this latter view, free speech is an essential part of the kind of civic community that makes up the liberal state. It is an activity that forms us into citizens, and its value is disclosed in that kind of civic activity. The activity of voting also carries this symbolic sense of forming us into members of the civic community, of being not merely a right but also a basic good.

Welfare rights on this view would not be constitutional rights (except where they are required to preserve political equality) but would be legislatively created rights to promote some scheme of equality in terms of promoting solidarity. Welfare rights, that is, may be seen to be created rights whereby the civic community (the union) both symbolically expresses and actually manifests a concern for the well-being of its less fortunate members (a non-paternalistic concern, we might add).

Does this allow in the back door illegitimate arguments at the level of the democratic liberal state about, for example, the relative goodness of various styles of life? Welfare rights are justified not by appeal to arguments about which styles of life are better, but by appeal to policy arguments about the value of civic community. Indeed, welfare rights become unthinkable in a social and political order in which there is no civic community, no shared identity. One problem always facing democratic liberal societies has to do with their inherent pluralism. We accept that there will just be different churches, synagogues, and mosques, different ideals, different goals of life, and so on. What then remains in common? It is always difficult for such societies to see their shared identities. For that reason, democratic liberal social union must be able to project its ideals so it can see them.[18] It must find ways of expressing that its members do care for one another, even when the members are also necessarily to a large part strangers to one another. One such projection finds its expression in the provision of welfare rights. A system of welfare rights both expresses and helps to sustain the ideal of sharing in a social and political order. People connect with other people in it; their symbolic significance lies in their allowing strangers in a civic community to express their identity with each other. It is not just a matter of compassion, as political rhetoric sometimes supposes, but a matter of civic community. (When you are down and out, who wishes to be treated with compassion? Isn't it better to be treated with respect?) What is disturbing to the disadvantaged is not the belief that people are not compassionate toward them but the feeling that nobody cares, that they are not part of the "club." It is their exclusion from full *citizenship* that is most bothersome. Not only must it be shown that the community cares for them; it must be done with respect for their status as citizens. What is at stake is not merely distribution of goods but also the sense of contribution of members of the civic community to some overall sense of shared identity (including the contribution from the disadvantaged, however that might be construed). Liberal social union requires that it demonstrate its ideals of community and sharing, and welfare rights, where they are justified, are strategies for demonstrating this kind of sharing.

What happens to property rights in this view? Libertarians from Nozick to Hayek, after all, have objected that any scheme involving coercive interference with property rights is an illegitimate interference with liberty. We may view property rights as valid claims to the use or benefit of things (in the broadest sense) and the right to exclude or include others from such use or benefit. How might we justify such rights? The utilitarian strategy—allowing individuals to have such rights would produce some maximal good—is out of the running. Another close cousin of the utilitarian view may be formulated in a rough way as follows: property is necessary to satisfy certain human needs (food, clothing, the desire to have a sphere of one's own); one may override, therefore, X's right to property if X's needs are already satisfied, and it is necessary to do so to satisfy Y's needs. Something like this view is, I suspect, at the heart of Rawls's theory; it certainly allows egalitarian considerations to enter the argumentative arena more easily. It is also clear that unless the concept of need is stretched quite a bit, it is difficult to see how a good deal of property may be construed as fulfilling "needs." Does this mean that, for example, most property owned by people in the developed and semi-developed lands is unjustified? (Or does a church in a poor area have no justified claim to, for example, its one medieval

III. Welfare Rights and Property Rights

painting? May the state expropriate it and sell it to provide for other more "basic" needs? Surely a religious service can proceed just as well with a photo-reprint of a Giotto as with the original.) One could expand, I think, on a number of other counterintuitive examples; I shall leave it as an assumption of my view that the "need" conception of property will not work.

Another conception would be one that saw property as not a means to the satisfaction of some other interest but as an embodiment of freedom and thus in some sense an end in itself. This is the view in which, naturally enough, those of libertarian inclinations will most likely find themselves at home. This view has a good pedigree (Locke, Hegel, and Nozick, among others). Unfortunately, this "tradition" has invested itself with Locke's idea of the original acquisition of property, the gist of which is that if one "mixes" one's labor with something that was previously unowned (and that could become something owned), then one converts it into one's own property. This is a flaw in the tradition, I think, and for a simple reason: Why should it be the case that one *acquires* the thing and not simply *loses* one's labor? The idea of "mixing" one's labor as giving one title to something is, I suspect, parasitic on some more basic intuitions. One would be that someone who takes the trouble to bring something new into the world "deserves" something in return. But why the thing itself? Why not instead, say, a medal? a certificate of appreciation from the locals? To say that it should be the thing itself as property rests on another basic intuition that there is something special about *property* that is lacking in a round of applause or a pat on the back. But what is so special about property?

Consider Robert Nozick's invocation of what he calls the "Lockean Proviso" in his libertarian theory of the limits on property rights. Nozick argues that one may not acquire the total supply of things that are necessary for life such that others are left in a worse-off state than they would be in a state of nature (that is the Proviso). He hints that this limitation belongs to "considerations internal to the theory of property, to its theory of acquisition and appropriation,"[19] but he apparently leaves it up to the reader to speculate as to what these considerations might be. Is it because one needs it?[20] Surely not. But why then?

Maybe another look at the "embodiment of freedom" conception of property without its trappings in the Lockean idea of acquisition would help us to see the point of the Proviso. What is wrong with acquiring the total supply of things that are necessary for life is what is wrong with all such monopolies: the *point* of property rights is to protect individual independence and to enable individual autonomy. Property rights give an individual a certain irreplaceable sphere of independence vis-à-vis others and the state; they protect one from being dependent on the sympathy of others or of the government. Such rights would then help to enable the ideal of development of people into autonomous individuals. Monopolies of important goods are one of the greatest threats to such independence. Prohibition of such monopolies is thus "internal" to the idea of property but only in the sense that the idea of property is located internally within some ideal of social union. To revert again to Hegelian terms: a conception of property rights whose result is the creation of such monopolies is one whose "concept" contradicts its "actuality"; it would be something that it is practically inconsistent to hold, since in such a world the right to property would come to be valued little at all (except by the few who had it).

The point of property rights is the same as the point of other rights. They provide a measure of security for the individual from interference by others. Without rights an individual is dependent on the sympathy of others, in particular of the people who staff the offices of authority. Rights are *protections* of our sense of self-respect, our dignity. To determine what rights individuals have, we must know what it is they are protecting. The point of property rights is to protect individual independence, not to give unimpeded right of way to the individual's will; these rights may be limited when the self-respect of individuals is at stake.

This is not an argument that property is an absolutely necessary element of human freedom (or a transcendental condition of the possibility of the realization of human freedom). It is more of a kind of interpretive argument that property is a specification of the abstract ideal of freedom. It is a form that freedom takes. What, however, exactly is the argument? It is found in the claim that postulation of a right to property best explains certain things. It can be understood only as an attempt to answer certain problems. It is well to try to bring these to the surface.

The postulation of a right to property is best understood in terms of the historical locus of the problems that it is supposed to resolve. Con-

III. Welfare Rights and Property Rights 157

sider the postulation of a *natural* right to property. Locke and others of his time spoke of the natural rights to life, liberty, and property (or estate) as if it were self-evident that these were the natural rights (and the only ones). They are of course *not* self-evident. Why then did enlightened people take them to be so? The ideas were formulated against the background of the debate between James I and the parliament in England as to the nature of the sovereign. The king, James I, under the influence of imported French theories about sovereignty argued that he and he alone had final and absolute power (like a god) over his subjects, that he was temporally answerable to nobody but himself. As we know, there was somewhat of a disagreement among various factions of the English people about this issue, which was settled after a brief scuffle. The Lockean triumvirate of the natural rights can be better understood when it is realized that they set limits to such claims of power: they *protected* individuals against the encroachments of the "sovereign." The sovereign after all can threaten basically three types of things: he can put you to death (no, one has a right to life); he can enslave you or arbitrarily imprison you (no, one has a right to liberty); or he can confiscate your holdings (no, one has a right to property). The natural right to property then is one defense against encroachments by a sovereign—and, by extrapolation, just a powerful other—on one's sphere of action.

A different conception of the relation of the state to its citizens would either not lead to a view of these rights as self-evident or require some kind of special justification for them. For example, in a more or less Aristotelian-Thomistic view of the relation, one would see the state as providing for the realization of certain basic human virtues and interests; a right to property would be justified (if at all) in terms of its role in promoting human flourishing. Contrast this with the views of the young Marx, who saw property as an incorporation of human alienation and thus preventing human flourishing—a reverse image of the same picture.

The *natural* right to property (not just the right to property *per se*) is thus intelligible only within the context of a view of individuals' needing to defend themselves against the arbitrary power of the state or of stronger others; in such a context, it does perhaps *seem* self-evident that these are the natural rights. Under the presupposition of such a state/citizen relationship property rights are justified as forms of freedom; they make freedom possible. But as we have seen, this is itself justified by the deeper principle of respect for persons, and it assumes concrete form in types of social union. In this respect, property would be no more a natural right than *habeas corpus* or the right to due process of law. Each would be justified as a legitimate protection of individuals against the arbitrary power of a sovereign. This just gives us all the more reason to eschew the language of natural rights in favor of that of basic rights.

IV
The State, Society, and the Constitution

I have taken the difference between the social state and the political state to be, abstractly put, that the social state would be justified by showing that it provides for the satisfaction of certain key interests in society, whereas the political state as the union of itself and the social state provides for the further conditions of respecting individual dignity. This distinction of state and society is, however, in one sense not a necessary one at all. Like all such distinctions, it is a reconstruction of a form of life, an explanation of how a form of life is possible. It may be objected that such a reconstruction is therefore doomed, if not to failure, to a kind of fatal one-sidedness of its own. Marxists, for example, might object that this form of life is itself only an 'appearance' of something more fundamental, namely, the mature development of a capitalist economy. Non-Marxist historicists might simply object that at best it captures a particular period of time, well or badly, but *only* a particular period.

Let us pursue the historicist objection. If we follow (at least as a starting point for discussion) Max Weber's well known condition for there being a state, namely, that there be an organized monopoly of force, then it is certainly true that states need not exist. Some historians have argued, for example, that in medieval Europe there was nothing corresponding to what we would nowadays call a *state*, although there was certainly enough the phenomenon of *rulership*.[21] The ordering of that time consisted of unseparated orders of rulership and incorporated life. Individuals found their social and political existence within this order according to their status. There was no one concentration of unitary power but rather a series of linking duties and privileges of vassals to masters, master to vassals, masters to each other, and so on. We need

IV. The State, Society, and the Constitution

not trace this out in any detail but simply note that it was a form of life in which the distinction of state and society would not play any helpful role in explanation.

Henry Maine's dictum that modern law is the passage from status to contract captures part of what happened. Before Maine had come up with this idea, however, one of Hegel's followers, Lorenz von Stein (a jurist by training), had presented a very similar notion.[22] The passage was from a social ordering without a state in which the relationships between individuals were structured according to *privilege* to a social ordering in which human *rights* became the principle that ordered the relationships between individuals. The state had already begun to form, but the French revolution brought this historical movement to its first historical completion; in it, society and state separated. The principle of the new social order was not that of 'status' and 'privilege' but of the autonomous individual existing (ideally) in a condition of equality with other autonomous individuals—of people in a condition of equality before the law, each having the freedom to pursue his or her own idea of the proper life.

The new demand of this freedom was, of course, independence from the old order of status and privilege, and its motor was individual *interest*. The concretization of this was the right to acquisition and property. So, von Stein argued, this required the construction of an independent state to secure the interests in legal order, possession, and acquisition. The state was a social body, justified by the social interests that it protected. This was liberalism taking its embodied form. This new movement, however, created a social opposition of classes, specifically, between those who came to own the means of production and those who had only their labor to sell. (Von Stein argued this point, incidentally, before Marx, and there is apparently some reason to think that Marx took many of his ideas from von Stein.[23])

As von Stein saw matters in 1850, the future of the *liberal* state lay in its becoming *social democracy*. Class distinctions were sharpening; the legitimacy of the state did not rest merely on its constitution but on its ability to solve the "social question" (of providing for the common welfare, of regulating and assisting the economy, and so on—in short, of answering to the interests in society).[24] The justifying purpose of the state, so von Stein predicted, would henceforth be to balance these competing interests, in particular through administrative social reform (equal opportunity programs, educational reform, and the like). The dilemma, as he saw it, was to avoid the powerlessness of a merely legalistic appeal to the constitution, while also avoiding the state's simply becoming an administrative apparatus for handling social questions and ceasing to be a democracy.[25]

We can try to rephrase von Stein's points in the following way. The separation of state and society was the result of a social movement in which the principle of individual autonomy replaced the old ideas of status and privilege. Rights, not privileges, became the fundamental political ideals and the linchpins of political rhetoric. In its historical inception, the state is a *social* state, but in the further actualization of its principle, the state must become a more general kind of thing, a *political* state mediating the interests of the society out of which it is derived. The fundamental political problem, on this view, for the future of the liberal state is to keep the state from being corrupted by the social interests that it is to mediate. (Another reader of Hegel, namely, Marx, held that this problem was insoluble; the state is always a social state — in our sense. Specifically, in Marx's sense, it is an organ for the oppression of one or more classes by one class: in modern times, the oppression and domination of the working class and its natural allies by the bourgeoisie.) Von Stein's general point was that within the framework of the present, the so-called 'political' principles of liberty and equality were 'social' principles, expressions, as I would put it, of a new form of mutual acknowledgment. The *state* comes to be seen as an agency, a particular organ for securing those principles. (Marx tried to give the principles a yet deeper explanation, namely, as expressions of an underlying economic order, thus opening the way for his and Lenin's view of the state as an organ ruling in the interests of one class.) *If* these principles are to be secured and protected, *then* the state necessarily becomes a political entity. Given, that is, a social order whose mainspring is interest, whose principles revolve around autonomy and property, a state is necessary; given other orderings, namely, that of medieval central Europe, it is not. The *philosophical* problem of the state becomes the reflection, as Hegel and von Stein saw it, of the *political* problem facing the liberal state: that of constructing an adequate conceptual picture of the state in these terms. It is, to switch to Hegelian terminology, that of conceiving of the "uni-

IV. The State, Society, and the Constitution

versality" of the state over and against the "particularity" of society. This could only be achieved in the transformation of the liberal state into the democratic liberal state. The association of property owners must develop into the community of fairness.

The state is justified in two ways: it is justified as the social state and as the political state. Together, these form the state *per se* as distinct from society. In a real, existential sense, the state is not one 'entity' neatly distinct from another 'entity,' society. It is staffed by individuals who come from society, who bring their own interests and outlooks with them, and who can try—and most likely will, if the principle of interest holds—to use it to their own interests. How do we conceive of the relation between the state and its agents? This must go beyond merely an exhortation to the agents of the state to perform their official obligations. It is part of von Stein's problem of "social democracy." The state had come to be conceived as an *agency* for the satisfaction of social interests, but this need not make it (or keep it) a democracy, as von Stein noted. As he saw it, history stood at a crossroads only partially foreseen by Hegel: either the liberal state learned to handle the "social" question that had arisen as a result of the forces that had brought it about (while maintaining itself as a liberal state and a democracy), or the state would come to be the object of class conflict—a battle over who 'had' the state in their own power. As von Stein saw it, this is the basic problem of modern politics, to see if it is possible in theory and in practice to preserve the liberal democratic nature of the state in the face of such social conflict or to succumb to an unending struggle by various classes for state power. The liberal state thus generated problems that were resolvable only by its becoming a *democratic* liberal state.

In a work on constitutional interpretation, John Hart Ely has argued that, for the writers of the American Constitution, the fundamental political (and conceptual) problem was something very similar to this: if the state is necessary, then how do we keep the interests of the rulers and ruled from separating?[26] Ely reads the history and structure of the United States Constitution as an answer to this question. The solution to be found there, so Ely argues, is institutionally to bind together the interests of the two groups (rulers and ruled) so that the rulers cannot separate their interests from those whom they rule—the result being that it would be impossible for the rulers to disadvantage others without disadvantaging themselves. This takes several forms, the most obvious of which are making the rulers be "citizens," that is, subject to the laws that they pass, and endowing the ruled with the ballot, a way of removing those from power whose interests diverge in some unacceptable way from the ruled.

As Ely rightly argues, this is not enough, for it will not serve to protect unpopular minorities whose interests differ from that of the majority. To do that, a two-pronged strategy was devised. First, a bill of rights was added on to the Constitution, thus putting some things that would be likely candidates for abuse out of reach for the rulers (although, as Ely notes, many of these safeguards turn out to be largely procedural). Second, government—and to an extent, society—is to be structured so that a variety of opinions will be heard, and dominating majority coalitions will be difficult to form. Ely calls this a "strategy for pluralism."[27] (It is interesting to contrast this strategy with the one discussed in Chapter Two, namely, the construction of a concept of sovereignty as an answer to problems of pluralism.) This second strategy tries to bind the interests of those without political power to those with it—a theory, as Ely puts it, of virtual representation.[28] This rests on the assumption that the people in power will not treat others less well than they treat themselves if they are forced to inflict the same bad treatment on themselves by doing so.

It is these two desiderata—in general keeping the interests of the ruler and the ruled from separating, and in particular preventing the majority coalition's interests from separating from those of the minority —that give content to the duty of representation. From this, one can derive both the concepts of popular government and strategies for the protection of minorities. Popular government—government by the ballot—is necessary to implement the first desideratum, and the system of checks and balances in the structure of government and in society— the strategy of pluralism—is to implement the second. Government may be said to be representative (at least minimally) when both these desiderata are met.

This dovetails at first glance neatly with the line of argument that I have been pushing about the nature of a democratic liberal state and the constitutional questions inherent in it. Earlier I argued that certain forms of legal positivism could be understood as an attack on the notion of sovereignty and a defense of the liberal state; I suggested further that in a liberal state there will be the *appearance* of positivism as the state assumes a position of neutrality vis-à-vis questions of the good life. We can now see deeper reasons for this. If the principle of respect for autonomy is recognized as an expression of respect for individual dignity, then the distinction of state and society—with society's principle being that of interest—becomes necessary. The complex of concepts associated with this idea gives rise to the problems of conflicts of interests between ruler and ruled. Switching back to Hegelian language, this is the problem of the state's maintaining its "universality" over and against society's "particularity." The neutrality of the state is the answer to this. (By "neutrality," I do not mean the same thing that is spoken of in the constitutional jurisprudence of so-called "neutral principles."[29]) Positivism is a plausible (but inadequate, one-sided) reconstruction of this neutrality, just as the theory of sovereignty is a plausible (but inadequate pure and simple) reconstruction of the bases of authority in a pluralistic society once that authority begins to become unified and centralized in the modern state. To this end, the constitution should not, by and large, be anything like a final statement of social values, held to be valid for all time (or at least from now on), frozen out of the political process; rather, it should be a statement and expression of liberal democratic political principle. That is, it should largely concern itself with reinforcing representation, with the *processes* by which the laws that govern society are made. It tries to ensure procedural fairness in the resolution of individual disputes and to ensure a broad participation in the processes of government and in the distribution of goods that the government has authority to distribute. It does not, as it were, dictate *outcomes* so much as it structures the *process* by which outcomes are decided. On the other hand, the process would be unjust when those who are in power block off channels of political change or when the rulers disadvantage a minority out of mere hostility to it by denying it (especially) protections that others get. It is not unjust simply when it results in decisions that one may feel to be wrong. This is of course the opposite of a view that sees the goal of the state as protecting and promoting certain basic values or ensuring that the "one, true religion" stay in force.[30] (We should, however, avoid Ely's faulty inference from this and claim than this is *all* that constitutional interpretation is about. More on that shortly.)

In this regard, we can distinguish a *public* sense of fairness from the *private* sense that we discussed earlier. (I am not, incidentally, claiming that this exhausts in any way all the senses of "fairness.") The private sense had to do with informed consent and with eliciting reliance. But membership in the state (being a citizen) is not a contractual matter; it is a constitutional affair. The relationship is different, and the sense of fairness must be in some subtle way also different. A state treats its citizens fairly when it treats them as political equals, with all that such a conception entails. More basically, it treats them fairly when it treats them with *dignity*. This entails not merely letting them formally have their say but actually listening to them. Think of the protest movements by feminists and minority groups: their complaint is often not that their speech is restricted, but that the powers that be do not actually listen or take their complaints seriously. One of the greatest insults is the awareness that nobody is listening and nobody cares. This is insulting because it carries the implicit message that you do not belong, that you do not have full membership in the civic community.

It might seem that this has things entirely backward. One derives a sense of social union, so it might seem, from applying the principle of fairness, not the other way around. That principle is usually taken to be something like, "When one benefits from a moderately just social arrangement, then one is obligated to repay the benefit in some fashion," where 'repaying' is shorthand for 'doing one's fair part.' However, figuring out how to apply the principle is notoriously difficult, since it obviously does not have a straightforward application across the board. Consider the problems of what economists call positive externalities. You and I live next door to each other in an as yet undeveloped area close to the city. The location is not considered particularly choice. I buy up all the available land around us, give part of it to the state to become a natural wildlife preserve, and develop a popular Olde Towne Shopping Mall on the rest. Because of the mixture of nature and pseudo-quaint shopping possibilities now surrounding your home, the value of your house is greatly enhanced. You were getting ready to sell your house before I did this, and you are now able to command a much better price for it than you would have been able to command previously. You have no obligation, however, to share your extra profits with me. An example of a negative externality will also do: Because of my negligent mis-

IV. The State, Society, and the Constitution

management, my firm closes, throwing hundreds of people out of work in the community in which you are selling your house. You therefore get less for it than you would otherwise. Must I compensate you for your lost revenue? Finally, just consider the problem of unsolicited gifts: I send you an unsolicited gift every day in the mail for a week. At the end of the week, I ask for a gift from you. You are not obligated to repay in kind.

What is it that makes the straightforward application of a principle of fairness troubling here? The missing feature seems to be the notion of citizenship. In the theory of social unions, the public sense of fairness is a principle that is derived from the demands of equal citizenship, not vice versa. The principle applies to those cases that concern our status as citizens, whereas none of the examples of gift giving or of externalities touch on us in that status. It is unfair not to do one's part as a citizen of the civic community; it is not unfair simply to benefit from externalities. The principle of fairness, in its public sense, expresses the ideal of equal citizenship; it is not an independent principle, waiting to be applied to associations of mutual benefit (that would make it a principle of "society"). Moreover, the principle of fairness has its hold in the motivations of equal citizens; its natural home is in the kind of character proper to a liberal social union. The principle of fairness in its public sense expresses a shared understanding of who we are, not merely a sense of what is due to us in mutually beneficial schemes.

From the public sense of fairness, one can also infer a sense of the proper virtues of public officials; they would be morally required to have or develop a kind of open-mindedness and sensitivity to complaints and demands from the citizenry that exceed the duties of any private citizen. The dialectic of state and society results not merely in constitutional and political arrangements but also in characteristics of virtue on the part of public officials, in the way in which principles of trust and good faith in the private sphere imply certain virtues on the part of private citizens. One way in which an individual's dignity can be injured is when he or she is belittled because of some group to which he or she belongs. Thus, public officials must not give the impression of belittling any group *per se*. (The fact that public officials are sometimes called on the carpet for doing so is often just attributed to "politics" or perhaps "hypocrisy" on the part of those doing the accusing. This misses the point, I think:

officials as representatives of a democratic liberal state must embody the virtues appropriate to that order, the basic principle of which is that the state respect and protect the dignity of individuals. This is not done when the officials of the state wittingly or unwittingly display contempt for people as members of certain types of groups.[31])

This point should not be misunderstood as simply an advocacy of "process" as opposed to "substance" in adjudicative matters. Some have argued (Ely among them—it is one of his major theses) that the relative priority of process over outcome entails a particular view of separation of powers, namely, that questions of "substance," of political "principle," are in a democracy to be left to the legislative body, whereas questions of correct procedure are the province of the judicial branch. The upshot of such views is always that judges *must* and *can* avoid all issues of substance, leaving such issues to the legislative branch. The role of judges is then only to decide if the specified procedures in the cases at hand were followed. This implication is, I think, unwarranted. The importance of "process" and "procedure" can be justified only by a deeper appeal to substantive issues, such as the principle of respecting individual dignity. In fact, one cannot make judgments about which kinds of processes are just without first deciding some rather basic substantive issues.

Several reasons can be given for this. First, there is the issue of why process and procedure should be important at all. The kind of justification of this that I have so far given clearly rests on conceptions of substance. Process itself is not a self-evident value. We can imagine something like the following argument (I have heard versions of it given in various peoples' democracies). Where the representatives of the people are sufficiently in touch with those whom they represent—because of similarity of class background, unavailability of opportunities for corruption, or whatever—there is no need for much procedure or certainly not the procedural mania of the "bourgeois" democracies. The interests of governor and governed will not (it is usually asserted, *cannot*) diverge. Now, independently of how one even views the likelihood of such a state of affairs, it points up that we must decide if procedure is to be valued only instrumentally, as a means to an end (and where this end can be achieved without this means, it wanes in importance), or if an emphasis on procedure is an essential component of what the just social and political order would be. If it is the latter, then the claims of procedure them-

IV. The State, Society, and the Constitution 167

selves rest on resolving fundamental substantive issues about what form the social and political order will take.

Second, one cannot neatly carve up the issues so that the major judicial duty is to avoid issues of substance by sticking simply to issues of process. Suppose one tried the following strategy for doing so. On the foundational level one accepts a process over an outcome view because of decisions that are themselves substantive, but, having done that, one need not make on the *judicial* level any more decisions of substance. However, on the foundational level, one does not argue so much for procedure *per se* as for something like *fair* procedure. The determination on the non-foundational level of what counts as fair procedure will thus itself depend on substantive notions, since one cannot decide whether a procedure is fair until one decides substantive issues like what counts as taking undue advantage of someone. For example: Is not having the money to purchase the help of legal counsel fair? How does one answer that question in the abstract? Fairness of procedure is itself a substantive notion, for one cannot determine if a procedure is fair until one determines things like what rights people have, the violation of which would invalidate any claim to fairness on the part of process.

Third, an appeal to procedure on its own will not help. The notion of procedure alone does not specifically determine any answer. What kind of procedure? Adjudicative or representative?[32] If the latter, then *who* gets to vote? Criminals? Children? Adults over eighteen or twenty-one? Only property-owning adult white males? Incompetents? Surely one of the most contentious issues of democratic theory is precisely the question of who gets the vote — who, that is, will be allowed to make up the active members of the political community. To decide that issue, one must again appeal to substantive ideas. "Representation reinforcing procedure" (Ely's term) is, I think, the correct idea, but it is not a purely formal idea, either in its foundations or in its applications. The justification of the idea, as I have presented it here, rests on von Stein's conception of the democratic liberal state as trying to preserve its independence from society, to avoid its takeover by one interest group or class. That is not a self-evident notion (if it were, why should one argue for it?), nor a non-controversial one. (Marxists, for example, hold it to be out and out false.) "Representation" itself is not a concept that permits a purely formal treatment. Is a person's right to representation exhausted by the vote? The theory of "virtual representation" would have little point if it were. Even laws prohibiting unjust discrimination depend on a prior identification of which groups are prevented from exercising basic rights. Arsonists do not, I take it, deserve special constitutional protection since the practice of arson is not a basic right. Laws burdening people on grounds of race or sex, however, would be examples of unjust discrimination for the reason that they do touch on basic rights.

Finally it might seem that even in the type of cases that I have mentioned, procedure is what really counts. In cases like legislation that has racist consequences, what is improper—"unconstitutional"—about such legislation is the nature of the *justification* given for it, not in the *consequences* conceived independently of the justification.[33] This argument still makes some substantive, non-procedural assumptions. This kind of restriction on process—that legislation enacted for unacceptable reasons be itself unacceptable—is justified by the idea that nobody would have, as it were, a right to violate anybody's rights (not even a legislature). Thus it too rests on some conceptions of what basic rights people have.

Perhaps it is well to stop and review the kinds of argumentative moves that have led us to this conclusion, for they contrast well with social contractarian and other similar arguments. The crucial principle is that of respect for persons. When that principle is integrated into the framework of other principles that make democratic liberal social union possible, one arrives at a distinction of state and society. The ideal of the autonomous individual was incompatible with the complex of principles that formed the network of the old order, specifically, with privilege and status. The ideal, however, generated a new set of problems. As Hegel and von Stein saw, this necessitated not merely a redrawing of the conceptual map but also a social and political revolution. It is when one reaches this level that arguments about basic rights begin, namely, as arguments about concrete realizations of these basic ideals. On the constitutional (that is, state) level, one infers basic rights as those claims that are necessary for an individual to participate as a political equal and that are necessary to protect minorities from being systematically excluded from the decision-making process. They are not "natural" rights that precede the political order; they are basic rights that are inferred from it. Voting can be justified as a basic right (although not the only

IV. The State, Society, and the Constitution 169

one) because it is a key element in binding the interests of those in power with those out of it. The right to vote is a basic and not a (legislatively) created right both because of this reason and because of the general consideration that the legislators may be presumed to have an interest in the status quo (in, that is, staying in power) and thus an interest in denying or limiting the vote to those who would naturally be against them.[34]

Contrast this view of a strategy for pluralism with an alternative approach, specifically, the one that Hegel himself took.[35] One might try to ensure that the interests of all will be taken into account by specifying in advance (in the constitution) what those interests are and giving them a place in the legislature or judiciary (somewhere, that is, in the governmental apparatus of the state). Hegel thought that this was possible by looking at the basic kinds of social classes out of which society was constructed (the *Stände*, the estates when they are taken into the political order), and ensuring that those interests get a hearing on the state level. They become entitled to representation as a class. Thus, the landowning class, the merchant class, and so on, all find in the state their representation as a class. Since each class has particular interests, not all of which are compatible, how can one maintain the so-called universality of the state with such an arrangement at its heart? To solve this problem, Hegel was compelled to find a *universal class*, one whose interests were identical with the interests of the state as a "universal." (There are also systematic reasons for this, which we need not go into here, that have to do with Hegel's need to organize his categories into 'triplets.') He thought that he found it in the class of civil servants, the bureaucrats, whose interest was simply in neutrally applying the rules of the administrative apparatus of the state, independently of their content. Presumably, by acting in the interests of the state (their 'employer'), they would offset the disintegrating forces of the more 'particular' classes.

The problems with this view are both practical and theoretical. It would seem reasonable to doubt that we could in this way actually define in advance what people's interests are. If nothing else, this gives no representation to newly forming groups (for example, feminists, newly immigrated racial minorities). And even if one also wrote *their* interests into the constitution, it seems reasonable to assume that there would always be newer ones. More importantly, it does not recognize a person's right to form a conception of what their own interest is, since it would define in advance what these interests might be, for example, as a bourgeois, as a worker, and so on. This makes the state inevitably into an authoritarian, not a liberal, state. Hegel's solution has much in common with a kind of outcome-oriented approach: one defines in advance certain goods or interests and puts them outside the give and take of the political process. This, however, corrupts the 'neutrality' of the state (its "universality"); it confuses the political state with the social state. (Politically such a solution may sometimes prove to be the only feasible one. Where there are, for example, warring factions in a civil conflict, a constitutional arrangement that specifies in advance that the interests of X and Y groups will be represented may be the only way to reach agreement. And, of course, as an example of how this model can be put to bad uses, one can think of the U.S. Constitution in its first form, which wrote the interests of the slave-owning class into the document itself.)

A number of other approaches are, of course, easily imaginable. There could be a variety of, for example, "philosopher king" approaches. One might try to educate the representatives or adopt some selection process so that only well-meaning, intelligent, good-hearted people would be in power, people who would never leave the interests of others out of account (or if they did, would immediately regret it and reverse themselves, presumably, as a result of self-criticism or criticism from without). I shall not go into why this view is unsound.

If it is to live up to its ideal, the liberal state must then be construed according to some such strategy for pluralism as a way of limiting and structuring the kind of social influences on the state and the way in which its decisions are made. It is natural that this strategy will need to assume various forms. As its principle, the liberal state rests on a respect for individual dignity, which I have interpreted as also calling in important ways for respect for individual autonomy. The *constitutional* strategy is to constitute the state so that the interests of ruler and ruled do not separate and minorities are not excluded from participation in the political process by majority coalitions or simple hostility from powerful interests. A *legislative* strategy is to create new, enforceable rights and the like that counteract other formations of social, economic, and political power. Overall, we can call such strategies for pluralism *balance of power* strategies, using the terms in a broader sense than Montesquieu used them, namely, not merely to denote a structure of government where the legislative, the judicial and the executive branches play off against one another, but also to denote a structure of society. (It is not implausible to read a good bit of American legal history as implementing this strategy in various ways.[36]) The justifying rationale is one of preventing some people from accumulating more say over others than is legitimate. This can obviously take many forms: welfare systems, jobs programs, regulation, educational grants, requirements of full disclosure, and so on. Harkening back to some arguments that were made earlier, I would say that the abstract political goal is to protect the dignity of individuals—in large part, but not wholly, by providing the context in which each person may make an autonomous choice.[37] More basically, it is to express the shared self-understandings we have by being members of the community of fairness.

V
Real Rights and Ideal Rights

The claim that individuals have such and such rights is justified by claiming that rights are the best explanation of why we should treat each other in certain ways. Rights are not the basic items out of which we construct the ideal political and social order. Rather, we begin with some sense of social and political order and ask ourselves what is necessary to resolve certain kinds of dilemmas found in that order. These dilemmas are both practical and philosophical. Philosophical problems about this revolve around problems of possibility; they arise when some basic concepts of the relevant social order are seen to conflict with other basic concepts, when it is an issue if both sets of concepts are equally compossible. For example: if one holds to the idea of the dignity of individuals (coming from the Judaeo-Christian tradition), then it is not at all clear that one can also hold to the idea of sovereignty.

This is not a view to the effect that all rights are relative to the society in which one lives. The abstract claims of morality become realized as rights only when one has a political and social order from which one can infer them as explanations of how to achieve those abstract aims. This is not to deny the temptation of the stronger claim about rights, namely, that *either* rights are independent of the political

172   *Basic Principles, Basic Rights, and the State*

and social order *or* they are simply relative to what a particular state or society says that they are (with the horrendous consequences which that implies). I am denying that this is indeed the alternative with which we presented. are First, there can be abstract demands of morality that one can justify outside of the political order—politics is not all that there is to life—and one can condemn a state's actions as immoral. Second, there is no reason to believe *a priori* that what a society *says* about rights is in fact consistent with its spirit. The assumption that a society's expressions of its spirit are always consistent or are even adequate to that spirit is most likely a false assumption to make. It took American society a few hundred years to acknowledge that racial inequality was inconsistent with its deepest ideals. It is not clear that it has yet to acknowledge this fully. Ideal (democratic liberal) rights may be inferred only from the idea of an ideal (democratic liberal) state and social order. This ideal, however, cannot be imported from the outside. It is to be found within the spirit of the social and political order itself. Thus, one can argue that certain states are better or worse than others *as* democratic liberal states, and one can criticize other states for not being so.

Now it might seem that rather than beginning, as contractarians (and even non-contractarians like Nozick) do, with certain basic rights as axiomatic primitives, as it were, and then constructing the ideal form of society and/or state from that, I am suggesting that we do the reverse: begin with the ideals found in our society (and/or state) and construct the basic rights out of that—to which it might be replied that there are a whole host of well-known objections, not the least of which is the general one that such a view inevitably sacrifices individuals to some social ideal and for that reason is practically and theoretically incompatible with liberal ideals.[38]

This depends on how one understands the concept of an ideal social and political ordering and its relation to the practical conditions of its realization. We can distinguish two ways of thinking about this, which we can call the instrumentalist and the interpretivist approaches. The instrumentalist approach holds that a liberal democratic social and political order is an end in itself, that it is itself a primary ideal, *tout court*. On this view, one would infer the basic rights through a kind of 'means-ends' or 'functionalist' analysis. Basic rights would be understood in terms of their political function, as perhaps necessary means to the

V. Real Rights and Ideal Rights

smooth functioning of a liberal democratic political order. They would be evaluated according to their effectiveness in bringing about this end. In trying to decide what individuals were at liberty to do, we would have to decide if the liberty to do X is important to the democratic process (or damaging or neutral). The liberties of individuals would then be purely relative to at least some conception (social or scientific? technocratic?) of how well they contributed to the democratic process. Liberty on this view would be a grant from the state in light of some considerations about its functional role. Liberty would not be so much a right in any strong sense as a kind of *authorization* by the state to do (or forbear from doing) something. This would be incompatible with liberal society, because it would put an individual's rights at the mercy of calculations as to their effectiveness in furthering some goal (however laudatory the goal might be).

The interpretivist model would consist in taking certain very abstract ideals—the spirit of a culture—and arguing for this or that realization in a social and political ordering. This Hegelian approach holds that these abstract ideals, such as respect for the dignity of individuals, acquire usable content only in the context of concrete institutions and forms of life, in particular in what we have called forms of social union. The abstract ideals are themselves extrapolated from concrete social unions. Consider Hegel's own examples of such abstract ideals (what he calls Abstract Right): property, as an embodiment of freedom; contract;[39] and the right to punish when one person wrongs another. Each of the abstract ideals can take many different kinds of specifications, depending on how a given culture understands a whole set of other things. (This is true, of course, of many other sets of ideals. A "good marriage," for example, is an ideal whose specifications obviously depend on a whole set of other, cultural, assumptions.)

Hegel tended to read history in part as a history of evolving conceptions of the basic abstract principles of "right." Not just any conception is as good as any other—although some were as good as could be, given the times. Later practical realizations and philosophical statements of certain ideals (such as rights) are rationally justified if they resolve dilemmas found in some earlier period. Moreover, these new solutions must respond to the older ones, showing them to be defective in ways that the proponents of the original conceptions could in principle accept. For example, the early liberal notion of natural rights rationally answers the problems inherent in the idea of sovereignty. Proponents of sovereignty could in principle see the defects in the notion and see how the idea of natural rights avoids those defects while answering the problems inherent in the original. For Hegel, the rationality of a political conception lay in its answering not *all* problems but the problems with which it was confronted. We might then in a Hegelian spirit read democratic liberalism as an evolving conception of the principle of respecting the dignity of individuals. In terms of this evolving conception, it would be a mistake to single out one principle as capturing the liberal tradition's notion of respect for the dignity of individuals. Such has been the case with those theories of the liberal tradition that mistakenly identify respect for dignity with respect for autonomy. Such a conception ignores the other crucial elements of a democratic liberal social union, such as mutual trust and the shared ends of a democratic liberal society. These ideals do not occur in a historical vacuum or come ready-made on to the historical scene. They evolve as answers to basic problems found in the evolving tradition of liberalism itself. Moreover, liberalism as a political tradition can maintain itself only insofar as it is capable of generating such answers to the dilemmas found within its mode of social union.

From this standpoint, we would not view basic rights as means to some end but rather as a part of the explanation of how it is possible to maintain a democratic liberal social union. At a deep level, this rests on admittedly controversial interpretations of the spirit of the culture. A theory of democratic liberal social union does not, as it were, proceed from abstract concepts to more concrete realizations deductively—as if the abstract principles were first premises in an argument, the conclusion of which was a statement of, for example, particular duties. It is more like considering possible executions of a general recipe, which can be realized in many different ways but not just in *any* way. It would not therefore be correct to say that basic rights are merely relative to the political order; they can also provide anchoring points, general standards of criticism for an order that does not recognize them in terms of positive law. Basic rights are those claims in our possession of which society or the state ought to protect us. An abstract formulation of basic rights will then be inferred from considerations of general principles and general considerations of the nature of the state and society as realizations of certain types of ideals found within democratic liberal social union.[40]

V. Real Rights and Ideal Rights

Concrete basic rights—which ones are actually enforceable and which ones are not—are inferred from the given legal and political setup, and the former may be used as a basis of criticism of the latter. As our picture of the social and political order becomes more filled out, our conceptions of what are the basic rights become also more specific. The very abstract general basic rights—life, liberty, property, to name the most often cited ones—are justified by very general claims about the ideals of the political order. (I think that what gives them the appearance of being natural rights is that they look as if they were independent of all social and political orders because they are common to so many.) They begin acquiring more specification as we begin, for example, to fill out our picture of what an adequate constitution in the community of fairness would look like.

Deliberation about such matters is not simply a case of choosing the best means to a given set of ends; it is also about the ends themselves. Often problems of deliberation are not ones of simply finding the best means to an end but of specifying more concretely what would *count* as an appropriate specification of that end. As an analogy, consider the kinds of arguments that occur periodically in universities about what would be the proper curriculum. It is generally acknowledged that it should produce "well-educated students." But *only* well educated? Not also well prepared for the job market? Or is that already included in the idea of being well educated? (Or, conversely, is it antithetical or perhaps irrelevant to the idea?) Does a well-educated person know philosophy? its history? the contemporary debates? both? Is a knowledge of mathematical logic necessary to this? Does he or she know computer science in the information age? What about the history of the West? the East? both? One can go on practically forever (meetings on this often do). The point is to illustrate the claim that what is going on in such arguments is not simply a deduction of specific duties or goals from first principles. Nor is it simply an argument about what are the best means to reach a certain goal. The arguments that occur are about how best to specify the goal itself.

This can lead those weary of such things sometimes to shrug their shoulders and sigh, "It's all relative!" In a sense, they are right, but not in the sense that they intend. When we get down to specifying the ideals themselves, many more factors come into play than when we argue about the goals themselves. Philosophers are usually quite good at arguing about goals, ideals, and what is abstractly bound up with these things. Practical people (like politicians) are often quite good at arguing how best to specify the goals in concrete situations. Both frequently find the other's strengths to be baffling: "fuzzy-minded philosophers" and "shallow power-grubbers" are typical mutual charges. The strength of each, however, represents one side of really the same argument: each is concerned with the abstract ideals of a political and social order and with what would count as an appropriate specification of those abstract goals. Things do become more 'relative' (if that is the right word) when one reaches the level of specification. The analogy, however, with a recipe should remind us that it is not *purely* relative: not just anything counts as *chili con carne* or *coq au vin*—but there is room for substantial disagreement about just what counts as the "best" *chili con carne* or the "best" *coq au vin*. Things get even more relative when one talks about the "best" given the real possibilities at hand.

This is not an issue of "conceptual analysis" of the "concept" of rights. It is an attempt to try to *fit* the conception of basic rights into a larger context, the purpose being to provide an explanation of how a democratic liberal legal and social order is possible. I am of course not denying that people do speak of natural rights (reference to them is part of the culture to some extent, not just an item in philosophy books) in often quite sophisticated ways. Nor am I claiming that what they say when they do this is "nonsense" or something. What I have argued is that the notion of natural rights is not the best explanation for what makes a democratic liberal social union possible. However, like the idea of a social contract (with which it is naturally allied), the idea of a set of natural rights serves as a powerful political symbol, a metaphor for construing the political environment.[41] One need not deny the utility and the power of its symbolic uses in order to claim that it is an abstraction out of a larger context. The concept of a natural right is parasitic, so we might say, on the full-blown concept of rights in a just order.

VI
A Note on Crime and Punishment

All modern societies have some set of institutions that may be loosely characterized as institutions for criminal justice, that is, for the punish-

VI. A Note on Crime and Punishment

ment of crime. There are many political problems connected with these institutions, and it seems to be a constant factor in modern society that people are generally dissatisfied with how effective the institution is working. But that is not my concern here. The more general issues concern the two words used above, namely, "crime" and "punishment." The first issue is what might be called a conceptual or definitional problem: what exactly *is* a crime? The second issue is a question of justification: what justifies the deliberate infliction of pain, loss of liberty (or goods or money), and perhaps loss of life, since *per se* these things are normally taken to be evils? If individuals should not be allowed to do such things to each other, then how can the state be allowed to get away with it? The two issues are connected, at least, in that punishment is generally taken to be justified (if justified at all) only for crimes, not simply for wrongdoing in general. If we have no clear idea of crime, how can we say that punishment is justified? (More particularly, we might ask if there is any non-arbitrary distinction to be made between tort offenses and criminal offenses. Why should the state *punish* at all and not simply demand compensation for the victims?)

I do not wish to pretend that what I have to offer constitutes a full theory of criminal justice. It does not in fact even come close. Instead, I wish to sketch out some very general reflections on the basic elements of what would explain the possibility of a democratic liberal state's punishing people. The possibility of punishment in a liberal state is to be explained, so I will argue, on a basis of considerations of the requirements of equality of citizenship, rather than on some more general theory of deterrence or retribution.

I shall not go deeply into the theories of retribution and deterrence; there is already an extensive enough literature on both. These theories may, however, be characterized in the following rough fashion. (Although presented in such brief form, they may appear to even minimally sophisticated readers as mere caricatures of themselves.) Deterrence theories usually justify punishment as a means of preventing the occurrence of crime; retributive theories generally claim that punishment is deserved as an end in itself because of the wrongness of the act. Or, to use another familiar characterization, deterrence theories are often said to be forward-looking theories. They justify punishment of a crime in terms of its future consequences, typically, in that people like the wrongdoer will decide against such an act once they realize what will happen to them if they do it (not to mention that the punished wrongdoer will have second thoughts about doing it again, or maybe cannot do it again because he has been incarcerated or executed). Retributive theories are often said to be backward-looking theories, in that they do not look to the future consequences of punishment so much as they look to what the person *has done*; they see the punishment as justified in terms of the actor's deserving it because of some past act he committed.

It is easy to produce general answers to various questions concerning punishment on the basis of these two theories, and it is also easy to generate powerfully conflicting intuitions about these answers. We can illustrate this through the application of a kind of bare bones deterrence theory. Let us assume that punishment would be justified if it deterred criminal activity to an "acceptable point" (assuming that the notion of an "acceptable point" is determinable, which it probably is not).[42] If so, then distribution of punishment (who gets it) might be done on the basis of calculations about the relative efficacy of deterrent measures. One might, for example, for serious wrongdoing punish not only the guilty party but his or her family too, on the idea that wrongdoers would be likely less to engage in nasty acts if they had to reckon with bad consequences descending on others whom they care about.

The standard line of intuitions that run contrary to this centralize around objections to using people merely as means and to what looks like unjustified punishment of the innocent. Deterrence theory, so it is argued, does not punish people because they deserve it but in order to further some social goal; it uses them merely as a means to some other end and thus fails to respect them as persons. Because of this goal orientation, it must also at least be *open* to punishing innocent persons, if that would further the goal. There are a variety of standard rejoinders that deterrence theorists traditionally make in response to this type of objection. One standard rejoinder, which assumes many forms, is that punishing the innocent would cause more harm than good and would not therefore be allowed under a regime of deterrence. Detractors keep the symmetry intact by raising an equal number of standard objections to the rejoinder. They point out that, even so, it is a contingent fact that punishing the innocent would do more harm than good, and it only shows that deterrence theorists see nothing intrinsically wrong with

VI. A Note on Crime and Punishment

punishing innocent people, should the occasion call for it. There are other problems. Are the sufferings of the person being punished to be given equal weight with the advantages (presumably, the overall wellbeing) to be gained by further deterrence? Questions of severity raise special problems. What if—as seems likely to be often the case—the inclination to commit smaller crimes is greater than the inclination to commit larger crimes, that is, petty thievery being more tempting than cold-blooded murder? Smaller penalties might deter more serious crimes, whereas larger penalties might be required to deter relatively unserious crimes. I am not suggesting that all deterrence theories are of this simple-minded type; but even the highly sophisticated versions of it must be constructed so as to evade these very basic counterintuitions.

Retributive theories generally fare no better. They focus on the guilty party's *deserving* punishment. The idea is (again, roughly) that by doing something (presumably, *morally*) wrong, a person deserves punishment. This puts calculations of the goodness of punishment (its beneficial or harmful consequences for society as a whole) outside of consideration; the person simply deserves the punishment, whatever the consequences. A strict retributivist would then apparently have to hold that if, for example, it were shown that a system of punishment actually increased the likelihood of crime, and some alternative system (say, rehabilitation) actually decreased it, the criminal would still deserve punishment. Moreover, since we are punishing for moral wrongs, why not also punish for immoral thoughts? Presumably, accidentally tripping someone and causing them to break their arm is not morally as bad as intentionally doing it. Why then not punish for intending to do it but never getting around to actually doing it? Why not just punish for bad thoughts in general?

The existence of such starkly opposed theories, each answering to solid intuitions on its own and each foundering on equally solid counter-intuitions, is for those inclined to dialectical treatments usually evidence for some kind of 'one-sidedness' on the part of both theories. But even among those who would scarcely call themselves dialecticians, there are efforts to mix the two theories. One way (following the work of Hart and Rawls) is to see the aim of the institution of punishment as, say, deterrence and then to supplement this ideal of deterrence with other principles of retributive and distributive justice as constraints on the pursuit of this goal. Thus, it might be held that although we seek to deter crime through punishment, considerations of retributive justice constrain us to punish only the innocent and to have the punishment be proportional to the crime (giving people no more and no less ideally than what they deserve, given the rules). For those who wish to hold mixed theories, whether we have the institution of punishment is a matter of calculating the consequences of having it or not having it. However, once we have it, principles of justice come into play as to how its rules and effects will be put into practice. Let us call this the 'mix and match' approach to the deterrence/retributivist controversy.

The dialectical two-step of objection/counterobjection does not end there. Hard-line retributivists ask us to imagine some ghastly crime (a series of sexually motivated ax murders of children or something like that) and then accept counterfactually that no amount of punishment of any kind would deter it. Do we still want to say that the wrongdoer should not be punished? (We are supposed to shake our heads and answer, "No.") And how would we fix the concept of deterrence here? If one less crime per year is committed than would be done without a system of punishment, it is OK? If one more crime is committed per year with a system of punishment than without it, then should we not punish? Any theory of the 'mix and match' type must also answer to these intuitions.

We could go on. Rather than do that, though, I would like to shift the focus. A theory of punishment should make room, if possible, for both sets of intuitions; it should explain how it is possible that both sets of intuitions have their force. To try to do this, I want to take as clues to the construction of such a theory that it is the *state* that is typically said to be the agency that is justified in inflicting punishment. This will lead us away from seeing deterrence and retribution as the only two competing theories of the justification of punishment.

The key notions in justifying punishment are those of *citizenship* and *workable alternatives*. I would propose the following hypothesis: those violations of rights are punishable (as criminal offenses) if a system of punishment is the only *workable alternative* to ensure that people abide by the laws, and that criminalization of these offenses is necessary in order to provide for peaceful coexistence among members of a democratic liberal order. This would distinguish crimes from other types of

VI. A Note on Crime and Punishment

offenses in that crimes would be those offenses that threaten the peaceful coexistence of the democratic liberal civic community. It would not justify a system of punishment as a means of abolishing crime or reducing it to acceptable levels (assuming that we even could make sense of that). Rather, it justifies it as necessary to maintaining respect for and compliance with those prohibitions necessary for the existence of a peacefully coexisting (liberal) community, if it is the only workable alternative.

The notion of citizenship enters when we consider that the system of punishment is a way of showing that those who *flout* the rules will not be allowed by the civic community to get away with such things.[43] To break the law that (let us assume) we have an obligation to obey is to assume an unequal status in the world of citizens. Criminals violate the principle of equality of citizenship. They assume a special place in the social order, one in which they are not bound by the standards to which you and I are subject. This is not the same as saying that criminals are taking more than their fair share. Rather, it is saying that in breaking the law, they are expressing the view that, as citizens, they are something special, beyond the constraints that fall to you and me. Criminals, we might say, show contempt for others by their flouting the law, by their assuming a special place.[44] The criminal who harms you may not harm me; but he or she does show contempt for both of us in his or her criminal act. A system of punishment does not rest on the denial that people can commit crimes and show contempt for other citizens. It only says that they cannot do it with impunity. Note that in a democratic liberal order, when we bring criminals to court we give them equal protection of the law; we force them again to submit to the demands of equality of citizenship. Note too that what in fact many people find disturbing about the inadequacies of the present system of criminal justice system seems to be connected to this idea that the lawbreakers are somehow "getting away with it."

To see what this view is, we can begin by noting what it is not. It is not a moralistic theory of crime and punishment. A moralistic theory would equate the concept of crime with some kind of (grave?) moral offense and would justify punishment for it as somehow an affirmation of society's moral values (or a defense of them, or whatnot). This view is not without plausibility. Murder, for example, is a moral wrong, and hence it is easy to think that the state is justified in punishing it *because* it is a moral wrong. A liberal state, however, is not empowered to enforce morality *per se*. The intuitive connection between the immorality of crime (such as murder) and the state's right or obligation to punish it is broken when one considers that the connection does not exist between a whole host of everyday immoralities and an obligation to punish them. Alas, there are less than honorable people in the world, and they daily betray confidences, lie, cheat, and deceive. Most of the time we just chalk off to "life" our encounters with these types and go on our way. But why? Many things that these people do are, after all, *moral* wrongs. But do we really want to set up a system of punishment for this? Courts for broken hearts? Tribunals for bruised egos? Surely not. Life goes on, despite the presence of all the flimflam artists around us.

The intuitive connection between crime and immorality that seems clear in the one case and not so clear in the others is, I think, better captured by focusing not on the morality or immorality of the offense but on what the offense *threatens*, namely, the basic terms of peaceful cooperation. The rights that individuals have not to be harmed in "criminal" ways would then be derivative from the state's obligation to *protect* the terms of peaceful cooperation in a liberal order. Perhaps it could be put in this way. Individuals have a variety of rights not to be harmed, but the state has the obligation to protect them by the institution of criminal law and punishment only when those violations threaten the fabric of peaceful coexistence. Those violations would be the *public* ones; the others would be the *private* ones (a subclass of which would require compensation—leaving open here how that subclass is to be determined). In fact, one could go further and argue that on this hypothesis punishment for immorality alone would be unjustified. Punishment is justified when the basic terms of cooperation of a liberal society are violated. It is not justified when, for example, that society takes forms that one wishes it did not—when matrimonial practices change, when what is and is not exposed by current clothing is more than one thinks proper, or when people of sexual persuasions that are other than what some groups hold to be normal start being rather open about it. It is not justified in maintaining the current *status quo* of conventional morality in a given time-slice of a society. (It is interesting in this regard how many debates about punishing so-called immoral behavior turn also on trying to show some purported harm that the behavior causes.)

VI. A Note on Crime and Punishment

Nor would a threat to cherished institutions be enough to criminalize the actions that threaten them. They must be actions that threaten the fabric of a democratic liberal order, not the ones that threaten the institutions of the society (cherished or otherwise).

To classify something as a crime is to reassert the role of the social union with regard to certain principles. Without the concept of a social and political *order*, the concept of crime has no independent role to play. (Notice too that if one collapsed the categories of state and society into one, there would no longer be any clear rationale for maintaining a crime/tort distinction.) The concept of crime exemplifies the primacy of social union. By not letting people get away with flouting the basic terms of social cooperation, we reaffirm the element of solidarity and civic equality in the union. Those who violate the basic rules undermine this solidarity and equality; it is important that they not be allowed to do this with impunity. It is not that we *primarily* wish to minimize the occurrence of criminal behavior (which however is an important secondary goal). Nor is it that we wish to bring the universe into a kind of proper balance through some form of retribution (although that may appeal to some people within the society). It is rather that we wish to show that even what we term to be the acceptable level of criminal behavior cannot be done with impunity. The wrongdoers must at any point factor in the probability of being caught. It is after all not crime alone that excites the passions; it is crime and getting away with it.

If this theory were successful (after it was worked out more fully, being presented here only in its most abstract form), it would do two things: (1) it would separate crimes from torts in a non-arbitrary way; (2) it would provide a rationale for punishment, namely, as justified only if it is the only practical alternative to maintaining respect and compliance for those rules necessary for a peacefully coexisting liberal community. This brings together some of the intuitions that underlie the seemingly incompatible theories of deterrence and retribution. We punish people for what they have done (a backward-looking component of the hypothesis) in order to show the law-abiding that those who knowingly flout the law do not get away with it (a forward-looking component).

This does not even begin to answer all the interesting questions that we would want a theory of punishment to answer. There remain outstanding questions, for example, about the severity of punishment. Are there intrinsic limits to how much punishment is justified to maintain respect for the basic rules? The most obvious answer would be that a principle of proportionality must play some role here. But how? One way might be to adapt Nozick's idea of punishment as a form of communicative behavior: it tells the wrongdoer, "This is at least how wrong what you did is."[45] Since we would want, as it were, to tell the wrongdoer the truth, we would not want to exaggerate (or understate?) the message. Questions of assessing responsibility are left open by this, but some things, I would think, are ruled out. For example, we have seen that a common objection to deterrence theories is that they allow for the possibility of punishing innocent people. This view of punishment presented here is one that focuses on the civic community's not letting people *get away* with violating the basic rules of the society. It would leave room for questions of diminished responsibility lessening or even obviating punishment, since we will not be letting someone "get away" with something when they are not responsible for it. Likewise, we will have no reason in general to punish the innocent, since a refusal to punish the innocent is also not letting anybody get away with anything. But this is only a very general consideration. Much more would have to be said for the account to be finally satisfactory. I only intend to suggest that the theory of social union and the idea of the community of fairness also have a role to play in questions of crime and punishment and to give an idea of what that role is.

Notes

Introduction

1. There are exceptions. Bruce Ackerman's *Reconstructing American Law* (Cambridge, Mass.: Harvard University Press, 1984) takes up some of the classical debates about the nature of the state and the way in which this affects our conception of jurisprudence.

2. See Alasdair MacIntyre, *After Virtue* (South Bend, Ind.: Notre Dame University Press, 1981); Michael J. Sandel, *Liberalism and the Limits of Justice* (Cambridge, Eng.: Cambridge University Press, 1982); Charles Taylor, *Hegel and Modern Society* (Cambridge, Eng.: Cambridge University Press, 1979).

3. "If the state is confused with civil society, and if its specific end is laid down as the security and protection of property and personal freedom, then the interest of the individual as such becomes the ultimate end of their association, and it follows that membership of the state is something optional. But the state's relation to the individual is quite different from this. . . . Unification pure and simple is the true content and aim of the individual, and the individual's destiny is the living of a universal life" (G. W. F. Hegel, *Philosophy of Right*, trans. T. M. Knox [Oxford: Oxford University Press, 1952]. p. 156, §258 Remark).

4. I am translating Hegel's usage of *Anerkennung* as "acknowledgment." The more usual translation is "recognition." I am avoiding this translation, however, because of its ambiguity between a psychological sense of "recognition" ("I didn't recognize Tom yesterday") and the sense in which one country "recognizes" another ("The United States today recognized the government of Freedonia").

5. This view has an apparent affinity with Kant's own description of his philosophy as a "transcendental" philosophy concerned with the necessary conditions of the possibility of experience. I understand the difference between my view (the speculative one) and the Kantian view (the transcendental one) as being that I do not take anything that I say to be a *necessary* condition of experience (or anything else), nor do I take my solutions to be unique (in the sense of being the only ones possible). Kant's view prescribes for itself exactly the unique definitive status that I would deny to this theory (or, for that matter,

to any theory). The view presented here has more affinities with the view of philosophy presented by Robert Nozick than it does with Kant's views. Cf. Robert Nozick, *Philosophical Explanations* (Cambridge, Mass.: Harvard University Press, 1982), pp. 8-24.

Chapter One

1. Tom Beauchamp and I discussed these two conceptions in the "Introduction" to Tom L. Beauchamp and Terry P. Pinkard, eds., *Ethics and Public Policy* (Englewood Cliffs, N.J.: Prentice-Hall, 1983), pp. 8-11.
2. John Rawls, *A Theory of Justice* (Cambridge, Mass.: Harvard University Press, 1971), §78, p. 515.
3. On this distinction, see Gary Watson, "Free Agency," *Journal of Philosophy*, April 1975, pp. 205-220.
4. I take the basic idea of autonomy's being equivalent to authenticity and independence from Gerald Dworkin, "Autonomy and Behavior Control," *Hastings Center Report* 6 (Feb. 1976): 23-28. My analysis of these terms, however, differs from his. Whereas Dworkin imports Harry Frankfurt's distinction of first order and second order desires into his system in order to explain them, I use the distinction of valuation and desiring to explain them.
5. See Hannah Arendt, *Eichmann in Jerusalem* (New York: Viking Press, 1963); see also her "Thinking and Moral Considerations: A Lecture," *Social Research*, Spring/Summer 1984, pp. 7-38.
6. Hegel notes in his *Philosophy of Right*, trans. T. M. Knox (London: Oxford University Press, 1952): "The maxim: 'Ignore the consequences of actions' and the other: 'Judge actions by their consequences and make these the criterion of right and good' are both alike maxims of the abstract Understanding. The consequences, as the shape proper to the action and immanent within it, exhibit nothing but its nature and are simply the action itself; therefore the action can neither disavow nor ignore them. On the other hand, however, among the consequences there is also comprised something interposed from without and introduced by chance, and this is quite unrelated to the nature of the action itself" (§118, *Zusatz*). Hegel also says, "Since the subjective satisfaction of the individual himself (including the recognition which he receives by way of honour and fame) is also part and parcel of the achievement of ends of absolute worth, it follows that the demand that such an end alone shall appear as willed and attained, like the view that in willing, objective and subjective ends are mutually exclusive, is an empty dogmatism of the abstract Understanding" (§124).
7. Hegel makes this argument in his *Philosophy of Right*, See §§105-141. It is important as a reading of Hegelian ethics to distinguish this from another, better-known, argument by Hegel against Kant in his *Phenomenology of Spirit*,

trans. A. V. Miller (Oxford: Oxford University Press, 1977), see pp. 236–262. There he interprets the Kantian theory as one that holds that moral action is simply one that is self-consistent. Hegel's argument in the *Phenomenology* is that anything (for example, a regime of property or a regime of no property) can be rendered consistent, and for this reason the Kantian theory is empty. This has been widely and justly attacked as an accurate reading of Kant, since it ignores many crucial passages in the Kantian text, particularly those having to do with "contradictions in conception" and "contradictions in will." See Onora Nell, *Acting on Principle* (New York: Columbia University Press, 1980). However, this was Hegel's youthful reading of Kant, which he modified in his mature works. His later criticisms of Kantian morality (insofar as the section in the *Philosophy of Right* on *Moralität* can be taken as criticisms of Kant) did not fall back simply on the arguments about consistency but on the ineluctable abstractness of Kantian morality. By conceiving of the agent only as a "rational agent in general," Kantian moral theory was restricted to a moral doctrine of those duties that hold for everybody at all times. These cannot be anything but abstract. Hegel did not so much deny the capability of Kantian moral theory to generate content as he denied its ability to generate sufficiently determinate moral content. What holds for a rational agent in general will never be specific enough to generate any concrete sense of what ought to be done or how one balances the inevitable conflicts of duties. His mature criticism of Kantian ethics therefore sees it as consistent, having some content but not being able to deliver on its promise of generating determinate content simply by appeal to what must hold for a rational agent in general. He expresses this in his often oblique manner: "These specific duties, however, are not contained in the definition of duty itself; but since both of them are conditioned and restricted, they *eo ipso* bring about the transition to the higher sphere of the unconditioned, the sphere of duty. Duty itself in the moral self-consciousness is the essence or the universality of that consciousness, the way in which it is inwardly related to itself alone; all that is left to it, therefore, is abstract universality, and for its determinate character it has identity without content, or the abstractly positive, the indeterminate" (*Philosophy of Right*, §135).

8. This criticism also finds its locus in Hegel: "The universal quality of the action is the manifold content of the action as such, reduced to the simple form of universality. But the subject, an entity reflected into himself and so particular in correlation with the particularity of his object, has in his end his own particular content, and this content is the soul of the action and determines its character. The fact that this moment of the particularity of the agent is contained and realized in the action constitutes subjective freedom in its more concrete sense, the right of the subject to find his satisfaction in the action" (*Philosophy of Right*, §121).

9. Bernard Williams comes to similar Hegelian conclusions in his *Ethics and the Limits of Philosophy* (Cambridge, Mass.: Harvard University Press, 1985).

10. The phrase "the thin theory of the self" is a play on Rawls's "thin theory of the good." Cf. Rawls, *A Theory of Justice*, §60.

11. This point is made quite forcefully by Gerald Dworkin in "Moral Autonomy" in H. T. Engelhardt, Jr., and Daniel Callahan, eds., *Morals, Science, and Society* (Hastings on the Hudson, N.Y.: Hastings Center, 1978), pp. 156–171.

12. I am using "ethos" as equivalent to Hegel's use of "*Sittlichkeit*," although this does not quite capture the sense of the expression. However, no other English term does better. I am using "spirit" in what I take to be its basic Hegelian sense minus the metaphysical associations that Hegel gave it. I am not using it to denote any kind of metaphysical entity, as he did. For some, this might, of course, disqualify the usage as being "Hegelian." Not much hangs on that, so I shall not belabor the point.

13. See Rawls, *A Theory of Justice*, §79.

14. See *ibid.*, p. 536.

15. This analogy is similar to one that Alasdair MacIntyre makes in *After Virtue* (South Bend, Ind.: Notre Dame University Press, 1981), p. 188, although he is making a slightly different point with it.

16. I would guess that one of the reasons that virtue does not occupy a central place in so much modern ethical theory is that it cannot be broken down into rules, and, in the shadow of Kant, modern ethical theory is virtually committed to being a theory of the moral rules.

17. "And thus it appears that, though understanding is capable of being instructed, and of being equipped with rules, judgment is a peculiar talent which can be practiced only, and cannot be taught.... For although an abundance of rules borrowed from the insight of others may indeed be proffered to, and as it were grafted upon, a limited understanding, the power of rightly employing them must belong to the learner himself; and in the absence of such a natural gift no rule that may be prescribed to him for this purpose can ensure against misuse" (Immanuel Kant, *Critique of Pure Reason*, trans. Norman Kemp Smith [London: Macmillan, 1964], pp. 177–178 [A133-B172].

18. This is not a virtue necessarily of intellectuals. An ethicist, for example, might not be a virtuous person, since he or she might be lacking in a large measure of that capacity. Note also how we rarely see people whose behavior is hidebound by rules as being particularly virtuous people.

19. This should not be taken as saying that the common good in a culture will be one that is to everyone's advantage in a narrow sense. Individuals can identify with these goods without their being necessarily to their own advantage;

one might, for example, believe that one's culture ought to further the arts or the sciences without that necessarily being to one's own advantage (unless one redefines the notion of "being to one's advantage" so that almost anything that one endorses will turn out to be *ipso facto* to one's advantage). The point is that there can be goods within my culture that I recognize as goods, around which I try to fashion my sense of self, but that are not to my advantage in any narrow sense.

20. Kant says, for example, in the *Groundwork of the Metaphysics of Morals*, trans. H. J. Paton (New York: Harper and Row, 1964), p. 107: "Our own will, provided it were to act only under the condition of being able to make universal law by means of its maxims—this ideal will which can be ours is the proper object of reverence; and the dignity of man consists precisely in his capacity to make universal law, although only on condition of being himself also subject to the law he makes."

21. Most prominent here would apparently be Robert Nozick, *Anarchy, State, and Utopia* (New York: Basic Books, 1975), given his Kantian principle of justice, "From each as they choose, to each as they are chosen" (p. 160). However, it is no straightforward matter ascribing this view *tout court* to Nozick. In his *Philosophical Explanations* (Cambridge, Mass.: Harvard University Press, 1982), Nozick claims that it is the capacity to be a *self*, an *I*, that is basic, and thus respect for people's choices is important only because it is responsive to the intrinsic value of these selves. Nevertheless, it is this move to respect for choice that gives some credence to social contract theory. Contract theorists (Rawls is a prime example) do not typically claim that all choices should be respected, but they do this by constructing an ideal choice situation in which we 'rationally' choose to put some things out of bounds. Why, though, should such idealized choice situations have any legitimacy as to how we actually ought to decide, unless we had already accepted some ideal of respect for choice in the first place? The difference between contractarians and libertarians in this regard just comes down to whether one respects *actual* choices individuals make (the ones they really make in libertarian society) or *hypothetical* choices individuals make (the ones they make in Rawls's Original Position). Both seem to be agreeing that respect for persons is respect for choice; they seem to be quibbling only about which choices count.

22. It is important to substitute the phrase "use merely as a means" for Kant's own "use as a means." We use each other as means in a variety of ordinary and justifiable ways, as when I ask a clerk in a store to show me a wristwatch. What would justify this on Kantian grounds would be that the clerk consents to the practice (although even this might not be the full story; one might also want a further characterization of the practice to which the clerk is consenting).

23. Kant, *Groundwork of the Metaphysics of Morals*, p. 97.

24. This point is argued forcefully by Robert E. Goodin in *Political Theory and Public Policy* (Chicago: University of Chicago Press, 1982), pp. 73-94. Goodin attaches this to a version of utilitarianism, and it is there that his view diverges from the one presented here.

25. We respect the comatose for what they are, not for what they do or can do. It would not be logically impossible, however, for us to exclude from consideration the comatose as 'one of us.' To do that consistently, however, one would have to argue that such an exclusion would be consistent with the ideals of the spirit of our culture. I doubt that this argument could be made in the major cultures of the world today—but, as I said, it is not logically excluded. The idea that treating them as not 'one of us' would put us on the 'slippery slope' to something horrible need not be taken as a utilitarian idea. The 'slippery slope' argument may also concern the other values that are central to the spirit of a culture. Whether one is on the 'slippery slope' is not, however, an *a priori* matter; it is an empirical question to be answered as best one can with the facts at hand.

26. This means that the self that is valuable is a particular kind of self, namely, one that can form moral communities. It is an interesting question whether this is the only kind of self that is possible. Kantians, Hegelians, and all those interested in transcendental arguments in general have always argued that something like this is the *only* type of self that is possible. On the view expressed here, even if there were another kind of self—a self that achieved its consciousness of self outside of any community—then it would not necessarily be deserving of the same respect as the kinds of selves that we are. I suspect that such a self would not be possible, but the extensive literature on transcendental arguments shows that it would be a difficult task ever to show that.

27. Animals form an interesting boundary case. It is not inconceivable that humans could come to see animals—or perhaps some set of them, like primates or certain types of mammals—as 'one of us' under the appropriate point of view, such as "life on earth," even if the animals themselves were incapable of reciprocating. We would then have 'one-way' moral relationships with them. But in some ways, are not such one-way moral relationships the kind that we take toward the dead? Think of the apparently moral sanctions about desecrating graveyards. Nonetheless, such one-way moral relationships are only extensions of the more full-blown cases of two-way moral relationships; the former presuppose the latter.

28. Some people have insisted on yet another type of justice, *commutative* justice. This would concern the proper dealing between individuals and other individuals or between individuals and groups when there is no question of the distribution of social goods. The justice, for example, of keeping faith, of executing one's promises to another would be taken to be a matter of commutative

justice. Likewise, many of the general duties that we owe to all people, such as taking due care in our actions not to inflict needless harm on others or on their property would also be taken to be duties of commutative and not distributive justice. One finds an excellent discussion of the notion of commutative justice in John Finnis, *Natural Law and Natural Rights* (Oxford: Clarendon Press, 1980), pp. 161-197. One could, of course, draw all these lines differently. One might put compensatory and retributive justice under the more general heading of *rectificational* justice and distinguish compensatory and retributive justice in terms of the type of rectification offered, for example, a rectification of private wrongs or of public wrongs. Nothing in the present discussion, however, hangs on this, so it is not worth exploring in detail here.

29. Desert has two other crucial features to it that are not germane to this discussion. To say that X deserves y is to say that this desert offers a *prima facie* reason for awarding y to X. Desert also depends on some feature of the person involved (not on some feature of anything or anybody else) that provides the basis for claiming desert. The idea of desert shares these last two features with that of entitlement. However, it is important to note that there are two conceptions of desert that might be confused with each other. These are what Feinberg calls polar and non-polar conceptions of it. Polar conceptions of desert apply to those cases where one either deserves a good or deserves an evil. Deserved punishment would be an example; in such cases, one deserves either to be set free (if one is innocent) or to suffer the punishment (if one is guilty). Non-polar conceptions of desert apply to things like awards, prizes, or grades; if one has the requisite features, one deserves the benefit (for example, the award), but one does not deserve an evil if one lacks them. Here the requisite contrast is between either deserving y or not deserving y, not between deserving good or deserving evil, as in the polar case. Cf. Joel Feinberg, "Justice and Personal Desert," in his *Doing and Deserving* (Princeton, N.J.: Princeton University Press, 1974), pp. 55-94.

30. See Rawls, *A Theory of Justice*, §§12-13.

31. Robert Coles, *Children of Crisis: A Study of Courage and Fear* (New York: Dell Publishing Co., 1967).

32. An interesting discussion of this, particularly with regard to questions of moral blameworthiness, is found in Thomas Nagel's "Moral Luck" in his *Mortal Questions* (Cambridge, Eng.: Cambridge University Press, 1979), pp. 24-38.

33. Rawls calls such a system where the results of natural endowments determine the distribution of goods a system of "natural liberty" (Rawls, *A Theory of Justice*, pp. 65-75).

34. One finds this view expressed by Nozick in *Anarchy, State, and Utopia*, pp. 237-238.

35. This ideal often gives rise, I suspect, to the mistaken notion of desert as a basis of justice, in that it might be interpreted as calling for individuals and institutions to leave one to one's own wits—that one "deserves" to make of oneself what one can.

36. See Thomas Grey, "Property and Need: The Welfare State and Theories of Distributive Justice," *Stanford University Law Review* 28 (1976): 877–902.

37. Michael J. Sandel, *Liberalism and the Limits of Justice* (Cambridge, Eng.: Cambridge University Press, 1982), p. 88. I have profited much from Sandel's fine-grained reading of Rawls in my construction of the views here, particularly on the relation between desert and entitlement in Rawls's theory.

38. See Joel Feinberg, "Is There a Right to Be Born?," in James Rachels, ed., *Understanding Moral Philosophy* (Encino, Calif.: Dickenson Publishing Co., 1976), pp. 346–357. Feinberg there argues that there are rights that belong to the unborn (your first-born son may have a right to inherit your estate long before he is ever born) but that one of them is not the right to be born (you violate nobody's rights if you decide not to have a child at all).

39. Rawls, *A Theory of Justice*, p. 102.

40. See C. B. Macpherson, *The Political Theory of Possessive Individualism* (Oxford: Oxford University Press, 1962). See also his *Democratic Theory* (Oxford: Oxford University Press, 1973).

41. Rawls, *A Theory of Justice*, p. 64.

42. This criticism is made by Sandel in his *Liberalism and the Limits of Justice*.

43. See Rawls, *A Theory of Justice*, pp. 75–82. The interpretation of the difference principle as involving something like this sense of sharing is suggested by Rawls himself: "A further merit of the difference principle is that it provides an interpretation of the principle of fraternity. . . . The difference principle, however, does seem to correspond to a natural meaning of fraternity: namely, to the idea of not wanting to have greater advantages unless this is to the benefit of others who are less well off" (p. 105). It is noteworthy that Rawls speaks of this as "not wanting . . . ," a feature of personality, of individual virtue.

Chapter Two

1. This thesis should be distinguished from two others. The first is that morality has an influence on the shape of the law; this is true, no doubt, as a sociological or historical fact but does not show any kind of essential (analytical) connection between them. The second thesis would be that law is always capable of moral criticism; this is true, but hardly demonstrates the existence of an analytical connection between law and morality and is in fact completely consis-

tent with a denial of any such connection. I shall leave open as to what exactly the so-called analytical connection is since the line of argument that I am pursuing does not depend on any particular conception of how that connection is specified (for example, as relations of synonymy, as relations of implication between platonic meanings, or whatnot). On these different senses of the possible relations between law and ethics, see H. L. A. Hart, *Law, Liberty, and Morality* (London: Oxford University Press, 1963).

  2. John Austin, *Lectures on Jurisprudence* (London: John Murray, 1885).

  3. Cf. H. L. A. Hart, *The Concept of Law* (New York: Oxford University Press, 1965).

  4. See Martin Kriele's excellent account of the origin of the ideal of sovereignty in his *Einführung in die Staatslehre* (Reinbek bei Hamburg: Rowohlt Taschenbuch Verlag, 1975), pp. 47-65. I have adopted much of my discussion from Kriele and from Roman Schnur's *Die französischen Juristen im konfessionellen Bürgerkrieg des 16. Jahrhunderts* (Berlin: Duncker und Humblot, 1962).

  5. This is so at least according to Kriele, *Einführung in die Staatslehre*, p. 51, who cites Schnur as an authority. The passage cited in Schnur does not justify this, although it might be extrapolated from other parts of the text. In any event, something like this is Schnur's thesis too.

  6. I am ignoring, it is obvious, the ways in which many authors tried to legitimate the exercise of sovereign power through some kind of doctrine of natural law; instead, I am trying to draw out the rationale—the dialectic, as it were—of the doctrine of sovereignty.

  7. This is one way of expressing a more general point that crops up often in the present literature on rights, namely, that having basic rights means having them independently of the sympathy of others for how one exercises those rights. A system based on sovereignty is, of course, one where all "rights" depend on the sympathy of the sovereign.

  8. Marxism is a variant on this. By holding that values depend on the class nature of society, Marx was able to claim that no higher order system of values is possible in a society torn by class division. The only way out of this impasse is for one privileged class—the proletariat—to gain control of the state and rule in its own particular interest, which, so it turns out, will actually be in the interest of all humanity after the revolution has been secured.

  9. See G. W. F. Hegel, *Philosophy of Right*, trans. T. M. Knox (Oxford: Oxford University Press, 1952): "The state is universal in form, a form whose essential principle is thought. This explains why it was in the state that freedom of thought and science had their origin" (§270, p. 172).

  10. See again *ibid.*, §205, p. 132; §303, pp. 197-198.

11. See Hegel's own account of the separation of church and state (*ibid.*, §270).

12. H. L. A. Hart, "Are There Any Natural Rights?," *Philosophical Review* 64 (1955): 175-191.

13. Compare this view with Marx's objection that the liberal state was always an arm of one class—the bourgeoisie—for the oppression of another class—the proletariat.

14. One would wonder why it is valid in these cases; to answer that question, one would also have to specify just exactly what conception of democracy one is working with and why that conception is to be preferred to others. A "bourgeois" democrat and a Marxist-Leninist democrat will presumably divide over conceptions of democracy, the status of majority rule, and similar questions. The role that acceptance should play will vary no doubt because of the different background political assumptions that the so-called bourgeois and the Marxist-Leninist make.

15. See Hart, *The Concept of Law*, pp. 181-207.

16. A very interesting presentation of this debate, coming down on the side of Hegel, is offered by Wolfgang Schild, "Savigny und Hegel," *Anales de la Catedra Francisco Suarez* 18/19 (1978-79): 271-320.

17. Ronald Dworkin, *Taking Rights Seriously* (Cambridge, Mass: Harvard University Press, 1978) and *A Matter of Principle* (Cambridge, Mass.: Harvard University Press, 1985). Josef Esser, whose work antedated Dworkin's writings by several years, has argued much the same point in the way he distinguishes rules from principles. In fact, Esser's arguments go beyond much of what Dworkin has to say in this regard, offering various kinds of distinctions between types of principles that are lacking in Dworkin's own writings. See Josef Esser, *Grundsatz und Norm in der richterlichen Fortbildung des Privatrechts* (3d ed.; Tübingen: J. C. B. Mohr, 1974).

18. Dworkin distinguishes among three senses of "discretion," two of them being 'weak' senses: (1) discretion in the sense of being the final authority on something—a weak sense; (2) discretion in the sense of something's being a matter requiring judgment—also a weak sense; (3) discretion in the sense that one is not bound by any standards set by the authority in question. It is the third, strong, sense of "discretion" that is the object of his attack. See *Taking Rights Seriously*, pp. 31-33.

19. *Ibid.*, pp. 22, 82.

20. *Ibid.*, pp. 87-88.

21. See *ibid.*, pp. 87, 340; "No Right Answer?," *A Matter of Principle*, p. 82. The most concise statement of this is in his introduction to a book which he edited, *Philosophy of Law* (London: Oxford University Press, 1977): "According

to that theory, roughly summarized, controversial propositions of law are true just in case the political theory that supplies the best justification for noncontroversial propositions of law provides for the rights or duties which the controversial propositions describe" (p. 9).

22. Dworkin, *Taking Rights Seriously*, p. 40.
23. *Ibid.*, p. 87.
24. Esser, *Grundsatz und Norm*, p. 132.
25. Ronald Dworkin, "'Natural' Law Revisited," *University of Florida Law Review* 34 (1982): p. 187. This does not, however, exhaust the types of principles that will be found in a rule of law. Consider Esser's typology of principles: axiomatic, rhetorical, dogmatic, immanent, informative principles; constructive principles; and value principles (among others). See Esser, *Grundsatz und Norm*.
26. See Rudolf von Jhering, *Geist des römischen Rechts* (Darmstadt: Scientia Verlag Aalen, 1968; orig. pub. Leipzig, 1907), pp. 48–58.
27. Von Jhering: "Nothing is more off the mark than to judge the law as one would a philosophical system, merely from the point of view of its intellectual content, its logical ordering and unity. Even if from this standpoint, it nonetheless looks like a masterpiece, its true value is not determined by this. Its true value lies in its functions, i.e., in its practical employability. What is the use of a machine that gives the impression of being a work of art if it is useless as a machine?" (*ibid.*, p. 48).
28. One objection might occur: Do we not try to do that in moral *theory*? Is not moral theory very much like the law in that regard? Any quick look into the books and articles on moral philosophy written in the last few years shows an equally great concern with, as it were, philosophical draftsmanship. Principles are articulated and modified, conditions are added to block certain unwanted results, and so forth. Maybe the analogy with law and moral theory can be made, but even so, the point can be used to show simply another greater disanalogy: when people draft laws, the laws become obligatory, and this is one of the factors to be considered in reflecting on its possible formal realizability; fortunately, philosophical refinements of, for example, rule-utilitarianism do not. Even badly drafted laws remain in force; the best drafted philosophical views do not.
29. See Esser, *Grundsatz und Norm*, p. 51. Esser argues that this is in fact not an adequate characterization of the role that the continental judge actually plays, since the appeal to principle turns out to be just as important in the continental legal order. Martin Kriele has argued a similar thesis, claiming that although the dominant conceptions of the two types of judges in both systems are different, the actual practice of the two is highly similar. This is because both

are conceived within the standpoint of a democratic liberal society, and this demands that both types of judge attempt to be instruments of justice. See Martin Kriele, *Recht und praktische Vernunft* (Göttingen: Vandenhoeck und Ruprecht, 1979).

30. See Rawls's very helpful discussion of "justice as regularity" in his *A Theory of Justice* (Cambridge, Mass.: Harvard University Press, 1971), pp. 235-239.

31. See Robert Nozick's short criticism of Dworkin on these grounds in his *Philosophical Explanations* (Cambridge, Mass.: Harvard University Press, 1982), p. 478n.

32. See *ibid.*, pp. 8-11.

33. Interestingly enough, this is an analogy that Dworkin himself has taken up as offering the best account of his earlier claims about principles. See "How Law Is Like Literature" in Dworkin, *A Matter of Principle*, pp. 146-166.

34. See George Dennis O'Brien's "Does Hegel Have a Philosophy of History?" for an account of Hegel's philosophy of history along these lines, in Michael Inwood, ed., *Hegel* (Oxford: Oxford University Press, 1985), pp. 174-198. Of course, Hegel held that we must see history as progressive. O'Brien makes an analogy with this and the history of science. We see succeeding scientific theories as improving on their predecessors. Put in its Hegelian mode (this is not quite the way O'Brien discusses it), this would have the corollary that we can only understand the rational superiority of one theory to another in terms of the problems that the later theory solved, problems that must have been apparent to the earlier theories but that were irresolvable in the terms of the earlier theories. On Hegelian terms, the rational superiority of some things is only to be understood historically. (Hegel did not hold this to be true of art, religion, or for that matter philosophy, the three forms of "absolute spirit," which he took to embody truths independent of their particular historical actualizations.) O'Brien distinguishes between the minimal part of Hegel's philosophy of history—the notion that "when an idea is presented in a scientific or historical mode of thought it bears an internal connection to possible futures which will emend, or change, or incorporate the idea. Now, this is not to say that anyone will actually pick up the option"—and the "stronger" part of Hegel's philosophy of history—the notion that "historical consciousness has an ontological grounding and *will* assert itself. History is not a game human beings could choose to absent themselves from" (p. 197). The question for any Hegelian philosophy of history is whether resolutions of problems must be progressive. What if people had decided that the difficulties in Newton's mechanics had been answered by something like alchemy rather than by Einsteinian relativity theory? What if medieval feudalism had been answered by barbarism rather than the great liberal revolutions? The Hegelian answer to this question must wait for another time.

Chapter Three

1. The metaphor of boundaries and the crossing of boundaries to capture the moral issue in question comes from Robert Nozick in *Anarchy, State, and Utopia* (New York: Basic Books, 1974), p. 57.

2. Charles Fried proposes something not far from this: "The law of property defines the boundaries of our rightful possessions, while the law of torts seeks to make us whole against violations of those boundaries, as well as against violations of the natural boundaries of our physical person. Contract law ratifies and enforces our joint ventures beyond those boundaries. Thus the law of torts and the law of property recognize our rights as individuals in our persons, in our labor, and in some definite portion of the external world, while the law of contracts facilitates our disposing of these rights on terms that seem best to us" (Charles Fried, *Contract as Promise* [Cambridge, Mass.: Harvard University Press, 1981], pp. 1–2).

3. Grant Gilmore, *The Death of Contract* (Columbus: Ohio State University Press, 1974), p. 90.

4. See Anthony Kronman, "Contract Law and Distributive Justice," *Yale Law Journal* 89 (1980): 472–511.

5. The distinction is quite analogous to Nozick's distinction between 'end-state' and 'historical' conceptions of justice. See Nozick, *Anarchy, State, and Utopia*, pp. 153–163. It is not, however, analogous to the distinction of consequentialist versus non-consequentialist views.

6. Historically, some have argued, American law has vacillated in and out of such a view. Morton Horwitz has argued that, in the eighteenth century, the duties imposed by the common law were regarded as prior to any obligations incurred by private agreement and were seen as overriding or nullifying the latter. It was only in the nineteenth century, so Horwitz claims, that the gap between contractual and non-contractual duties began to grow. Contract law had existed prior to the nineteenth century, but not in the form in which we now know it; it was subordinate to property law and functioned mainly to transfer title to the things for which the contract was made. In the eighteenth century, the fairness of the exchange was believed to put limits to contractual obligation: equity courts would refuse to enforce contracts in which what is called "consideration" was inadequate. See Morton Horwitz, *The Transformation of American Law* (Cambridge, Mass.: Harvard University Press, 1977).

7. Compiling just a list of the writings in which utilitarianism has been attacked on these grounds would be a hopelessly long task (and not really a very fruitful one). The contemporary *locus classicus* of all such objections, nonetheless, may be said to be Rawls's *A Theory of Justice*. I am here giving only the abbreviated version of some of these criticisms. The more detailed versions have

thus far not convinced the utilitarians; the shorter version is bound not do so either. Why that is the case is a matter for speculation, at another time.

8. Hegel's argument occurs in two sections of his *Phenomenology of Spirit*, called "The Truth of Enlightenment" and "Absolute Freedom and Terror" (*Phenomenology of Spirit*, trans. A. V. Miller [Oxford: Oxford University Press, 1971], pp. 349–363). The appeal to utility emerges, Hegel argues, when the traditional unreflective world collapses under the weight of the kind of self-reflective culture of modernity. Reflection breeds skepticism. In such a state of affairs, not only are traditional religious ethics thrown into question, but appeals to any tradition lose their hold. (Hegel characterizes such a skeptical state of affairs as the culture of vanity: since each person cannot refer to any objective goods, the basis of individual value is personal wit and success, parading under the masquerade of public service. See p. 320.) The appeal to utility enters as the rationalistic answer to the question of value in a fragmented world. It offers a better explanation of ethical categories since it can pretend to rational treatment (as Hegel puts it, it is the result of "rational insight"). Although eighteenth century materialism tried to replace the traditional source of ethics with one based on some version of the natural order, in Hegel's view it fared no better than traditional appeals to faith. It simply substituted the abstraction of matter for the abstractions of faith. The better explanation of the value of things will be their role in promoting or hindering human happiness—their utility. While utility appears as a rational solution and as something concrete (after all, we each have wants and interests), it turns out to be just as much of an abstraction as the solutions found in traditional faith and materialism. It is captured in the Rousseauian idea of "universal freedom, which would separate itself in this way into its constituent parts and by the very fact of doing so would have made itself into an *existing* Substance, would thereby be free from *particular* individuality, and would aportion the *plurality* of individuals to its various constituent parts" (p. 358, translation slightly altered). This ignores the reality of individuals, "for where the self is merely *represented* and is present only as an idea, there it is not *actual*; where it is represented by proxy, it *is not*" (p. 359). Hegel does not argue that it is impossible to demand sacrifices of individuals, only that theories like utilitarianism cannot justify this sacrifice. Such sacrifice can be justified if the individual can see a point in the sacrifice (as we might put it: if the sacrifice is *fair*). It can be fair only if the people involved can legitimately identify with the political order. This occurs in a community in which our identities are not fragmented from the social unions in which we live. In such a state of affairs, in Hegel's terms, the relation between the individual will and the universal will is no longer antithetical: "It does not lose itself in that will, for pure knowing and willing is much more *it* than is that atomic point of consciousness" (p. 363).

9. Hegel, *Phenomenology of Spirit*, p. 360.

10. John Findlay says, "The values of justice and injustice may be held to be the fruits of the *disjunction of persons*" (J. N. Findlay, *Values and Intentions* [London: George Allen and Unwin, 1961], p. 293). Findlay also claims that "the values of justice and injustice *are* connected with the *exclusiveness of persons*" (p. 294, my emphasis). Rawls uses similar terminology, when he says that "Utilitarianism does not take seriously the distinction between persons" (John Rawls, *A Theory of Justice* [Cambridge, Mass.: Harvard University Press, 1971], p. 27).

11. John Finnis, *Natural Law and Natural Rights* (Oxford: Clarendon Press, 1980), p. 113.

12. John Rawls, *A Theory of Justice*, p. 30. Rawls of course claims that his theory is a non-teleological one, not a non-consequentialist one. A non-teleological theory is one that justifies its first principles independently of some specific conception of goodness, whereas non-consequentialism is a doctrine that holds that the moral status of our actions is independent of their consequences.

13. As Rawls puts it, "it is natural to think that rationality is maximizing something and that in morals it must be maximizing the good. Indeed, it is tempting to suppose that it is self-evident that things should be arranged so as to lead to the most good" (*ibid.*, pp. 24-25).

14. There is another underlying appeal to utilitarianism that I shall not go into here. In a pluralistic society in which it is difficult to find any agreement on the nature of the good, the idea that there is at least one thing that is good—happiness—can come to seem very plausible. Utilitarianism would thus take the place of a full blooded Aristotelianism; it would be what is left of the Aristotelian notion of well-being once it is stripped of any idea of basic human capacities and powers. It would not be surprising then that people like Mill would try to reintroduce certain Aristotelian elements into utilitarianism.

15. There is a longstanding principle in ethics that holds that we have a greater duty to avoid doing harm than we have a duty to do good; or in the language of philosophical ethicists, our duties of non-maleficence are stronger than our duties of beneficence. This is one way of interpreting the claim that our primary duty is not to maximize good. However, this principle is probably not nearly so universally held as its proponents often present it as being. It seems to be the case that various kinds of perfectionist schemes implicitly reject this as a reactionary principle, an ideological mask for an attempt to prevent revolution; Maurice Merleau-Ponty at one point in his career seemed to advocate such a view. See Maurice Merleau-Ponty, *Humanism and Terror*, trans. John O'Neill (Boston: Beacon Press, 1969).

16. See Rawls, *A Theory of Justice*.

17. *Ibid.*, pp. 87-88.
18. See Kronman, "Contract Law and Distributive Justice."
19. Kronman, *ibid.*, p. 503.
20. *Ibid.*
21. *Ibid.*, p. 504.
22. "The law of property defines the boundaries of our rightful possessions, while the law of torts seeks to make us whole against violations of those boundaries, as well as against violations of the natural boundaries of our physical person. Contract law ratifies and enforces our joint ventures beyond those boundaries . . . and the will theory of contract, which sees contractual obligations as essentially self-imposed, is a fair implication of liberal individualism" (Fried, *Contract as Promise*, pp. 1-2).
23. *Ibid.*, p. 97.
24. See *ibid.*, p. 21.
25. See Horwitz, *The Transformation of American Law*.
26. On this new type of social expectation and its relation to the rise of the market, see Robert Heilbronner, *The Worldly Philosophers* (New York: Simon and Schuster, 1970), pp. 22-23.
27. This was Oliver Wendell Holmes's view (at least as Gilmore presents it). Holmes saw consideration as that for which parties bargained; for a benefit or detriment to be legally recognized, it must be the case that (in Holmes's words) "the parties must have dealt with it on that footing" (quoted in Gilmore, *The Death of Contract*, p. 19). Consideration must be that which is exchanged for the promise, and the parties must view it as such. This has good claim to being the formal doctrine it is supposed to be, since it says nothing about the adequacy of consideration.
28. Gilmore, *The Death of Contract*, p. 65.
29. Gilmore cites several decisions by Justice Benjamin Cardozo to support this point. See *ibid.*
30. *Ibid.*, p. 70. Gilmore refers there to the "Restatement" on contracts.
31. *Ibid.*, p. 95.
32. This is a theme developed by F. A. Hayek. See especially his *The Constitution of Liberty* (Chicago: University of Chicago Press, 1960).
33. There is one other related set of strategies that ought to be mentioned. We could call these egalitarian and libertarian theories of distribution. An egalitarian theory will be one that focuses on the distribution of burdens and benefits in liberal society and sees an equal distribution of these as good in itself, and the burden of proof is on those who wish to depart from equality. A well-known example is Rawls's system with his "difference principle," namely, that the distribution of social goods is to be equal unless an inequality works to the benefit of

the worst-off group. The difference principle gives those who bear the burden of proof just the argument that they need to depart from equality. But absent that argument or one like it, any egalitarian must continue to distribute and redistribute toward equality. The libertarian view, on the other hand, would claim that a state should not interfere with voluntary transactions between consenting adults, and the burden of proof is on those who wish to justify such coercive interference. A well-known example is Robert Nozick's endorsement of a 'process' rather than an 'end-state' view of entitlements. Note that neither theory rules out such interference with equality or liberty; each only states that the *burden of proof* is on those who wish to justify such departures from equality or liberty. However, it is not clear that the two theories, interpreted in this way, really would come down to radically different conclusions (as they in fact seem to in both Rawls's and Nozick's presentations of them). What would be a good reason for departing from equality? Well, preserving liberty might be a good one (Nozickian examples turn on this very plausible intuition). What might be a good reason for limiting liberty in the libertarian sense? Well, preservation of equality might be just the reason one was looking for. We could explain the ability of both egalitarians and libertarians to play off equally powerful intuitions by noting that both sorts of intuitions are equally powerful in our liberal democratic culture. Moreover, once all the intuitions have been taken into account, the end result of both types of theories might not actually look that much different. This suggests that perhaps the principles of equality and liberty are just interpretations of some more basic principle, such as respect for persons, and are not themselves ground-level principles that must be chosen in opposition to each other. Indeed, since democratic liberalism is the form of social union in which the two intuitions may coexist peacefully, it would be misleading (or at least not very helpful) to fret about whether democratic liberalism a purely "egalitarian" or "libertarian" theory.

34. The classical locus for this point of view is Aristotle in his *Politics*. A more modern expression is G. W. F. Hegel, particularly in his *Philosophy of Right*. One finds contemporary expression in Klaus Hartmann, *Politische Philosophie* (Munich: Karl Alber Verlag, 1981).

35. See Duncan Kennedy, "Form and Substance in Private Law Adjudication," *Harvard Law Review* 89 (1976): 1685–1778. The *locus classicus* of such views is Roberto Unger's *Knowledge and Politics* (New York: Free Press, 1975).

36. Jay Katz argues that such a view is intrinsic to the problems surrounding issues concerning informed consent in the medical context. See Jay Katz, "Informed Consent—A Fairy Tale? Law's Vision," *University of Pittsburgh Law Review* 39 (1977): 137–174.

37. See Finnis, *Natural Law and Natural Rights*, chap. 7.

38. See David Lyon's discussion of this in his "Human Rights and the General Welfare" in *Philosophy and Public Affairs* 6, no. 2 (Winter 1977): 113-129.

39. See the interesting discussion of betrayal in Judith Shklar's *Ordinary Vices* (Cambridge, Mass.: Harvard University Press, 1984), pp. 138-191. Shklar notes that the violation of trust is not the mere thwarting of legitimate expectations—disappointment—but something deeper. See pp. 151-152. Treason, she also notes, is almost always considered one of the most terrible crimes a person can commit.

40. See *ibid.*, pp. 166-173.

41. See the case of *Raffles v. Wichelhaus* (2 H.&C. 906, 159 Eng. Rep. 375), where a person contracts to buy cotton shipped on a boat called "Peerless." Unknown to both parties, there are two ships called "Peerless," each of which is sailing at a different time. Neither party understands that the other party is referring to a different boat. *Raffles v. Wichelhaus* is reprinted in E. Allen Farnsworth and William F. Young, *Cases and Materials on Contracts* (Mineola, N.Y.: Foundation Press, 1980), pp. 693-695.

42. The German *Civil Code Book* (*Bürgerliches Gesetzbuch*) explicitly recognizes this in one of its (for German jurists) most interesting parts, §242: "The debtor is bound to effect performance according to the requirements of good faith [*Treu und Glauben*], common habits being duly taken into consideration." (The translation is E. J. Cohn's in his "Civil Law," p. 59.) Cohn argues that §242 has partially filled the role in German law that equity fills in Anglo-American law (see p. 62). The role of this stated "rule" of law as a "principle" has not been lost on German jurists. As a sample, see Karl Larenz, *Richtiges Recht* (Munich: C. H. Beck, 1979), pp. 80-87; Martin Kriele, *Recht und praktische Vernunft* (Göttingen: Vandenhoeck und Ruprecht, 1979), pp. 85-86.

43. See Tom L. Beauchamp and Ruth Faden, *A History and Theory of Informed Consent* (Oxford: Oxford University Press, 1986).

44. *Meinhard v. Salmon*, 249 N.Y. 458 (1928).

45. *Ibid.*

46. *Ibid.*

47. *Ibid.*

48. Nozick, *Anarchy, State, and Utopia*, pp. 93-95.

49. *Williams v. Walker-Thomas Furniture Co.*, 121 U.S. App. D.C. 315, 350 F. 2d 445 (D.C. Cir. 1965), as partially reprinted in Farnsworth and Young, *Cases and Materials on Contracts*, pp. 504-509.

50. Quoted in Pierre C. Dostert, "Appellate Statement of Unconscionability: Civil Legal Aid at Work," *American Bar Association Journal* 54 (Dec. 1968): 1184, taken from an as yet unpublished casebook edited by Richard Danzig, *An Introduction to the Law of Private Agreement*.

51. *Williams v. Walker-Thomas Furniture Co.* in Farnsworth and Young, *Cases and Materials on Contracts*, p. 505.
52. *Ibid.*, pp. 506–507.
53. *Ibid.*, pp. 507–508.
54. If we apply the same line of reasoning as we have so far followed, we should be forced to the conclusion that what constitutes legitimate reliance and what makes an action faulty will depend on the nature of the interaction. Cardozo is almost always an excellent guide in these matters. A landmark case in which Cardozo wrote the majority opinion, *Hynes v. New York Central Railroad*, 231 N.Y. 229 (1921), illustrates this idea. A young boy was killed when a cross-arm from a high tension pole fell and knocked him into the Hudson River. The New York Central Railroad had put up and maintained the pole. At the time of the accident the boy was standing on a makeshift diving board attached to a structure owned by the New York Central Railroad; the diving board, however, extended into the airspace over the Hudson River, a "public" space. In getting to this point, the boy had "trespassed" on New York Central Railroad's property, and in the New York law of the day, landowners owed no duty of care to trespassers. Yet when struck, the boy was no longer, as it were, trespassing but standing in a public space. The narrow legal issue then might have seemed to turn on whether the boy was at the time of the accident standing in a public space and thus deserving of "due care" from the railroad, or whether he was a "trespasser" to whom the railroad owed no such duty. Cardozo noted that American society easily tolerated such activities on the part of adolescent boys and that in fact the railroad had tolerated this activity. Yet society (and, correspondingly, the law) held that landowners should not be liable for injuries incurred by trespassers. Cardozo argued that in this case there was indeed a duty of care—not because landowners owed trespassers due care as a general rule but because the mores of the society—and the railroad—tolerated this form of behavior. Cardozo thus deftly avoided making landowners responsible for all harm caused but nonetheless maintained the general idea that eliciting reliance does give one responsibility and that the determination of this requires reference to the mores of a given culture. See G. Edward White's discussion of Cardozo's role in this case in his *Tort Law in America* (New York: Oxford University Press, 1980), pp. 121–123.
55. Nozick, *Anarchy, State, and Utopia*, pp. 93–95.
56. This is a criterion of efficiency taken from Richard Posner. Posner goes further than Nozick and elevates the principle of efficiency to defining completely the justice of the distribution of resources. A distribution is efficient, Posner argues, if it is wealth-maximizing, and it is wealth-maximizing if it puts the good in question into the hands of those who value it most. The best way of measuring this value, so Posner argues, is to ask who would pay the most for it.

If, for example, one has a dispute over some entitlement—say, to build a polluting factory or to have pollution free air—one must ask, "Who would be willing to pay the most for the entitlement?" Posner has done this in a variety of different articles and books. For a representative view of his position, see Richard Posner, *The Economics of Justice* (Cambridge, Mass.: Harvard University Press, 1981). For the more detailed and definitive statement, see his *Economic Analysis of Law* (Boston: Little, Brown and Co., 1977). It is wise to check which edition one has, since Posner keeps revising the book in significant ways.

57. Charles Fried, *An Anatomy of Value* (Cambridge, Mass.: Harvard University Press, 1970), see chap. 11.

58. This two-pronged way of construing the principle of beneficence is drawn from the excellent discussion of it in Tom L. Beauchamp and James F. Childress, *Principles of Biomedical Ethics* (New York: Oxford University Press, 1979), pp. 135–167.

59. See also *ibid.*, pp. 145–152, for an excellent discussion of this in the biomedical context.

60. See Richard Posner, "The Ethical and Political Basis of Wealth Maximization," chap. 4 of *The Economics of Justice*, pp. 88–115.

61. Ronald Dworkin, "Why Efficiency?," *Hofstra Law Review* 8 (1980): 563–565, reprinted in Dworkin, *A Matter of Principle* (Cambridge, Mass.: Harvard University Press, 1985), pp. 267–289.

Chapter Four

1. See G. W. F. Hegel, *Philosophy of Right*, trans. T. M. Knox (London: Oxford University Press, 1952), §183: "In the course of the actual attainment of selfish ends . . . there is formed a system of complete interdependence, wherein the livelihood, happiness and legal status of one man is interwoven with the livelihood, happiness and rights of all. On this system, individual happiness, &c., depend, and only in this connected system are they actualized and secured. This system may be prima facie regarded as the external state, the state based on need, the state as the understanding conceives it [*Verstandesstaat*]."

2. See Robert Nozick, *Anarchy, State, and Utopia* (New York: Basic Books, 1974), pp. 54–119. Unfortunately, my brief summary cannot do justice to the breadth and subtlety of Nozick's arguments about this.

3. This has been argued by Eric von Magnus, "Risk, State, and Nozick," *Midwest Studies in Philosophy* 7 (1982): 121–132.

4. See Nozick, *Anarchy, State, and Utopia*, pp. 280–292.

5. It should be noted that Nozick explicitly takes as his aim the reduction of the political to the non-political. My argument is that he fails.

6. G. W. F. Hegel, *Phenomenology of Spirit*, trans. A. V. Miller (Oxford: Oxford University Press, 1977), pp. 111-119.

7. This is only partially the Hobbesian model of society that it appears to be. There are, for example, a whole host of human relations that fall outside of this model of society. For example, there is the family (where the 'glue' is certainly neither—merely?—self-interest nor is it "political"). There are others: love, friendship, teacher-pupil relations, mentor-apprentice relations, all of which fall outside these categories. I am not advancing a Hobbesian theory of "human nature"; I am only tracing out a sketch of how one might view certain embodiments of principles such as autonomy in social (in this restricted sense of "social") relations.

8. See Klaus Hartmann, *Politische Philosophie* (Munich: Karl Alber, 1981), pp. 61-68.

9. It might be objected that this view simply recapitulates a longstanding error in political philosophy, that of viewing the relation between an individual and the state as being one of *citizenship*, instead of simply as individuals' being related to some kind of agency. Alexander Bickel, for one, has argued something like this and pointed out the dangers: "A relationship between government and the governed that turns on citizenship can always be dissolved or denied. Citizenship is a legal construct, an abstraction, a theory. No matter what the safeguards, it is at best something given and given to some and not to others, and it can be taken away" (Alexander Bickel, "Citizen or Person?: What Is Not Granted Cannot Be Taken Away," in Alexander Bickel, *The Morality of Consent* [New Haven, Conn.: Yale University Press, 1975], p. 53). What I have argued, however, is not that the relation between an individual and the state is exhausted by the concept of citizenship but that this is the essential makeup of the core of the political state. The dangers of a view that sees the relationship between the individual and the state as exhausted by the concept of citizenship are manifold. The main danger is that it would give the state the right to define which group of people count as "citizens" and then treat all the non-citizens within its territory as it pleased (denying them rights, due process, and so forth). Such actually happened in the U.S. Supreme Court decision of *Dred Scott*, where a black slave was declared not to be a "citizen" and therefore liable to remain in slavery, falling outside of the boundary of the protection of the laws owed to such "citizens" (see Bickel, "Citizen or Person?," pp. 36-40). I do not think that such dangers would be consistent with the views presented here. The political state is justified as a protection of human dignity; the individual does not lose this claim simply by not being a citizen of a state. Presumably, a state would have an obligation to treat all people with the respect commensurate with their dignity even though it need not treat "aliens" the same as it treats its "citizens" (it can deny aliens the vote, set up separate passport checks at borders, and so on).

What it cannot do is treat them with less dignity; it may not, for example, deny them "equal protection of the laws." I would think—although I do not have a full blown argument to show it—that a just state may not arbitrarily remove citizenship from its members, as the Soviets did with Alexander Solzhenitsyn. The state is not a "club" that can eject its members for bad behavior.

Michael Walzer argues in his *Spheres of Justice* (New York: Basic Books, 1983) that citizenship is the primary good to be distributed in a state. It follows for Walzer that the right to choose an admissions policy (whom to allow into the state) is a basic right—in fact, may be *the* basic political right of the members of a state; Walzer actually speaks of countries—nation-states—as "national clubs or families" (p. 42). Walzer does think, however, that there are some moral restrictions on this. He holds that we have a moral duty to let in those who are like us ("ethnic relatives," as he calls them [p. 41]); this comes from the duty of mutual aid. He also explicitly claims that one must give all immigrants the possibility of being naturalized, and that any "determination of aliens and guests by an exclusive band of citizens . . . is not communal freedom but oppression" (p. 62). These restrictions do not fit in terribly well with his other claims, for example, "the distribution of membership is not pervasively subject to the constraints of justice" (p. 61); he hedges this by saying that "self-determination in the sphere of membership is not absolute" (p. 62). If his claims are to be kept coherent with each other, even Walzer must admit that self-respect is at least *as* primary a good as membership. Indeed, to the extent that it functions as a limitation on the right to treat members differently from non-members, it is more important than membership.

10. For a similar view, see Günther Maluschke, *Philosophische Grundlagen des demokratischen Verfassungsstaates* (Munich: Karl Alber, 1982), pp. 317–343.

11. John Rawls, *A Theory of Justice* (Cambridge, Mass.: Harvard University Press, 1971), chap. 2. In a later publication, Rawls makes this point more forcefully and distinguishes his view from Nozick's precisely on the point of "inalienable" rights. See Rawls, "Social Unity and Primary Goods," in Amartya Sen and Bernard Williams, eds., *Utilitarianism and Beyond* (Cambridge, Eng.: Cambridge University Press, 1982), p. 171ff.

12. Martin Kriele, *Einführung in die Staatslehre* (Reinbek bei Hamburg: Rowohlt Taschenbuch Verlag, 1975), pp. 151–156.

13. One familiar objection to this is the libertarian counterclaim that any restriction on a person's right to choose what he or she thinks is in his or her own interest (and that does not violate another's rights) is an affront to his or her dignity. This is, however, ultimately an indefensible position. The constitutional order is based on the abstract principle of respect for persons and for that reason

excludes some things as beyond choice, those things that are necessary for each person to be able to participate as a political equal.

This argument should not be confused with an argument for paternalism, where by "paternalism" I understand the coercive interference by the state with individual actions such that a person is prohibited from doing something (or required to do it) on the grounds that it is good for them not to do it (or to do it). Thus, so the argument might run, if the state can put some things out of bounds for free choice, why then can it not put many more things—for paternalistic reasons—out of bounds?

This, however, would simply confuse the types of arguments being used. Paternalistic arguments turn on whether something is in one's interests; arguments about non-waivable consitutional rights turn on the conditions for defining and maintaining a just social and political order, not on the interests of individuals. The justification of a right as a constitutional right turns on its being necessary for the person's standing as a political equal; paternalistic arguments turn on whether something is or is not in someone's interests.

Nor is the constitutional argument the same as a moralistic argument. An argument of the latter type might try to prohibit a certain kind of behavior that a majority find offensive on grounds that it is "sinful." One's status, however, as a sinner or saint is irrelevant to one's status as a political equal. The stains (or lack thereof) on one's soul make no appearance in arguments about one's political status in a just order.

14. The point is also made by Robert E. Goodin, *Political Theory and Public Policy* (Chicago: University of Chicago Press, 1982), pp. 73-94.

15. This kind of dialectical strategy is Hegelian in inspiration. New categories (and the principles inherent in them) are introduced in order to make up for deficiencies in the previous ones. (Thus, for example, the "political" state is introduced to make up for the deficiencies of the "social" state.) The deficiencies are ones of explanation of how a form of life is possible. As such, the argument moves in a way similar to Rawls's idea of reflective equilibrium: we take certain basic ideas for granted and try to reconstruct them in a theory. This is a kind of "regressive" dialectic; we begin with a form of life and "regress" from it to its basic conditions as explanations of how it might be possible. (Although this has some affinities with what have been called transcendental arguments, it has, I think, more in common with what Hegel called "speculative" arguments. We have not shown that these categories are the only ones that would explain the possibility of this form of life. We have offered only one speculative theory—more like a set of hypotheses than a set of logical conditions—among potentially many.)

I have treated this difference between regressive and progressive dialectic as they appear in Hegel's work in "The Logic of Hegel's *Logic*," *Journal of the History of Philosophy* 17, no. 4 (Oct. 1979): 431–433 (reprinted in Michael Inwood, ed., *Hegel* [Oxford: Oxford University Press, 1985], pp. 85–109). In a progressive dialectic, one begins from some basic concepts and systematically introduces new content; in the regressive dialectic, one assumes something to be reconstructed and justifies one's categories as steps toward a complete reconstruction of what one has taken for granted as in need of explanation. In ethical theory, a progressive dialectic would be one that began with some basic concept (for example, a self-legislating will or an autonomous person) and showed how moral content followed from that. The regressive method is the one I have used; one shows that the explanation is incomplete because something (for example, political rights) has been left out. The idea comes from Kant's distinction of an analytic (regressive) method and a synthetic (progressive) method in his *Prolegomena to Any Future Metaphysics*, trans. Peter G. Lucas (Manchester: Manchester University Press, 1959), pp. 4, 5n. In any dialectical argument, it will be, of course, difficult to distinguish the two. This is the point, as I see it, of Rawls's helpful notion of "reflective equilibrium." Whether one is "regressing" or "progressing" depends on where one is going in the process of seeking equilibrium. If one is correcting one's intuitions because of their incompatibility with key features of the theory, then one is progressing; if one is modifying the theory because of basic intuitions, then one is regressing. I see this, incidentally, as another piece of (admittedly small) evidence of the affinity of Rawls's and Kant's views (an affinity that Rawls has claimed but that is often disputed). On these points about explanation and social categories, see also Klaus Hartmann, "Ideen zu einen neuem systematischen Verständnis der Hegelschen Rechtsphilosophie," *Perspektiven der Philosophie*, 2, Amsterdam, 167–200.

16. See Karl Marx, "Critique of Hegel's *Philosophy of Right*," in David McClellan, ed. and trans., *Karl Marx: Selected Writings* (Oxford: Oxford University Press, 1977), pp. 26–31.

17. Both Hartmann and Maluschke argue that a doctrine of separation of powers is incompatible with a strict reading of Hegel's theory. See Maluschke, *Philosophische Grundlagen*, pp. 299–305, and Hartmann, *Politische Philosophie*, pp. 209–211.

18. Norbert Hornstein suggested to me this way of putting the matter.

19. Nozick, *Anarchy, State, and Utopia*, pp. 180–181.

20. Thomas Grey argues that this is indeed the point of the "Proviso" in Thomas Grey, "Property and Need: The Welfare State and Theories of Distributive Justice," *Stanford University Law Review* 28 (1976): 888–889.

21. For an overview of some of the literature and how it applies to these kinds of concerns, see E.-W. Böckenförde, "Die Entstehung des Staates als Vorgang der Säkularisation" and "Die Bedeutung der Unterscheidung von Staat

und Gesellschaft im demokratischen Sozialstaat der Gegenwart," both in E.-W. Böckenförde, *Staat, Gesellschaft, Freiheit* (Frankfurt am Main: Suhrkamp, 1976).

22. The basic work in which Lorenz von Stein presented these theses was his *Geschichte der sozialen Bewegung in Frankreich von 1789 bis auf unsere Tage* (Leipzig: no pub., 1850), reprinted in 1921 in an edition edited by G. Salomon (Munich: Drei Masken Verlag, 1921). See also Maluschke, *Philosophische Grundlagen*, pp. 317–336, and Klaus Hartmann, "Reiner Begriff und Tätiges Leben," in Roman Schnur, ed., *Staat und Gesellschaft: Studien über Lorenz von Stein* (Berlin: Duncker und Humblot, 1978). See also E.-W. Böckenförde, "Lorenz von Stein als Theoretiker der Bewegung von Staat und Gesellschaft zum Sozialstaat," in Böckenförde, *Staat, Gesellschaft, Freiheit*.

23. See Böckenförde's discussion of this in "Lorenz von Stein." See Lorenz von Stein's work *Proletariat und Gesellschaft*, the first edition of which was published in 1842, two years before Marx's celebrated "Paris Manuscripts" of 1844. The second, greatly expanded, edition of *Proletariat und Gesellschaft* was published in 1848. See the reprint of the 1848 edition edited by Manfred Hahn (Munich: Wilhelm Fink Verlag, 1971).

24. The German term for this conception of the state as having obligations to society, *der Sozialstaat*, should not be confused with the conception of the "social state" that I am employing here.

25. Would this be a kind of historical explanation of why someone like Rawls would offer *social* principles of justice and then simply identify the state with the government and explain the state as "the association consisting of equal citizens" and the government as "the citizen's agent . . . which satisfies the demands of their public conception of justice" (Rawls, *A Theory of Justice*, p. 212, §34)?

26. John Hart Ely, *Democracy and Distrust: A Theory of Judicial Review* (Cambridge, Mass.: Harvard University Press, 1980), see pp. 77–88.

27. *Ibid.*, p. 80.

28. See *ibid.*, pp. 82–86.

29. See *ibid.*, pp. 54–55.

30. Robert Nozick has objected (in *Anarchy, State, and Utopia*, pp. 169–172) that taxation of earnings from labor is on a par with forced labor, since it comes down to the government's demanding that people work X hours *gratis* for the government, and that is close enough to forced labor to count as forced labor. For Nozick, the question of whether the government has a right to tax is really the question of whether forced labor by the government is justified (the answer is, of course, no). Nozick's argument deserves more treatment than I can give it, but the intuitive objection is that *somehow* paying money and rendering services are different (just *how* they are different is, of course, difficult to say, and that's why Nozick's point hits home). Judges are, for example, in breach of

contract cases prone not to require specific performance but instead to award monetary damages. Consider Hegel's quite different claim about the state's right to tax. The state, Hegel says, "lays claim only to a single form of riches, namely, money. . . . [I]n fact, however, money is not one particular type of wealth amongst others, but the universal form of all types so far as they are expressed in an external embodiment and so can be taken as 'things'. Only by being translated into terms of this extreme culmination of externality can services exacted by the state be fixed quantitatively and so justly and equitably" (*Philosophy of Right*, §299). Hegel goes on to note that this distinction can only be made when the "principle of subjective freedom" is recognized. If the state should demand the services of someone, it should also be able to distinguish the quality of the service from a similar but worse (or better) service. (But is four hours of writing by Walker Percy on a par with four hours of writing by the local porno king? How many hours of Walker Percy's writing is worth two hours of mime by Marcel Marceau? How could one possibly come up with a metric that would allow one even to begin answering such questions?) This inclines me to say that if the state is justified at all in such things, it would be in taxing for money and not services or labor—thus breaking the link between taxation and forced labor that Nozick makes. Of course, it can be replied that the state is not justified at all in doing such things (although the strong analogy with forced labor will not perhaps serve as the justification). Part of the appeal of Nozick's claim lies, I think, in the theory of the state with which it is connected. For Nozick, the state is a protective organization (a social state in our sense); it is like a corporation in which one owns stock. Now surely it would be outrageous if, after buying stock in a corporation (say, General Motors), one received a notice to the effect that one had to send yet more money to General Motors because the management had decided that some people somewhere were due a bit more in life than they actually had, that the General Motors management would determine who these people were, and that the penalty for failing to comply was some terrible punishment to be inflicted by duly registered agents of the corporation, just as it would be outrageous if the corporation were to demand that each shareholder put in two hours of labor per week, without pay, at a General Motors plant (taxation on a par with forced labor?). If the state were *only* a corporation, then Nozick's analogy might hold. If it is not (or is more than a corporation), then the strength of the analogy weakens.

31. Of course, there are problems with defining just what counts as belonging to a group and greater problems in defining what kinds of groups merit special attention. If one says that the poor are lazy and shiftless, and just want to live off the hard earned wealth of the more industrious, is one insulting a group? But what of people who find trivial things insulting? See Ely, *Democracy and Dis-*

trust, pp. 145-170, for a discussion of the more concrete problems facing such a test for which groups merit special scrutiny.

32. On this point, see Laurence H. Tribe, "The Puzzling Persistence of Process-Based Constitutional Theories," *Yale Law Journal* 89 (1980): 1063.

33. See Ronald Dworkin, "The Forum of Principle," *New York University Law Review* 56 (1981): 469, reprinted in Ronald Dworkin, *A Matter of Principle* (Cambridge, Mass.: Harvard University Press, 1985), pp. 33-71.

34. This is only one strategy for maintaining the state's "universality" vis-à-vis society. Keeping the interests of the rulers from separating from those of the ruled is, as it were, a political solution, looking at the problem from the standpoint of the state. We can also look at it from the standpoint of society. Does the liberal state have the right to promote certain virtues on the part of the citizenry, namely, those necessary for the maintenance of a liberal community? One thinks of the virtues, for example, of tolerance and respect for others. A liberal order cannot long survive where these virtues are absent. (How long can it last where there is, for example, profound and widespread anti-semitism or racism? intolerance for minority views or contempt for legal procedure? One thinks in this regard of the sad example of Weimar Germany.) However one decides the issue (I lean toward thinking that it does have the right), certain things do not follow. First, it would not follow that the state has a right to *punish* people for lacking those virtues. There are many things that the state might have a right to promote (well-maintained highways, for example) but for the absence of which would have no right to punish someone. Second, it does not follow that the state has a right to promote virtue in general; it would follow that it had the right to promote *only* those virtues necessary for maintaining liberality among citizens (tolerance and so on). The liberal state is not a generalized moral policeman. To maintain that the state has a right to promote liberal virtues is just to say that the state has the right to promote a liberal *social* as well as *political* order. To put it another way: the appearance of complete neutrality of the state is only that—an *appearance* of the deeper level of principle on which it is founded.

35. Hegel discusses this in his *Philosophy of Right*. See especially §§205 and 303 for his discussion of the universal class. §§301-302 gives the arguments for "constitutionalizing" the estates. He discusses the aptitude of civil servants for such a "universal" task in §§289-297. Hegel's argument about the aptitude of civil servants is reminiscent of the argument in American jurisprudence about the role of judges. Some optimistic legal realists, for example, argue that the judge is most capable of making correct policy in many areas, since he or she stands "outside" the give and take of political debate. Of course, others argue that judges are the least capable of doing this. Without ignoring the complexities of legal interpretation, I think that it would be fair to say that a "policy-making"

view of judges would be inconsistent with the views I have so far advanced, since it would violate the neutrality of the state by removing important matters from representational concerns. Of course, that is exactly why many of those who argue for such a policy-making view want to give judges that power, namely, a distrust of the *outcomes* that representative government comes up with. That was also Hegel's reason (I think). This leaves, incidentally, room for different margins of interpretative power for judges in civil matters (for example, tort and contract) than in constitutional matters. Compare Ely's views on this (*Democracy and Distrust*, pp. 67-69).

36. Ely, to some extent, reads constitutional history this way. Lawrence Friedman, in his *A History of American Law* (New York: Simon and Schuster, 1973), sees much of the development of American law as based on a distrust of large accumulations of power, whether it be by the trusts, the judiciary, or whatever. The strategy, he notes, has always been to offset this by regulation, antitrust laws, and similar methods.

37. A liberal strategy for pluralism that tries to show respect for the dignity of individuals will also be one that allows a wide latitude to individuals in what they may do so as not to allow claims of treason to enter into what are otherwise good faith dealings. Part of the intent of the framers of the American constitutional system was to prevent the kind of political backbiting that tried to portray good faith political opposition as treasonous activity. See Judith Shklar, *Ordinary Vices* (Cambridge, Mass.: Harvard University Press, 1984), pp. 178-190.

38. At least in some places, Rawls talks as if this view of the relation of rights and an ideal picture of society was his own view. He says, for example, that a theory of justice, "when fully presented, expresses an underlying conception of human society, that is, a conception of the person, of the relations between persons, and of the general structure and ends of social cooperation. . . . [J]ustice as fairness does this by bringing together certain general features of any society that it seems one would, on due reflection, wish to live in and want to shape our interests and character." See John Rawls, "Reply to Alexander and Musgrave," *Quarterly Journal of Economics* 88 (Nov. 1974): 633, reprinted in part as "A Contractarian Theory of Social Justice" in Tom L. Beauchamp and Terry P. Pinkard, eds., *Ethics and Public Policy* (Englewood Cliffs, N.J.: Prentice-Hall, 1983), see p. 148.

39. We might be more tempted to say only 'promise keeping' and make contract a special case of that, even though Hegel quite explicitly rejected that view. Perhaps "free and binding exchange" would capture Hegel's point. See Hegel, *Philosophy of Right*, §79.

40. Charles Taylor makes a similar point: "The citizen republic is to be valued not just as a guarantee of general utility, or as a bulwark of rights. It may

even endanger these in certain circumstances. We value it also because we hold the form of life in which men govern themselves, and decide their own fate through common deliberation, is higher than the one in which they live as subjects of even an enlightened despotism" (Charles Taylor, "The Diversity of Goods," in Sen and Williams, eds., *Utilitarianism and Beyond*, p. 143).

41. See Simeon McIntosh for a forceful defense and presentation of this view of reading the constitution (Simeon McIntosh, "Legal Hermeneutics: A Philosophical Critique," *Oklahoma Law Review* 35, no. 1 [Winter 1982]: 61–71).

42. See Nozick, *Anarchy, State, and Utopia*, pp. 61–62.

43. Hyman Gross, whose theory is highly similar to the one presented here, calls it an "anti-impunity" theory: wrongdoers should not be allowed to break the law with *impunity*. See Hyman Gross, *A Theory of Criminal Justice* (New York: Oxford University Press, 1979), pp. 400–412.

44. I take this nice phrase about the criminal's showing contempt for others from David Luban.

45. See Robert Nozick, *Philosophical Explanations* (Cambridge, Mass.: Harvard University Press, 1982), pp. 370–374.

Index

Ackerman, Bruce, 185
Acknowledgment, xv, 15, 36, 37, 48, 53, 96, 97, 106, 108, 112, 136, 142, 143, 149, 160
Altruism, 100, 104, 106, 110
American Uniform Commercial Code, 109, 113
Arendt, Hannah, 13, 148, 186
Aristotle, xiii, xviii, 7, 61, 201; Aristotelian, 7, 199; Aristotelian-Hegelian model of history of philosophy, xvii, xviii, xix; Aristotelian-Thomistic, 157
Austin, John, 54, 55, 56, 57, 58, 59, 60, 62, 65, 70, 71, 74, 193
Authenticity, 12, 186
Autonomy, xii, xviii, 5-15, 11-21, 25, 31-36, 84, 90, 99, 103, 108, 109-111, 114, 120-122, 133-135, 142, 149-150, 156, 160, 163, 170, 174, 188, 205, 208; action-oriented conception, 4, 14; and anonymity, 7, 20, 21, 22; autonomous choice, 10, 11, 13, 32, 33, 34, 51, 111, 121, 171; autonomous person, 5, 6, 10, 12, 14, 142, 208; and conception of self, 6-8; and independence, 11-12, 15; Kantian conception, 3, 5-8, 11-12, 18-20; in relation to freedom, 4-6, 11-15; respect for autonomy, 31, 142, 163; and self-legislation, 5, 22-23; will-oriented conception, 4, 14

Balance of power, 170
Beauchamp, Tom L., 186, 202, 204, 212
Beneficence, 77, 130, 199, 204
Bentham, Jeremy, 85
Bickel, Alexander, 205
Bill of rights, 162
Böckenförde, E.-W., 208, 209
Bodin, Jean, 58

Bureaucrat: and judges, 72-73; and universal class, 62, 169

Callahan, Daniel, 188
Cardozo, Justice Benjamin, 114, 115, 200, 203
Character: character identity, 9-10, 27; character-predicates, 14; conception of character, 7; ideals of character, 23, 142; and social union, 27-28; and virtues, 27-28, 108, 110, 212
Childress, James F., 204
Choice: autonomous choice, 10, 11, 13, 32, 33, 34, 51, 111, 121, 171; free choice, 4, 10, 11, 12, 13, 15, 33; respect for choice, 32-38, 43, 91, 103-104, 108, 114, 134, 143, 189
Citizen, 47, 144
Citizenship, 47, 144, 153-154, 165, 177-184
Cohn, E. J., 202
Coke, Edward, 148
Coles, Robert, 41, 191
Common good, 3, 17, 18, 19, 21, 30, 32, 45, 48, 49, 50, 99, 102, 103, 104, 106, 188
Community: civic community, 145, 149, 151, 152, 153, 154, 164, 165, 181, 184; community of fairness, 50, 51, 70, 145, 151, 161, 171, 175, 184
Compensation, 87, 95, 177; damages, 83, 90, 93, 95, 103, 110, 111, 128; in formation of minimal state, 140-141; for imposition of risk, 124-130
Confucian, 12
Consensus building, 152, 153
Consent, 32, 33, 35, 80, 133, 140, 201; informed consent, 117-121; as justifying imposition of risk, 122-126

215

Constitution, 145, 148, 159; constitutional interpretation, 161-171
Contract, 81-96; consideration in contract, 91-94; contractarian, 45, 151, 168, 172, 189, 212; contractual obligation, 80, 93; outcome-oriented justification, 81, 82, 83, 87, 89, 90, 92, 95, 101, 105; process-oriented justification, 81, 90, 91, 95, 100, 101; as promise, 89-91; quasi-contract, 117
Crime, 176-184; crime and tort, 177, 183; crimes, 38, 177, 179, 180, 181, 183, 202

Danzig, Richard, 202
Democratic liberalism, 32, 51, 70, 174, 201; democratic liberal state, 145, 151, 152, 153, 161, 162, 166, 167, 172, 177; and Dworkin's conception of the law, 70-71; and Rawlsian conception of justice, 47-48
Deneuve, Catherine, 39
Deontology, 16
Desert, 39-44, 48-50, 191, 192
Deterrence, 177, 178, 179, 180, 183, 184
Dialectic, 71, 149, 179, 180, 207, 208
Dignity, 32, 33, 34, 35, 36, 37, 38, 43, 44, 48, 51, 111, 112, 113, 133, 135, 142, 143, 144, 145, 149, 150, 151, 156, 158, 163, 164, 165, 166, 170, 171, 173, 174, 189, 205, 206, 212
Dominant protective agency, 139, 140
Dostert, Pierre, 202
Dworkin, Gerald, 12, 186, 188
Dworkin, Ronald, 53, 65, 66, 67, 68, 69, 70, 71, 131, 194, 195, 196, 204, 211

Egalitarian, 127, 152, 154, 200, 201
Eichmann, Adolf, 11, 186
Einstein, Albert: Einsteinian, 29, 196
Ely, John Hart, 161, 162, 163, 209, 210, 212
Engelhardt, H. T., Jr., 188
Entitlement, 39, 40, 42, 44, 48, 49, 191, 192, 201, 204
Equality: moral equality, 69, 70, 148; political equality, 145, 150, 152, 153
Esser, Josef, 53, 65, 68, 72, 194, 195
Ethics: as distinct from morality, 15-17, 20-21; and ethos, 23-24, 29-31; foundationalist and non-foundationalist models, 24-26; and ideals of society, 98-99; and interest, 97-99; and judgment, 20, 27, 28, 131; and relativism, 29-30
Ethos, 23, 24, 30, 31, 77, 113
Exploitation, 101, 118-120

Faden, Ruth, 202
Fairness, 50-51, 70, 88, 106, 112, 114, 115, 120, 145, 151, 161, 163, 171, 175, 184, 197; private sense, 116-117; public sense, 164-167
Farnsworth, E. Allan, 202, 203
Fate, sharing, in the Rawlsian sense, 44-48
Feinberg, Joel, 191, 192
Findlay, John, 84, 199
Finnis, John, 85, 99, 101, 102, 103, 104, 114, 191, 199, 201
Frankfurt, Harry, 186
Fraternity, 106, 192
Frederick the Great, 73
Freedom: and conception of self, 10, 13; Kantian model of freedom, 23; and property, 155-158; in relation to autonomy, 4-6, 11-15; and valuation, 10-12; as willing the proper objects of the will, 23, 31
Freedonia, 185
Fried, Charles, 89, 90, 91, 127, 197, 204
Friedman, Lawrence, 212

Gilmore, Grant, 80, 93, 94, 95
Goodin, Robert E., 190, 207
Grant, Cary, 39
Grey, Thomas, 192, 208
Gross, Hyman, 213

Habeas corpus, 148, 158
Hahn, Manfred, 209
Hart, H. L. A., 54, 55, 56, 57, 58, 59, 60, 62, 63, 64, 65, 66, 68, 69, 70, 71, 74, 179, 193, 194
Hartmann, Klaus, 201, 205, 208, 209
Hayek, F. A., 154, 200
Hegel, G. W. F., xiv, xv, 16, 17, 20, 21, 23, 62, 65, 70, 84, 97, 113, 125, 136, 138, 139, 141, 143, 155, 159, 160, 161, 168, 169, 170, 173, 174, 185, 186, 187, 188,

193, 194, 196, 198, 199, 201, 204, 205, 207, 208, 210, 211, 212; Hegelian, 17, 18, 23, 54, 78, 111, 126, 130, 136, 151, 152, 156, 160, 163, 173, 174, 186, 188, 190, 196, 207
Heilbronner, Robert, 200
Heteronomy, 5, 19
Hornstein, Norbert, 208
Horwitz, Morton, 92, 93, 197, 200

Individualism, 94, 100, 106, 110, 192, 200; radical individualist, 43, 44, 47, 50, 51, 70, 106, 107, 108, 128, 143
Instrumentalist, 172
Insurance, 127, 128
Interest: and moral evaluation, 97–99; as principle of society, 141–145
Inwood, Michael, 196, 208

James I, 157
Judge, conception of, 66–67, 72–73
Justice: commutative justice, 102; compensatory justice, 38; distributive justice and contract, 87–91; and pluralism, 49–51; retributive justice, 38, 177–180; as specifying type of community, 50–51

Kant, Immanuel, xii, xvii, 4, 5, 6, 7, 15, 16, 19, 20, 21, 23, 24, 28, 32, 33, 34, 85, 133, 185, 186, 187, 188, 189, 208; Kantian, xv, xviii, 3, 5, 6, 7, 8, 11, 12, 15, 16, 17, 18, 19, 20, 21, 22, 23, 24, 32, 33, 34, 36, 43, 133, 134, 150, 185, 187, 189, 190; Kantian-critical model of history of philosophy, xvii
Katz, Jay, 201
Kennedy, Duncan, 99, 100, 101, 103, 104, 106, 201
Knox, T. M., 185, 186, 193, 204
Kriele, Martin, 148, 193, 195, 196, 202, 206
Kronman, Anthony, 88, 89, 90, 91, 197, 200

Larenz, Karl, 202
Libertarian, 38, 77, 103, 104, 111, 115, 122, 123, 124, 125, 135, 142, 152, 154, 155, 189, 200, 201, 206
Locke, John, 155, 157
Lotteries, 39–44

Luban, David, 213
Lucas, Peter G., 208
Lyons, David, 202

MacIntyre, Alisdair, 185, 188
Macpherson, C. B., 44, 192
Magna Charta, 148
Maine, Henry, 159
Maluschke, Günther, 206, 208, 209
Marceau, Marcel, 210
Market, 29, 40, 41, 92, 93, 94, 95, 107, 110, 112, 113, 120, 175, 200
Marx, Karl, 29, 38, 157, 159, 160, 193, 194, 208, 209; Marxism, 13, 14, 71, 158, 193; Marxist-Leninist, 194
Master and slave, 143
Maximin, 45, 146, 147
McClellan, David, 208
McIntosh, Simeon, 213
Meinhard v. Salmon, 114, 202
Membership, 27, 150, 164, 185, 206
Michel de L'Hopital, 58, 61, 69, 104, 147
Miller, A. V., 187, 198, 205
Morality: abstract morality, 16, 17, 29, 31, 37; as distinct from ethics, 15–17, 20–21; Kantian conception, 15–17; and law, 96–99; moral imagination, 24–25; *Moralität*, 187; moral judgments, 14

Nagel, Thomas, 191
Nell, Onora, 187
Newton, Isaac, 29, 196
Non-consequentialism, 85, 199
Notstaat, 138
Noumenal, 6
Nozick, Robert, xi, xii, 38, 115, 116, 122, 123, 124, 125, 127, 138, 139, 140, 141, 154, 155, 172, 184, 186, 189, 191, 196, 197, 201, 202, 203, 204, 206, 208, 209, 210, 213

O'Brien, George Dennis, 196
Obligation: civil obligation, 79–80, 88–90, 96–97, 101–103; legal obligation, 54, 66
O'Neill, John, 199
Original Position, 45, 47, 48, 88, 146, 147, 189

Paton, H. J., 189
Percy, Walker, 210
Pinkard, Terry, 186, 212
Plato, xiii, 13, 61
Pluralism, 162, 163, 169, 170, 199, 212; and common good, 18-19, 31; and democratic liberalism, 32; and distributive justice, 49-51; as leading to a conception of sovereignty, 58-59; and rights, 60-61; and rule of law, 77; strategy for pluralism, 61, 63, 162, 169, 170, 212; and welfare rights, 153-154
Positivism, 22, 53, 54, 60, 61, 63, 64, 65, 68, 69, 70, 71, 72, 162, 163
Posner, Richard, 203, 204
Principle: and abstract morality, 31; balancing principles, 17, 31, 109, 121-136; and common good, 49; and form of life, 75; and pluralism, 49-51; principle-based theories of law, 53, 65, 68, 71; and rules, 66-68; and social union, 78, 96-99; source of principles, 24-25
Privileges, 148, 158, 160
Property, 154-158
Public, 35, 49, 67, 117, 137, 141, 145, 149, 152, 153, 164, 165, 182, 186, 190, 191, 198, 202, 203, 207, 209, 212
Punishment, 176-184; and impunity, 181, 183, 213

Rational agent, 5, 6, 7, 19, 20, 21, 25, 106, 187
Rawls, John, xi, xii, xv, 5, 7, 25, 26, 27, 40, 41, 42, 43, 44, 45, 46, 48, 49, 50, 84, 85, 87, 88, 89, 127, 132, 146, 147, 154, 179, 186, 188, 189, 191, 192, 196, 197, 199, 200, 201, 206, 207, 208, 209, 212; Rawlsian, xiii, xv, xviii, 27, 43, 44, 46, 47, 48, 49, 50, 127, 146, 147
Recipe, 132-134, 174, 176
Relativism, 29
Reliance, 83, 95, 107, 108, 109, 110, 111, 112, 114, 115, 116, 121, 164, 203
Representation, 162, 163, 167, 168, 169; reinforcing representation, 163; virtual representation, 162
Respect: respect for choice, 32, 33, 35, 43, 91, 103, 104, 107, 108, 111, 114, 143, 189; respect for persons, 5, 25, 31, 32, 33, 35, 36, 43, 89, 90, 91, 97, 107, 111, 112, 118, 143, 144, 146, 149, 150, 158, 168, 189, 201, 206
Retribution, 38, 177, 178, 179, 180, 183, 191
Revolution, 60, 84, 159, 168, 193, 196, 199
Rights: basic rights, 140, 145, 148-150, 175; civil rights, 146, 147, 148; economically modeled rights, 145; human rights, 148, 159; liberty-rights, 100, 104; natural rights, 71, 139, 149, 157, 158, 174, 175, 176, 191, 194, 199, 201; politically modeled rights, 145; political rights, 138, 140, 141, 145, 208; private rights, 141, 149; right to vote, 140, 149, 169; welfare rights, 151, 153, 154
Risk: libertarian theory of, 122-125; normal and extraordinary, 127; risk/benefit, 131
Rose, Pete, 41
Rousseau, Jean-Jacques, 13, 84, 198
Rule of law, 53, 68, 73, 74, 75, 77, 78, 107, 195

Sandel, Michael J., 185, 192
Savigny, Karl Friedrich von, 64, 65
Schild, Wolfgang, 194
Schnabel, Artur, 37
Schnur, Roman, 193, 209
Self: autonomous self, 6-8; essential self, 7, 8, 9, 10, 12, 13, 19, 20; ideal self, 13, 14; Kantian model of self, 5-7, 19, 21; self-choice, 5; self-consciousness, 20, 31, 35, 36, 97, 187; self-definitions, 31; self-determination, 5, 6, 18; and social union, 27
Self-interest, 29, 46, 50, 101, 150
Self-legislation, 6, 16, 18, 19, 21, 23, 32, 208
Self-respect, 36, 37, 48, 87, 156, 206; and self-esteem, 37
Sen, Amartya, 206, 213
Sharing, 43, 44, 45, 46, 47, 48, 49, 50, 96, 99, 100, 104, 106, 112, 120, 127, 152, 153, 154, 192
Shklar, Judith, 202, 212
Smith, Norman Kemp, 188
Social categories, 17, 24, 25, 27, 30, 208

Social democracy, 159
Social union: conception, 25-31; Rawlsian conception, 25-27
Solidarity, 152, 153, 183
Solzhenitsyn, Alexander, 206
Sovereignty, 53, 58, 59, 60, 61, 62, 65, 70, 104, 148, 149, 157, 162, 163, 171, 174, 193
Spirit, 17-18, 23-25, 29-31, 75, 113, 172-174
State: democratic liberal state, 145, 151, 152, 153, 161, 162, 166, 167, 172, 177; liberal state, 29, 62, 69, 70, 72, 145, 151, 152, 153, 159, 160, 161, 162, 163, 166, 167, 170, 172, 177, 182, 194, 211; minimal state, 138, 140, 141; *Notstaat*, 138; as organized monopoly of force, 158; political state, 130, 141, 144, 145, 149, 150, 151, 158, 160, 161, 170, 205; social state, 138, 142, 144, 145, 149, 150, 151, 158, 160, 161, 170, 210; state based on need, 138, 204
State of nature, 139, 140, 149, 155

Taylor, Charles, 185, 212, 213
Terms of cooperation, 77, 78, 104, 111, 182
Tolerances, 60

Tort, 76, 80, 82, 87, 90, 95, 102, 110, 121, 127, 128, 177, 183, 197, 200, 203, 212
Tribe, Laurence, 211

Unger, Roberto, 201
Universal class, 62, 169, 211
Utilitarianism, 16, 17, 18, 21, 24, 82, 83, 84, 85, 86, 87, 98, 99, 105, 126, 130, 131, 142, 154, 190, 197, 198, 199, 206, 213; preference-utilitarianism, 84; rule-utilitarianism, 195

Valuation, 8, 10, 14, 31, 96, 186
Virtue, 27-28, 108-109, 165-166
Von Jhering, Rudolf, 72, 121, 195
Von Magnus, Eric, 204
Von Stein, Lorenz, 159, 160, 161, 167, 168, 209
Vote, 72, 140, 141, 143, 148, 149, 153, 167, 168, 169, 205

Walzer, Michael, 206
Watson, Gary, 186
Wealth-maximizing, 203
Weber, Max, 63, 64, 72, 158
White, G. Edward, 203
Williams, Bernard, 188, 206